FAVORITE BRAND NAME™

BAKING

Publications International, Ltd.

Favorite Brand Name Recipes at www.fbnr.com

Contents

Introduction

*D*o you have a secret urge to bake homemade treats? Are you interested in making a big impression with family and friends? Whatever the reason, now is the time to discover the pleasures of fun and easy baking.

Jam-packed with a fabulous assortment of over 300 recipes for breads, cakes, cookies, desserts and pies, this book is designed for the busy cook. Many of the delicious creations start with convenient mixes and prepared doughs. Other tasty treats use a minimum of easy-to-find ingredients and streamlined preparation steps. Best of all, you'll have time to relax while your recipe is baking. Even those with the most hectic schedules can easily prepare these dazzling and delicious recipes.

The following guidelines are chockful of tips and hints for successful baking. Be sure to read this section before you begin. Both the novice and experienced baker will find helpful information to make their time in the kitchen easier and more enjoyable.

Baking Basics

- Read the entire recipe before you begin to be sure you have all the necessary ingredients and utensils.

- Remove butter and cream cheese from the refrigerator to soften, if necessary.

- Always use the pan size suggested in the recipe. Prepare pans as directed.

- Measure the ingredients accurately and assemble them in the order they are listed in the recipe.

- Always check for doneness at the minimum baking time given in the recipe.

- Adjust oven racks and preheat the oven. Check oven temperature with an oven thermometer to make sure the temperature is accurate.

Measuring

Measuring Dry Ingredients: Always use standard measuring spoons and cups. Fill the appropriate measuring spoon or cup to overflowing and level it off with a metal spatula or flat edge of a knife. When measuring flour, lightly spoon it into the measuring cup and then level it off. Do not tap or bang the measuring cup since this will pack the flour.

Measuring Liquid Ingredients: Use a standard glass or plastic measuring cup with a pouring spout. Place the cup on a flat surface, fill to the desired mark and check the measurement at eye level. When measuring sticky liquids, such as honey and molasses, grease the measuring cup or spray it with nonstick cooking spray before filling; this ensures that the sticky liquid will not cling.

Common Weights and Measures

Dash = less than ⅛ teaspoon

½ **tablespoon** = 1½ teaspoons

1 tablespoon = 3 teaspoons

2 tablespoons = ⅛ cup

¼ **cup** = 4 tablespoons

⅓ **cup** = 5 tablespoons plus 1 teaspoon

½ **cup** = 8 tablespoons

¾ **cup** = 12 tablespoons

1 cup = 16 tablespoons

½ **pint** = 1 cup or 8 fluid ounces

1 pint = 2 cups or 16 fluid ounces

1 quart = 4 cups or 2 pints or 32 fluid ounces

1 gallon = 16 cups or 4 quarts

1 pound = 16 ounces

General Substitutions

If you don't have:	Use:
1 teaspoon baking powder	¼ teaspoon baking soda plus ½ teaspoon cream of tarter
½ cup firmly packed brown sugar	½ cup granulated sugar mixed with 2 tablespoons molasses
1 ounce (1 square) unsweetened baking chocolate	3 tablespoons unsweetened cocoa plus 1 tablespoon shortening
3 ounces (3 squares) semisweet baking chocolate	3 ounces (½ cup) semisweet chocolate chips
1 cup sweetened whipped cream	4½ ounces thawed frozen whipped topping
1 cup buttermilk	1 tablespoon lemon juice or vinegar plus milk to equal 1 cup (stir; let stand 5 minutes)
1 tablespoon cornstarch	2 tablespoons all-purpose flour or 2 teaspoons arrowroot
½ cup corn syrup	1¼ cups granulated sugar plus ¼ cup water
1 cup honey	1¼ cups granulated sugar plus ¼ cup water
1 whole egg	2 egg yolks plus 1 teaspoon cold water
1 teaspoon vinegar	2 teaspoons lemon juice
1 cup whole milk	1 cup skim milk plus 2 tablespoons melted butter
1 cup sour cream	1 cup plain yogurt

How Much of This = That

Almonds, blanched, slivered	4 ounces = 1 cup
Butter	2 cups = 1 pound or 4 sticks
	1 cup = ½ pound or 2 sticks
	½ cup = 1 stick or 8 tablespoons
	¼ cup = ½ stick or 4 tablespoons
Chocolate	1 (6-ounce) package chocolate chips = 1 cup chips *or* 6 (1-ounce) squares semisweet chocolate
Cocoa, unsweetened	1 (8-ounce) can = 2 cups
Coconut, flaked	3½ ounces = 1⅓ cups
Cream cheese	1 (3-ounce) package = 6 tablespoons
	1 (8-ounce) package = 1 cup
Flour, all purpose	1 pound = 3½ to 4 cups
Honey, liquid	16 ounces = 1⅓ cups
Milk	
Evaporated	1 (5-ounce) can = ⅔ cup
	1 (12-ounce) can = 1⅔ cups
Sweetened, condensed	1 (14-ounce) can = 1¼ cups
Shortening	1 pound = 2½ cups
Sugar	
Granulated	1 pound = 2½ cups
Brown, packed	1 pound = 2¼ cups
Powdered	1 pound = 3¾ to 4 cups, unsifted

Cranberry Cheesecake Muffins
(page 13)

Coffee-Time Breads

❧ ❧ ❧

Want the family to wake up to the tantalizing aroma of home-baked bread and freshly brewed coffee? Is it your turn for office treats? Looking for a tasty brunch delight? In this chapter you'll find an easy-to-bake sweet bread for every occasion.

Try Cranberry Cheesecake Muffins (page 13), Blueberry Orange Muffins (page 30) or Gooey Caramel and Chocolate Pecan Rolls (page 34). There's only one thing better than the aroma of fresh-baked bread, and that's being able to make it quickly and easily.

Peachy Cinnamon Coffeecake

1 can (8¼ ounces) juice pack sliced yellow cling peaches

1 package DUNCAN HINES® Bakery-Style Cinnamon Swirl Muffin Mix

1 egg

1. Preheat oven to 400°F. Grease 8-inch square or 9-inch round pan.

2. Drain peaches, reserving juice. Add water to reserved juice to equal ¾ cup liquid. Chop peaches.

3. Combine muffin mix, egg and ¾ cup peach liquid in medium bowl; fold in peaches. Pour batter into pan. Knead swirl packet 10 seconds before opening. Squeeze contents onto top of batter and swirl with knife. Sprinkle topping over batter. Bake at 400°F for 28 to 33 minutes for 8-inch pan (or 20 to 25 minutes for 9-inch pan) or until golden. Serve warm.

Makes 9 servings

Hearty Breakfast Rolls

1 (8-ounce) package refrigerated crescent dinner rolls

2 tablespoons strawberry or apricot preserves

6 slices OSCAR MAYER® Smoked Ham

¾ cup VELVEETA® Shredded Pasteurized Process Cheese Food

Preheat oven to 350°F.

Unroll dough into two rectangles; firmly press perforations together to seal. Spread rectangles with preserves; top with ham and process cheese food.

Roll up each rectangle, starting at narrow end; seal edge. Cut each roll into four slices. Place, cut side down, in greased 8-inch pie plate or round cake pan.

Bake 25 to 30 minutes or until golden brown. *Makes 8 servings*

Prep Time: 15 minutes
Cook Time: 30 minutes

Peachy Cinnamon Coffeecake

Orange Brunch Muffins

3 cups all-purpose baking mix

¾ cup all-purpose flour

⅔ cup granulated sugar

2 large eggs, lightly beaten

½ cup plain yogurt

½ cup orange juice

1 tablespoon grated orange peel

2 cups (12-ounce package) NESTLÉ® TOLL HOUSE® Premium White Morsels, divided

½ cup chopped macadamia nuts or walnuts

Preheat oven to 375°F. Grease or paper-line 18 muffin cups.

Combine baking mix, flour and sugar in large bowl. Add eggs, yogurt, juice and orange peel; stir just until blended. Stir in *1⅓ cups* morsels. Spoon into prepared muffin cups, filling ¾ full. Sprinkle with nuts.

Bake for 18 to 22 minutes or until wooden pick inserted into centers comes out clean. Cool in pans for 10 minutes; remove to wire racks to cool slightly.

Microwave *remaining* morsels in small, *heavy-duty* plastic bag on MEDIUM-HIGH (70%) power for 1 minute; knead.

Microwave at additional 10- to 20-second intervals, kneading until smooth. Cut tiny corner from bag; squeeze to drizzle over muffins. Serve warm.

Makes 18 muffins

Cook's Tip: *Standard size muffin pans have cups that are 2½ or 2¾ inches in diameter; giant muffin pans have 4-inch diameter cups.*

Banana-Nana Pecan Bread

1 cup QUAKER® Oats (quick or old fashioned, uncooked)

½ cup chopped pecans

3 tablespoons margarine or butter, melted

2 tablespoons firmly packed brown sugar

1 (14-ounce) package banana bread quick bread mix

1 cup water

½ cup mashed ripe banana

2 eggs, lightly beaten

3 tablespoons vegetable oil

Heat oven to 375°F. Grease and flour bottom only of 9×5-inch loaf pan. Combine oats, pecans, margarine and sugar; mix well. Reserve ½ cup oat mixture for topping; set aside. In bowl, combine remaining oat mixture, quick bread mix, water, banana, eggs and oil. Mix just until dry ingredients are moistened. Pour into prepared pan. Sprinkle top of loaf with reserved oat mixture. Bake 50 to 55 minutes or until wooden pick inserted in center comes out clean. Cool 10 minutes in pan; remove to wire rack. Cool.   *Makes 12 servings*

Cranberry Cheesecake Muffins

1 package (3 ounces) cream cheese, softened

4 tablespoons sugar, divided

1 cup reduced-fat (2%) milk

⅓ cup vegetable oil

1 egg

1 package (about 15 ounces) cranberry quick bread mix

1. Preheat oven to 400°F. Grease 12 muffin cups.

2. Beat cream cheese and 2 tablespoons sugar in small bowl until well blended.

3. Beat milk, oil and egg in large bowl until blended. Stir in quick bread mix just until dry ingredients are moistened.

4. Fill muffin cups ¼ full with batter. Drop 1 teaspoon cream cheese mixture into center of each cup. Spoon remaining batter over cream cheese mixture.

5. Sprinkle batter with remaining 2 tablespoons sugar. Bake 17 to 22 minutes or until golden brown. Cool 5 minutes. Remove from muffin cups to wire rack to cool.   *Makes 12 muffins*

Prep and Bake Time: 30 minutes

Cherry and Almond Coffeecake

1 sheet (½ of 17¼-ounce package) frozen puff pastry

1 package (3 ounces) cream cheese, softened

⅓ cup plus 2 tablespoons powdered sugar, divided

1 egg, separated

¼ teaspoon almond extract

1 tablespoon water

½ cup dried cherries or cranberries, coarsely chopped

½ cup sliced almonds, divided

1. Thaw pastry sheet according to package directions.

2. Preheat the oven to 375°F. Spray baking sheet with nonstick cooking spray.

3. Combine cream cheese, ⅓ cup powdered sugar, egg yolk and almond extract in large bowl. Beat with electric mixer at medium speed until smooth; set aside. In separate small bowl, mix egg white and water; set aside.

4. On lightly floured board, roll out pastry into 14×10-inch rectangle. Spread cream cheese mixture over dough leaving a 1-inch border. Sprinkle evenly with cherries. Reserve 2 tablespoons almonds; sprinkle remaining almonds over cherries.

5. Starting at one of the long sides, loosely roll up dough jelly-roll style. Place roll on the baking sheet, seam side down. Form into circle, pinching ends together. Using scissors, cut at 1-inch intervals from the outside of the ring toward (but not through) the center. Twist each section half a turn, allowing filling to show.

6. Brush top of ring with egg white mixture. Sprinkle with reserved almonds. Bake 25 to 30 minutes or until light brown. Using large spatula, carefully remove ring to wire rack. Cool 15 minutes; sprinkle with remaining 2 tablespoons powdered sugar.

Makes 1 (12-inch) coffeecake

Cherry and Almond Coffeecake

Cranberry Pecan Muffins

1½ cups fresh or frozen cranberries

¼ cup light corn syrup

1 package DUNCAN HINES®
Bakery-Style Cinnamon Swirl
Muffin Mix

1 egg

¾ cup water or milk

½ cup chopped pecans

1. Preheat oven to 400°F. Place 14 (2½-inch) paper liners in muffin cups. Place cranberries and corn syrup in heavy saucepan. Cook on medium heat, stirring occasionally, until cranberries pop and mixture is slightly thickened. Drain cranberries in strainer; set aside.

2. Empty muffin mix into medium bowl. Break up any lumps. Add egg and water. Stir until moistened, about 50 strokes. Stir in cranberries and pecans. Knead swirl packet from Mix for 10 seconds before opening. Cut off 1 end of swirl packet. Squeeze contents over top of batter. Swirl into batter with knife or spatula. *Do not completely mix in.* Spoon batter into muffin cups (see Cook's Tip). Sprinkle with contents of topping packet from

Mix. Bake at 400°F for 18 to 22 minutes or until toothpick inserted into centers comes out clean. Cool in pans 5 to 10 minutes. Serve warm or cool completely.   *Makes 14 muffins*

Cook's Tip: *Fill an equal number of muffin cups in each muffin pan with batter. For more even baking, fill empty muffin cups with ½ inch of water.*

Cranberry Pecan Muffins

Orange Cinnamon Swirl Bread

Bread

    1 package DUNCAN HINES®
        Bakery-Style Cinnamon Swirl
        Muffin Mix

    1 egg

    ⅔ cup orange juice

    1 tablespoon grated orange peel

Orange Glaze

    ½ cup confectioners' sugar

    2 to 3 teaspoons orange juice

    1 teaspoon grated orange peel

    Quartered orange slices, for
        garnish (optional)

1. Preheat oven to 350°F. Grease and flour 8½×4½×2½-inch loaf pan.

2. For bread, combine muffin mix and contents of topping packet from mix in large bowl. Break up any lumps. Add egg, ⅔ cup orange juice and 1 tablespoon orange peel. Stir until moistened, about 50 strokes. Knead swirl packet from Mix for 10 seconds before opening. Squeeze contents on top of batter. Swirl into batter with knife or spatula, folding from bottom of bowl to get an even swirl. *Do not completely mix in.* Pour into pan.

Bake at 350°F 55 to 60 minutes or until toothpick inserted in center comes out clean. Cool in pan 10 minutes. Loosen loaf from pan. Invert onto cooling rack. Turn right side up. Cool completely.

3. For orange glaze, place confectioners' sugar in small bowl. Add orange juice, 1 teaspoon at a time, stirring until smooth and desired consistency. Stir in 1 teaspoon orange peel. Drizzle over loaf. Garnish with orange slices, if desired.

Makes 1 loaf (12 slices)

Cook's Tip: If glaze becomes too thin, add more confectioners' sugar. If glaze is too thick, add more orange juice.

Orange Cinnamon Swirl Bread

Banana Brunch Coffee Cake

2 ripe, medium DOLE® Bananas

1 package (18.25 ounces) yellow cake mix

1 package (3.4 ounces) instant vanilla pudding mix (4 servings)

4 eggs

½ cup vegetable oil

1 teaspoon vanilla extract

½ cup chopped almonds

⅓ cup packed brown sugar

1 teaspoon ground cinnamon

½ teaspoon ground nutmeg

• Purée bananas in blender (1 cup). Combine bananas, cake mix, pudding mix, eggs, oil and vanilla in large mixing bowl. Mix well and beat at medium speed 8 minutes, scraping side of bowl occasionally.

• Combine almonds, brown sugar, cinnamon and nutmeg. Pour one-half cake batter into greased 3-quart Bundt pan. Sprinkle with almond mixture. Cover with remaining batter. Insert knife in batter and swirl in figure eight patterns through layers. (Be sure not to over mix layers.)

• Bake at 300°F 55 to 60 minutes. Cool in pan on wire rack 10 minutes. Invert onto rack to complete cooling. Dust with powdered sugar when cool, if desired. Garnish with sliced bananas, raspberries and fresh mint, if desired.

Makes 12 servings

Prep Time: 15 minutes
Bake Time: 60 minutes

Cook's Tip: *If you buy bananas tinged with green, let them ripen at room temperature. You can keep fully ripe bananas in the refrigerator for a few days—the skin will darken but the inside will taste delicious.*

Honey-Bran Muffins

1 cup FIBER ONE® cereal

1 cup milk or orange juice

¼ cup vegetable oil

1 egg

1¼ cups GOLD MEDAL® all-purpose flour

¼ cup sugar

¼ cup honey

2 teaspoons baking powder

½ teaspoon salt

1. Heat oven to 400°F. Grease bottoms only of 12 regular-size muffin cups or use paper liners in each muffin cup.

2. Crush cereal.* Stir together cereal and milk in large bowl; let stand 5 minutes. Beat in oil and egg with spoon. Stir in remaining ingredients just until flour is moistened. Divide batter evenly among muffin cups.

3. Bake 20 to 25 minutes or until light brown. Immediately remove from pan.

Makes 12 muffins

*Place cereal in plastic bag or between sheets of waxed paper and crush with rolling pin. Or, crush in blender or food processor.

Prep Time: 15 minutes
Bake Time: 25 minutes

Breakfast Blondies

2 cups (12 ounces) chopped dried fruits, such as mixture of cranberries or blueberries, cherries or strawberries, apricots, dates or raisins

2 cups (8 ounces) shredded JARLSBERG LITE™ cheese

1 (8½-ounce) package corn muffin mix

1 whole egg plus 1 egg white

½ cup fat-free (skim) milk

2 tablespoons cinnamon-sugar mixture

Preheat oven to 400°F.

Combine dried fruit, cheese and corn muffin mix; set aside.

Whisk together eggs and milk in large bowl. Add fruit mixture, stir together and allow to stand 3 minutes. Spoon evenly into nonstick 10×6-inch baking pan or regular baking pan sprayed with nonstick cooking spray. Sprinkle top with cinnamon-sugar.

Bake 25 minutes or until toothpick inserted in center comes out clean. Cut into squares. Serve warm or at room temperature.

Makes 12 blondies

Sausage Pinwheels

2 cups biscuit mix

½ cup milk

¼ cup butter or margarine, melted

1 pound BOB EVANS® Original Recipe Roll Sausage

Combine biscuit mix, milk and butter in large bowl until blended. Refrigerate 30 minutes. Divide dough into two portions. Roll out one portion on floured surface to ⅛-inch-thick rectangle, about 10×7 inches. Spread with half the sausage. Roll up lengthwise into long roll. Repeat with remaining dough and sausage. Place rolls in freezer until hard enough to cut easily. Preheat oven to 400°F. Cut rolls into thin slices. Place on baking sheets. Bake 15 minutes or until golden brown. Serve hot. Refrigerate leftovers.

Makes 48 pinwheels

Note: This recipe may be doubled. Refreeze after slicing. When ready to serve, thaw slices in refrigerator and bake.

Apple Pecan Muffins

½ cup water

1 egg, lightly beaten

¼ cup frozen apple juice concentrate, thawed, undiluted

2 tablespoons butter, melted

2 cups buttermilk baking mix

½ cup chopped pecans

¼ cup sugar

¼ teaspoon ground cinnamon

1. Preheat oven to 400°F. Grease 12 muffin cups.

2. Fit processor with steel blade. Place water, egg, apple juice and butter into work bowl. Process using on/off pulsing action 3 or 4 times to mix. Add baking mix, pecans, sugar and cinnamon; process using on/off pulsing action just until flour is moistened. *Do not overprocess.* Batter should be lumpy.

3. Spoon batter into muffin cups, filling each about ⅔ full. Bake until golden, 12 to 15 minutes. Serve warm.

Makes 1 dozen muffins

Sausage Pinwheels

Creamy Cinnamon Rolls

2 (1-pound) loaves frozen bread
    dough, thawed

⅔ cup (one-half 14-ounce can)
    EAGLE® BRAND Sweetened
    Condensed Milk* (NOT
    evaporated milk), divided

1 cup chopped pecans

2 teaspoons ground cinnamon

1 cup sifted powdered sugar

½ teaspoon vanilla extract

    Additional chopped pecans
    (optional)

*Use remaining Eagle Brand as a dip for fruit. Pour into storage container and store tightly covered in refrigerator for up to 1 week.

1. On lightly floured surface roll each bread dough loaf into 12×9-inch rectangle. Spread ⅓ cup Eagle Brand over dough rectangles. Sprinkle rectangles with 1 cup pecans and cinnamon. Roll up jelly-roll style starting from a short side. Cut each log into 6 slices.

2. Generously grease 13×9-inch baking pan. Place rolls cut sides down in pan. Cover loosely with greased waxed paper and then with plastic wrap. Chill overnight. Cover and chill remaining Eagle Brand.

3. To bake, let pan of rolls stand at room temperature for 30 minutes. Preheat oven to 350°F. Bake 30 to 35 minutes or until golden brown. Cool in pan 5 minutes; loosen edges and remove rolls from pan.

4. Meanwhile for frosting, in small bowl, combine powdered sugar, remaining ⅓ cup Eagle Brand and vanilla. Drizzle frosting on warm rolls. Sprinkle with additional chopped pecans.

Makes 12 rolls

Prep Time: 20 minutes
Bake Time: 30 to 35 minutes
Chill Time: Overnight
Cool Time: 5 minutes

Creamy Cinnamon Roll

Apple Streusel Mini Muffins

1 package (7 ounces) apple cinnamon muffin mix

¼ cup chopped pecans

2 tablespoons brown sugar

1 tablespoon flour

2 teaspoons butter, melted

½ cup shredded peeled apple

1. Preheat oven to 425°F. Coat 18 mini-muffin cups with nonstick cooking spray.

2. Combine pecans, brown sugar, flour and butter in small bowl.

3. Prepare muffin mix according to package directions. Stir in apple. Fill each muffin cup ⅔ full. Sprinkle approximately 1 teaspoon pecan mixture on top of each muffin. Bake 12 to 15 minutes or until golden brown. Cool slightly. Serve warm.

Makes 18 mini muffins

Variation: For regular-size muffins, grease six 2½-inch muffin cups. Prepare topping and batter as directed. Fill muffin cups ⅔ full of batter. Sprinkle approximately 1 tablespoon pecan mixture on each muffin. Bake 18 to 20 minutes or until golden brown. Makes 6 regular muffins.

Pineapple Crunch Coffee Cake

1¾ cups reduced-fat baking mix

½ cup wheat germ

½ cup plus 2 tablespoons fat-free (skim) milk

½ cup reduced-fat sour cream

¼ cup granulated sugar

1 egg

1 teaspoon vanilla

2 cans (8 ounces each) crushed pineapple in unsweetened pineapple juice, drained

⅓ cup packed dark brown sugar

⅓ cup uncooked old-fashioned or quick oats

Preheat oven 350°F. Coat 8-inch square baking dish with nonstick cooking spray.

Combine baking mix, wheat germ, milk, sour cream, granulated sugar, egg and vanilla in medium bowl. Stir to blend thoroughly. (Batter will be lumpy.) Spread batter in baking dish. Spoon pineapple evenly over batter. Sprinkle brown sugar and oats over pineapple.

Bake 30 minutes or until toothpick inserted in center comes out clean.

Makes 9 servings

Peanut Butter Chip & Banana Mini Muffins

2 cups all-purpose biscuit baking mix

¼ cup sugar

2 tablespoons butter or margarine, softened

1 egg

1 cup mashed very ripe bananas (2 to 3 medium)

1 cup REESE'S® Peanut Butter Chips

Quick Glaze (recipe follows, optional)

1. Heat oven to 400°F. Grease small muffin cups (1¾ inches in diameter).

2. Stir together baking mix, sugar, butter and egg in medium bowl; with fork, beat vigorously for 30 seconds. Stir in bananas and peanut butter chips. Fill muffin cups ⅔ full with batter.

3. Bake 12 to 15 minutes or until golden brown. Meanwhile, prepare Quick Glaze, if desired. Immediately remove muffins from pan; dip tops of warm muffins into glaze. Serve warm.

Makes about 4 dozen small muffins

Quick Glaze

1½ cups powdered sugar

2 tablespoons water

Stir together powdered sugar and water in small bowl until smooth and of desired consistency. Add additional water, ½ teaspoon at a time, if needed.

Makes about 1 cup

Cook's Tip: *Remove muffins from their cups immediately after baking and cool them on a wire rack. They are best served warm. Stored in an airtight food storage bag, muffins will stay fresh for several days.*

Pumpkin Bread

1 package (about 18 ounces) yellow cake mix

1 can (16 ounces) solid pack pumpkin

4 eggs

⅓ cup GRANDMA'S® Molasses

1 teaspoon cinnamon

1 teaspoon nutmeg

⅓ cup nuts, chopped (optional)

⅓ cup raisins (optional)

Preheat oven to 350°F. Grease two 9×5-inch loaf pans.

Combine all ingredients in a large bowl and mix well. Beat at medium speed 2 minutes. Pour into prepared pans. Bake 60 minutes or until toothpick inserted into center comes out clean.

Makes 2 loaves

Hint: Serve with cream cheese or preserves, or top with cream cheese frosting or ice cream.

Bacon Brunch Buns

1 loaf (1 pound) frozen bread dough

¼ cup unsalted butter or margarine, melted

2 tablespoons (½ package) HIDDEN VALLEY® Original Ranch® with Bacon salad dressing mix

1 cup (4 ounces) shredded Cheddar cheese

2 egg yolks

1½ tablespoons cold water

3 tablespoons sesame seeds

Thaw bread dough following package directions. Preheat oven to 375°F. On floured board, roll dough into rectangle about 18×7 inches. In small bowl, whisk together butter and salad dressing mix. Spread mixture on dough; sprinkle with cheese. Roll up tightly, jelly-roll style, pinching seam to seal. Cut into 16 slices. Place slices, cut side down, on greased jelly-roll pan. Cover with plastic wrap and let rise until doubled in bulk, about 1 hour. In small bowl, beat egg yolks and water; brush mixture over buns. Sprinkle with sesame seeds. Bake until golden brown, 25 to 30 minutes. Serve warm.

Makes 16 buns

Pumpkin Bread

Blueberry Orange Muffins

1 package DUNCAN HINES®
Bakery-Style Wild Maine
Blueberry Muffin Mix

½ cup orange juice

2 egg whites

1 teaspoon grated orange peel

1. Preheat oven to 400°F. Grease 2½-inch muffin cups (or use paper liners).

2. Rinse blueberries from Mix with cold water and drain.

3. Empty muffin mix into large bowl. Break up any lumps. Add orange juice, egg whites and orange peel. Stir until moistened, about 50 strokes. Fold blueberries gently into batter.

4. For large muffins, fill cups two-thirds full. Bake at 400°F 18 to 21 minutes or until toothpick inserted into centers comes out clean. (For medium muffins, fill cups half full. Bake at 400°F 16 to 19 minutes or until toothpick inserted into centers comes out clean.) Cool in pan 5 to 10 minutes. Carefully loosen muffins from pan. Remove to cooling racks. Serve warm or cool completely.

Makes 8 large or 12 medium muffins

Butterscotch Crescents

½ cup HERSHEY'S Butterscotch Chips

¼ cup MOUNDS® Sweetened Coconut Flakes

2 tablespoons finely chopped nuts

1 can (8 ounces) refrigerated quick crescent dinner rolls

Powdered sugar

1. Heat oven to 375°F.

2. Stir together butterscotch chips, coconut and nuts in small bowl. Unroll crescent roll dough to form eight triangles. Lightly sprinkle 1 heaping tablespoon butterscotch mixture on top of each; gently press into dough. Starting at short side of each triangle, roll dough to opposite point. Place rolls, point side down, on ungreased cookie sheet; curve into crescent shapes.

3. Bake 10 to 12 minutes or until golden brown. Sprinkle with powdered sugar. Serve warm.   *Makes 8 crescents*

Blueberry Orange Muffins

Streusel Coffeecake

32 CHIPS AHOY!® Chocolate Chip Cookies, divided

1 (18- to 18.5-ounce) package yellow or white cake mix

½ cup BREAKSTONE'S® or KNUDSEN® Sour Cream

½ cup PLANTERS® Pecans, chopped

½ cup BAKER'S® ANGEL FLAKE® Coconut

¼ cup packed brown sugar

1 teaspoon ground cinnamon

⅓ cup margarine or butter, melted

Powdered sugar glaze (optional)

1. Coarsely chop 20 cookies; finely crush remaining 12 cookies. Set aside.

2. Prepare cake mix batter according to package directions; blend in sour cream. Stir in chopped cookies. Pour batter into greased and floured 13×9-inch baking pan.

3. Mix cookie crumbs, pecans, coconut, brown sugar and cinnamon; stir in margarine or butter. Sprinkle over cake batter.

4. Bake at 350°F for 40 minutes or until toothpick inserted in center of cake comes out clean. Cool completely. Drizzle with powdered sugar glaze if desired. Cut into squares to serve. *Makes 24 servings*

Preparation Time: 25 minutes
Cook Time: 40 minutes
Cooling Time: 2 hours
Total Time: 3 hours and 5 minutes

Breakfast Blossoms

1 (12-ounce) can buttermilk biscuits (10 biscuits)

¾ cup SMUCKER'S® Strawberry Preserves

¼ teaspoon ground cinnamon

¼ teaspoon ground nutmeg

Grease ten 2½- or 3-inch muffin cups. Separate dough into 10 biscuits. Separate each biscuit into 3 even sections or leaves. Stand 3 sections evenly around side and bottom of cup, overlapping slightly. Press dough edges firmly together.

Combine preserves, cinnamon and nutmeg; place tablespoonful in center of each cup.

Bake at 375°F for 10 to 12 minutes or until lightly browned. Cool slightly before removing from pan. Serve warm.
Makes 10 rolls

Streusel Coffeecake

Gooey Caramel and Chocolate Pecan Rolls

2 loaves (1 pound each) frozen white bread dough

1 jar (12 ounces) caramel ice cream topping

⅔ cup coarsely chopped pecans

1 cup semisweet chocolate chips, divided

4 tablespoons butter, divided

1. Thaw bread dough according to package directions.

2. Preheat oven to 375°F. Divide caramel topping evenly between two 9-inch round cake pans; spread in thin layer. Sprinkle pecans evenly over caramel.

3. Microwave ⅔ cup chocolate chips and 2 tablespoons butter in medium microwavable bowl at HIGH for 30 seconds; stir. Microwave for 20 second intervals, if necessary, stirring until smooth; set aside.

4. On lightly floured surface, roll one loaf bread dough into 12×8-inch rectangle. Spread half chocolate mixture over dough. Beginning from the long side, roll up jelly-roll style to form 12-inch log, pinching seam to seal. Slice into 12 rolls; arrange cut side down in 1 prepared pan. Repeat with remaining dough and chocolate mixture.

5. Cover; let rise in warm place until nearly doubled, about 1 hour. Uncover; bake 20 to 25 minutes. Immediately invert onto serving plates.

6. Melt remaining ⅓ cup chocolate chips and 2 tablespoons butter in microwave as directed in step 3. Drizzle over warm rolls. *Makes 24 rolls*

Gooey Caramel and Chocolate Pecan Rolls

Cinnamon Chip Filled Crescents

2 cans (8 ounces each) refrigerated quick crescent dinner rolls

2 tablespoons butter or margarine, melted

1⅔ cups (10-ounce package) HERSHEY₅S Cinnamon Chips, divided

Cinnamon Chips Drizzle (recipe follows)

1. Heat oven to 375°F. Unroll dough; separate into 16 triangles.

2. Spread melted butter on each triangle. Sprinkle 1 cup cinnamon chips evenly over triangles; gently press chips into dough. Roll from shortest side of triangle to opposite point. Place, point side down, on ungreased cookie sheet; curve into crescent shape.

3. Bake 8 to 10 minutes or until golden brown. Drizzle with Cinnamon Chips Drizzle. *Makes 16 crescents*

Cinnamon Chips Drizzle: Place remaining ⅔ cup chips and 1½ teaspoons shortening (do not use butter, margarine, spread or oil) in small microwave-safe bowl. Microwave at HIGH 1 minute; stir until melted.

Breakfast Pizza

1 can (10 ounces) refrigerated pizza crust

1 package (7 ounces) prebrowned fully cooked sausage patties, thawed

3 eggs

½ cup milk

1 teaspoon dried Italian seasoning

2 cups (8 ounces) shredded pizza-style cheese

Salt and pepper

1. Preheat oven to 425°F. For crust, unroll pizza dough and pat onto bottom and up side of greased 12-inch pizza pan. Bake 5 minutes or until set, but not browned.

2. While crust is baking, cut sausages into ½-inch pieces. Whisk together eggs, milk and Italian seasoning in medium bowl until well blended. Season to taste with salt and pepper.

3. Spoon sausages over crust; sprinkle with cheese. Carefully pour egg mixture over sausage and cheese. Bake 15 to 20 minutes or until eggs are set and crust is golden. *Makes 6 servings*

Tip: For a special touch, serve this pizza with your favorite salsa.

Spring Break Blueberry Coffeecake

Topping

½ cup flaked coconut

¼ cup firmly packed brown sugar

2 tablespoons butter or margarine, softened

1 tablespoon all-purpose flour

Cake

1 package DUNCAN HINES® Bakery-Style Wild Maine Blueberry Muffin Mix

1 can (8 ounces) crushed pineapple with juice, undrained

1 egg

¼ cup water

1. Preheat oven to 350°F. Grease 9-inch square pan.

2. For topping, combine coconut, brown sugar, butter and flour in small bowl. Mix with fork until well blended. Set aside.

3. Rinse blueberries from Mix with cold water and drain.

4. For cake, place muffin mix in medium bowl. Break up any lumps. Add pineapple with juice, egg and water. Stir until moistened, about 50 strokes. Fold in blueberries. Spread in pan. Sprinkle reserved topping over batter. Bake at 350°F for 30 to 35 minutes or until toothpick inserted in center comes out clean. Serve warm or cool completely.

Makes 9 servings

Cook's Tip: *To keep blueberries from discoloring the batter, drain them on paper towels after rinsing.*

Cheddar and Apple Muffins

2 cups buttermilk baking mix

½ to 1 teaspoon ground red pepper

½ teaspoon salt

⅔ cup milk

1 egg, lightly beaten

1 medium apple, peeled, cored and grated

1 cup (4 ounces) shredded sharp Cheddar cheese

1. Preheat the oven to 375°F. Spray 12 (2½-inch) muffin cups with nonstick cooking spray.

2. Combine baking mix, red pepper and salt in large bowl. Add milk and egg; mix until just moistened. *Do not overmix.* Fold in apple and cheese.

3. Spoon batter into muffin cups until three-fourths full. Bake 20 to 25 minutes or until golden brown. Cool 5 minutes in pan. Loosen sides of muffins with knife; remove from pan to wire rack. Serve warm.   *Makes 1 dozen muffins*

Cran-Lemon Coffee Cake

1 package (about 18 ounces) yellow cake mix with pudding in the mix

1 cup water

3 eggs

⅓ cup butter, melted and cooled

¼ cup fresh lemon juice

1 tablespoon grated lemon peel

1½ cups coarsely chopped cranberries

Preheat oven to 350°F. Grease and flour 12-inch tube pan. Beat cake mix, water, eggs, butter, lemon juice and lemon peel in large bowl with electric mixer on low speed 2 minutes. Fold in cranberries. Spread batter evenly in prepared pan.

Bake about 55 minutes or until wooden pick inserted 1-inch from edge comes out clean. Cool on wire rack 10 minutes. Remove from pan; cool on wire rack. Coffee cake may be served warm or at room temperature.   *Makes 12 servings*

Cheddar and Apple Muffins

Cinnamon Honey Buns

¼ cup butter or margarine, softened
  and divided

½ cup honey, divided

¼ cup chopped toasted nuts

2 teaspoons ground cinnamon

1 loaf (1 pound) frozen bread dough,
  thawed

⅔ cup raisins

Grease 12 muffin cups with 1 tablespoon butter. To prepare honey-nut topping, mix together 1 tablespoon butter, ¼ cup honey and chopped nuts. Place 1 teaspoon topping in each muffin cup. To prepare filling, mix together remaining 2 tablespoons butter, remaining ¼ cup honey and cinnamon. Roll out bread dough onto floured surface into 18×8-inch rectangle. Spread filling evenly over dough. Sprinkle with raisins. Starting with long side, roll dough into log. Cut log into 12 slices. Place 1 slice, cut side up, into each prepared muffin cup. Set muffin pan in warm place; let dough rise 30 minutes. Place muffin pan on foil-lined baking sheet. Bake at 375°F 20 minutes or until buns are golden brown. Cool in pan 5 minutes. Invert muffin pan to remove buns.   *Makes 12 buns*

Favorite recipe from **National Honey Board**

Hearty Banana Carrot Muffins

2 ripe, medium DOLE® Bananas

1 package (14 ounces) oat bran
  muffin mix

¾ teaspoon ground ginger

1 medium DOLE® Carrot, shredded
  (½ cup)

⅓ cup light molasses

⅓ cup DOLE® Seedless or Golden
  Raisins

¼ cup chopped almonds

• Mash bananas with fork (1 cup).

• Combine muffin mix and ginger in large bowl. Add carrot, molasses, raisins and bananas. Stir just until moistened.

• Spoon batter into paper-lined muffin cups. Sprinkle tops with almonds.

• Bake at 425°F 12 to 14 minutes until browned.   *Makes 12 muffins*

Prep Time: 20 minutes
Bake Time: 14 minutes

Cinnamon Honey Buns

Newton Muffins

1¾ cups all-purpose flour

¼ cup sugar

1 tablespoon baking powder

⅓ cup margarine or butter, melted

1 egg, slightly beaten

¾ cup apple juice

10 Fat Free FIG or APPLE NEWTONS® Fruit Chewy Cookies, coarsely chopped

1. Mix flour, sugar and baking powder in medium bowl. Stir in margarine or butter, egg and apple juice just until blended. (Batter will be lumpy.) Stir in cookie pieces. Fill 12 greased 2½-inch muffin-pan cups.

2. Bake at 400°F for 15 to 20 minutes or until toothpick inserted into centers comes out clean. Serve warm or cold.

Makes 1 dozen muffins

Apricot-Filled Blueberry Biscuits

1 package (12 ounces) frozen blueberries, unthawed *or* 2½ cups fresh blueberries

2¼ cups all-purpose baking mix

⅔ cup milk

2 tablespoons sugar

1 teaspoon ground cinnamon

½ cup apricot jam

Preheat oven to 450°F. Reserve ½ cup blueberries for garnish. In large bowl combine baking mix, milk, sugar, cinnamon and remaining 2 cups blueberries. Stir just until soft dough forms. Turn dough onto surface dusted with baking mix; knead 5 times. Roll ½-inch thick; cut dough with 3-inch heart or other shaped cookie cutter. Place on ungreased cookie sheet. Gently reroll and cut out scraps; place on cookie sheet. Bake until golden brown, 8 to 10 minutes. To serve, slice biscuits horizontally in half. Spread apricot jam on bottom halves; cover with tops. Serve with reserved blueberries and whipped cream, if desired.

Makes 8 servings

*Favorite recipe from **North American Blueberry Council***

Colorful Streusel Coffee Cake

¾ cup (1½ sticks) butter or margarine, divided

1 cup granulated sugar

2 large eggs

1 teaspoon vanilla extract

2½ cups all-purpose flour, divided

1 teaspoon baking powder

1¾ cups "M&M's"® Chocolate Mini Baking Bits, divided

4 KUDOS® Milk Chocolate Granola Bars Peanut Butter, chopped

½ cup firmly packed light brown sugar

Preheat oven to 350°F. Grease 9-inch springform pan. In large bowl cream ½ cup butter and granulated sugar until light and fluffy; beat in eggs and vanilla. In medium bowl combine 2 cups flour and baking powder; blend into creamed mixture. *Do not overmix.* Stir in ¾ cup "M&M's"® Chocolate Mini Baking Bits. Spread batter into prepared pan. In separate bowl combine chopped KUDOS®, remaining ½ cup flour, brown sugar and ¼ cup melted butter to create streusel. Add remaining 1 cup "M&M's"® Chocolate Mini Baking Bits and toss to mix. Sprinkle streusel evenly over batter. Bake 35 to 40 minutes or until golden and firm to the touch. Cool completely before removing side of pan. Store in tightly covered container. *Makes 12 slices*

Cook's Tip: *Stir quick bread batter lightly—just until the dry ingredients are moistened. Don't worry about small lumps. Overmixing the batter results in a dense, tough bread.*

Fast Pesto Focaccia (page 54)

Savory Breads

❧ ❧ ❧

Searching for a savory muffin or scone to accompany a luncheon soup or salad? Looking for a yummy biscuit or specialty bread for a family feast? This collection of breads, includes a variety of tasty recipes such as biscuits, bread sticks, corn bread, focaccia and stromboli.

Start with a convenient mix and make it special by adding herbs, spices or cheese. Try Savory Pull Apart Biscuits (page 68), Biscuit Bread Italiano (page 46) or Cheddar Pepper Muffins (page 72) and score big points at every meal.

Ham and Cheese Corn Muffins

1 package (about 8 ounces) corn muffin mix

½ cup chopped deli ham

½ cup (2 ounces) shredded Swiss cheese

⅓ cup reduced-fat (2%) milk

1 egg

1 tablespoon Dijon mustard

1. Preheat oven to 400°F. Combine muffin mix, ham and cheese in medium bowl.

2. Combine milk, egg and mustard in 1-cup glass measure. Stir milk mixture into dry ingredients; mix just until moistened.

3. Fill 9 paper cup-lined 2¾-inch muffin cups two-thirds full with batter.

4. Bake 18 to 20 minutes or until light golden brown. Remove muffin pan to cooling rack. Let stand 5 minutes. Serve warm.   *Makes 9 muffins*

Serving Suggestion: For added flavor, serve Ham and Cheese Corn Muffins with honey-flavored butter. To prepare, stir together equal amounts of honey and softened butter.

Biscuit Bread Italiano

1½ cups buttermilk

1 egg

3 cups biscuit mix

1 cup (4 ounces) grated Cheddar cheese

1 can (2½ ounces) sliced ripe olives, drained

1 package (1½ ounces) LAWRY'S® Original-Style Spaghetti Sauce Spices & Seasonings

In large bowl, combine buttermilk and egg. Stir in remaining ingredients; mix well. Spoon into greased 9×5×2-inch loaf pan. Bake in 350°F oven 45 to 50 minutes. Turn out on rack to cool.

Makes 12 servings

Serving Suggestion: Serve with pasta dishes, it makes a nice change from garlic bread.

Hint: For a hearty snack or picnic fare, add 1½ cups chopped salami or pepperoni to the dough.

Hint: This bread can also be made into drop biscuits; reduce baking time to 30 minutes or until toothpick comes out clean.

Ham and Cheese Corn Muffins

Crispy Ranch Breadsticks

2 tablespoons dry ranch party dip mix
2 tablespoons sour cream
1 package (10 ounces) refrigerated pizza dough
Butter, melted

1. Preheat oven to 400°F. Grease baking sheets or line with parchment paper. Combine dip mix and sour cream in small bowl; set aside.

2. Unroll pizza dough on lightly floured work surface. Shape dough into 16×10-inch rectangle. Brush with melted butter. Spread dip mixture evenly over top of dough; cut into 24 (10-inch) strips. Shape into desired shapes.

3. Place breadsticks ½ inch apart on prepared baking sheets. Bake 10 minutes or until golden brown. Serve immediately or place on wire rack to cool.

Makes 24 breadsticks

Crispy Spiced Nut Breadsticks: Place 1 cup chopped pecans and 1 tablespoon vegetable oil in plastic bag; toss to coat. combine ¼ teaspoon chili powder, ¼ teaspoon ground cumin, ¼ teaspoon curry powder, ⅛ teaspoon ground cinnamon and dash of ground red pepper in small bowl. Add to nuts; toss to coat. Place nuts in small pan over medium heat and stir constantly until nuts are lightly toasted. Sprinkle nut mixture with 1 teaspoon garlic salt; cool to room temperature. Instead of spreading dough with sour cream mixture, sprinkle ½ cup very finely chopped spiced nuts over dough (store remaining nuts in tightly covered container). Cut into 24 (10-inch) strips). Shape into desired shapes. Bake as directed.

Cook's Tip: The type of surface of a baking sheet determines its browning characteristics. Shiny finishes promote even browning. Dark metal baking sheets absorb more heat and cause food to brown quickly. Nonstick finishes minimize sticking and make cleanup easier.

Top to Bottom:
Crispy Spiced Nut Breadsticks
and Crispy Ranch Breadsticks

Greek Spinach-Cheese Rolls

1 loaf (1 pound) frozen bread dough

1 package (10 ounces) frozen chopped spinach, thawed and squeezed dry

¾ cup (3 ounces) crumbled feta cheese

½ cup (2 ounces) shredded reduced-fat Monterey Jack cheese

4 green onions, thinly sliced

1 teaspoon dried dill weed

½ teaspoon garlic powder

½ teaspoon black pepper

1. Thaw bread dough according to package directions. Spray 15 muffin cups with nonstick cooking spray; set aside. Roll out dough on lightly floured surface to 15×9-inch rectangle. (If dough is springy and difficult to roll, cover with plastic wrap and let rest 5 minutes to relax.) Position dough so long edge runs parallel to edge of work surface.

2. Combine spinach, cheeses, green onions, dill weed, garlic powder and pepper in large bowl; mix well.

3. Sprinkle spinach mixture evenly over dough to within 1 inch of long edges. Starting at long edge, roll up snugly, pinching seam closed. Place seam side down; cut roll with serrated knife into 1-inch-wide slices. Place slices cut sides up in prepared muffin cups. Cover with plastic wrap; let stand 30 minutes in warm place until rolls are slightly puffy.

4. Preheat oven to 375°F. Bake 20 to 25 minutes or until golden. Serve warm or at room temperature. Rolls can be stored in refrigerator in airtight container up to 2 days. *Makes 15 rolls*

Greek Spinach-Cheese Rolls

Savory Rosemary Quick Bread

1¾ cups reduced-fat buttermilk baking mix

1 cup (4 ounces) shredded Cheddar cheese, divided

¾ cup skim milk

2 egg whites

1⅓ cups *French's® Taste Toppers™* French Fried Onions, divided

1 tablespoon sugar

1 tablespoon butter, melted

2 teaspoons chopped fresh rosemary *or* ½ teaspoon dried rosemary

Preheat oven to 375°F. Line 9-inch square baking pan with foil; spray with nonstick cooking spray.

Combine baking mix, ½ cup cheese, milk, egg whites, ⅔ cup **Taste Toppers**, sugar, butter and rosemary in large bowl; stir just until moistened. *Do not overmix.* Spread into prepared pan.

Bake 20 minutes or until toothpick inserted into center comes out clean. Sprinkle with remaining cheese and ⅔ cup **Taste Toppers**. Bake 1 minute or until cheese is melted and **Taste Toppers** are golden. Remove to wire rack; cool 5 minutes. Remove foil. Cut into squares. Serve warm or cool.   *Makes 8 servings*

Prep Time: 15 minutes
Cook Time: 21 minutes

Tunnel of Cheese Muffins

2 cups biscuit mix

5 slices bacon, crisply cooked and crumbled

¾ cup milk

1 egg, beaten

12 (½-inch) cubes Swiss cheese

Stir together biscuit mix and bacon in medium bowl. Add milk and egg, stirring just to mix. Spoon half of batter into 12 buttered muffin pan cups. Press one cheese cube in each cup. Top with remaining batter, covering cheese completely. Bake in preheated 400°F oven 25 minutes or until golden. Serve hot.

Makes 12 muffins

Favorite recipe from **Wisconsin Milk Marketing Board**

Sesame Italian Bread Sticks

¼ cup grated Parmesan cheese

3 tablespoons sesame seeds

2 teaspoons Italian seasoning

1 teaspoon kosher salt (optional)

12 frozen bread dough dinner rolls, thawed

¼ cup butter, melted

1. Preheat oven to 425°F. Spray large baking sheet with nonstick cooking spray.

2. In small bowl, combine cheese, sesame seeds and Italian seasoning and salt, if desired. Spread out on plate.

3. On lightly floured surface, roll each bread piece into a rope, about 8 inches long and ½ inch thick. Place on baking sheet and brush tops and sides with butter. Roll each buttered rope in seasoning, pressing seasoning into sides. Return ropes to baking sheet, placing 2 inches apart. Twist each rope 3 times pressing both ends of rope down on baking sheet. Bake 10 to 12 minutes, or until golden brown.

Makes 12 bread sticks

Mexican Corn Bread

¼ pound VELVEETA® Mexican Pasteurized Process Cheese Spread with Jalapeño Peppers, cubed

2 tablespoons milk

1 egg, beaten

1 (8½-ounce) package corn muffin mix

• Preheat oven to 350°F.

• Stir together process cheese spread and milk in saucepan over low heat until process cheese spread is melted. Add with egg to muffin mix, mixing just until moistened. Pour into greased 8-inch square pan.

• Bake 20 minutes.

Makes 6 to 8 servings

Variation: Substitute VELVEETA® Pasteurized Prepared Cheese Product for VELVEETA® Pasteurized Process Cheese Spread with Jalapeño Peppers.

Prep Time: 10 minutes
Cooking Time: 20 minutes

Southern Biscuit Muffins

2½ cups all-purpose flour

¼ cup sugar

1½ tablespoons baking powder

¾ cup cold butter

1 cup cold milk

Preheat oven to 400°F. Grease 12 (2½-inch) muffin cups. (These muffins brown better on the side and bottom when baked without paper liners.)

Combine flour, sugar and baking powder in large bowl. Cut in butter with pastry blender until mixture resembles coarse crumbs. Stir in milk just until flour mixture is moistened. Spoon evenly into prepared muffin cups.

Bake 20 minutes or until golden. Remove from pan. Cool on wire rack.

Makes 12 muffins

Cook's Tip: *These muffins taste like baking powder biscuits and are very quick and easy to make. Serve them with jelly, jam or honey.*

Fast Pesto Focaccia

1 can (10 ounces) pizza crust dough

2 tablespoons prepared pesto

4 sun-dried tomatoes packed in oil, drained

1. Preheat oven to 425°F. Lightly grease 8×8-inch pan. Unroll pizza dough; fold in half and pat into pan.

2. Spread pesto evenly over dough. Chop tomatoes or snip with kitchen scissors; sprinkle over pesto. Press tomatoes into dough. Make indentations in dough every 2 inches using wooden spoon handle.

3. Bake 10 to 12 minutes or until golden brown. Cut into squares and serve warm or at room temperature.

Makes 16 squares

Prep and Cook Time: 20 minutes

Southern Biscuit Muffin

Ham Stromboli

1 can (10 ounces) refrigerated pizza
  dough
1 tablespoon prepared mustard
½ pound thinly sliced deli ham
1 package (3½ ounces) sliced
  pepperoni
1 teaspoon dried Italian seasoning
2 cups (8 ounces) shredded part-skim
  mozzarella cheese

1. Preheat oven to 425°F. Unroll pizza
dough on greased jelly-roll pan; pat dough
into 12-inch square. Spread mustard over
dough to within ½ inch of edges. Layer
ham slices down center 6 inches of dough,
leaving 3-inch border on either side and
½-inch border at top and bottom. Top
ham with pepperoni slices. Sprinkle with
Italian seasonings and cheese.

2. Fold sides of dough over filling, pinching
center seam and each end to seal. Bake
15 to 20 minutes or until lightly browned.

Makes 6 servings

Prep & Cook Time: 22 minutes

Corn Bread Wedges

1 package corn bread mix
1 cup (4 ounces) finely grated sharp
  Cheddar cheese
¼ cup butter or margarine, softened
¼ teaspoon Worcestershire sauce
¼ teaspoon TABASCO® brand
  Pepper Sauce
1 egg white, stiffly beaten
  Paprika

Prepare corn bread according to package
directions and bake in 9-inch pie plate.
Meanwhile, combine cheese, butter,
Worcestershire sauce and TABASCO®
Sauce; beat until smooth. Fold in egg
white.

Cut cornbread into 8 wedges; spread
evenly with cheese mixture. Sprinkle with
paprika. Set oven to broil; broil about
4 minutes or until cheese topping melts
and becomes puffy and golden brown.

Makes 8 servings

Ham Stromboli

Southwestern Sausage Drop Biscuits

1 pound BOB EVANS® Zesty Hot
    Roll Sausage

3 cups all-purpose (biscuit) baking
    mix

1¼ cups (5 ounces) shredded sharp
    Cheddar cheese

1 cup seeded, diced fresh or drained
    canned tomatoes

1 cup chopped green onions

1 cup milk

¼ teaspoon paprika

    Dash cayenne pepper

    Butter (optional)

Preheat oven to 350°F. Crumble and cook
sausage in medium skillet until browned.
Drain on paper towels. Combine sausage
and remaining ingredients except butter in
large bowl; mix well. Shape dough into
2-inch balls; place on ungreased baking
sheet. Bake 12 minutes or until golden.
Serve hot with butter, if desired.
Refrigerate leftovers.

Makes about 2 dozen small biscuits

Quick Corn Bread with Chilies 'n' Cheese

1 package (12 to 16 ounces) corn
    bread or corn muffin mix

1 cup (4 ounces) shredded Monterey
    Jack cheese, divided

1 can (4 ounces) chopped green
    chilies, drained

1 envelope LIPTON® RECIPE
    SECRETS® Vegetable Soup Mix

Prepare corn bread mix according to
package directions; stir in ½ cup cheese,
chilies and vegetable soup mix. Pour
batter into lightly greased 8-inch baking
pan; bake as directed. While warm, top
with remaining ½ cup cheese. Cool
completely on wire rack. To serve, cut
into squares.   *Makes 16 servings*

Cheesy Focaccia

3 cups buttermilk baking mix

1 package (8 ounces) VELVEETA®
   Mild Cheddar Shredded
   Pasteurized Process Cheese Food

1 teaspoon dried basil leaves, crushed

¼ teaspoon dried oregano leaves,
   crushed

1 cup milk

6 tablespoons olive oil, divided

Preheat oven to 375°F.

Stir together baking mix, process cheese food and seasonings. Add milk; mix well.

Coat bottom of 15×10×1-inch jelly roll pan with 2 tablespoons olive oil. Pat dough evenly into pan with floured hands. Make indentations with fingertips at 1-inch intervals over entire surface of dough. Brush remaining olive oil evenly over dough.

Bake 20 minutes or until golden brown. Cut into rectangles; serve warm.

Makes approximately 3 dozen

Prep Time: 10 minutes
Cook Time: 20 minutes

Spicy Onion Bread

2 tablespoons instant minced onion

⅓ cup water

1½ cups biscuit mix

1 egg, slightly beaten

½ cup milk

½ teaspoon TABASCO® brand
   Pepper Sauce

2 tablespoons butter, melted

½ teaspoon caraway seeds (optional)

Preheat oven to 400°F. Soak instant minced onion in water 5 minutes. Combine biscuit mix, egg, milk and TABASCO® Sauce in large bowl and stir until blended. Stir in onion. Turn into greased 8-inch pie plate. Brush with melted butter. Sprinkle with caraway seeds. Bake 20 to 25 minutes or until golden brown. *Makes 8 servings*

Broccoli & Cheddar Muffins

3 cups buttermilk baking and
    pancake mix

2 eggs, lightly beaten

⅔ cup milk

1 teaspoon dried basil

1 cup (4 ounces) shredded Cheddar
    cheese

1 box (10 ounces) BIRDS EYE®
    frozen Chopped Broccoli, thawed
    and drained

• Preheat oven to 350°F. Combine baking mix, eggs, milk and basil. Mix until moistened. (Do not overmix.)

• Add cheese and broccoli; stir just to combine. Add salt and pepper to taste.

• Spray 12 muffin cups with nonstick cooking spray. Pour batter into muffin cups. Bake 25 to 30 minutes or until golden brown.

• Cool 5 minutes in pan. Loosen sides of muffins with knife; remove from pan and serve warm.

Makes 1 dozen large muffins

Southwestern Corn Muffins: Prepare 1 box corn muffin mix according to package directions; add ⅔ cup BIRDS EYE® frozen Corn and 1 teaspoon chili powder to batter. Mix well; bake according to package directions.

Prep Time: 5 to 10 minutes
Bake Time: 25 to 30 minutes

Cook's Tip: *Don't stir the batter too much—overmixing will make the muffins tough. (There should still be lumps in the batter; these will disappear during baking.)*

Broccoli & Cheddar Muffins

Country Biscuits

2 cups all-purpose flour
1 tablespoon baking powder
1 teaspoon salt
⅓ CRISCO® Stick or ⅓ cup
    CRISCO® all-vegetable
    shortening
¾ cup milk

1. Heat oven to 425°F. Combine flour, baking powder and salt in medium bowl. Cut in shortening using pastry blender (or two knives) to form coarse crumbs. Add milk. Mix with fork until dry mixture is moistened. Form dough into a ball.

2. Transfer dough to lightly floured surface. Knead gently 8 to 10 times. Roll out dough to ½-inch thickness. Cut with floured 2-inch round cutter. Place on ungreased baking sheet.

3. Bake at 425°F for 12 to 14 minutes or until golden. *Do not overbake.*

Makes 12 to 16 biscuits

Krispie Cheese Twists

½ cup grated Parmesan cheese
¾ teaspoon LAWRY'S® Seasoned
    Pepper
½ teaspoon LAWRY'S® Garlic Powder
    with Parsley
1 package (17¼ ounces) frozen puff
    pastry, thawed
1 egg white, lightly beaten

In small bowl, combine Parmesan cheese, Seasoned Pepper and Garlic Powder with Parsley. Unfold pastry sheets onto cutting board. Brush pastry lightly with egg white; sprinkle each sheet with ¼ cheese mixture. Lightly press into pastry, turn over; repeat. Cut into 1-inch strips; twist. Place on greased cookie sheet and bake in 350°F oven 15 minutes or until golden brown. *Makes 2 dozen twists*

Serving Suggestion: Great as an appetizer too!

Hint: To make 1 dozen, use one of the two packaged pastry sheets and reduce other ingredients by half.

Country Biscuits

Chinese Flatbreads

1 pound frozen white bread dough, thawed

Sesame oil

1½ to 2 teaspoons LAWRY'S® Garlic Salt

2 green onions, thinly sliced

2 teaspoons sesame seeds

On well-floured work surface, roll dough into rectangle, about 15×6 inches. Brush lightly with sesame oil. Sprinkle with Garlic Salt and green onions. Starting from long edge, roll dough up jelly-roll fashion. With serrated knife, cut dough into 1-inch slices and flatten each slice slightly by pressing with heel of hand. Arrange slices on baking sheet sprayed with nonstick cooking spray. Brush tops lightly with sesame oil and sprinkle with sesame seeds. Cover and let rise in warm place 30 minutes. Bake in 375°F oven 15 minutes or until golden.

Makes 4 servings

Hint: Breads can be baked ahead and frozen. Reheat 5 minutes in 350°F oven.

Tip: Serve as an accompaniment to oriental chicken salad or as an appetizer for company.

Oniony Corn Muffins

1 package (12 ounces) corn muffin mix

⅔ cup milk

1 egg

1 can (7 ounces) whole kernel corn, drained

1⅓ cups *French's® Taste Toppers*™ French Fried Onions, slightly crushed

Preheat oven to 400°F. Grease 12-cup muffin pan. Prepare corn muffin mix according to package directions using milk and egg. Stir in corn and *Taste Toppers*. Do not overmix.

Fill muffin cups using ¼ cup batter for each cup. Bake 15 minutes or until toothpick inserted into centers comes out clean. Cool in pan on wire rack 5 minutes. Loosen muffins from pan; remove and serve warm.

Makes 12 servings

Prep Time: 15 minutes
Bake Time: 15 minutes

Chinese Flatbreads

Last Minute Tomato Swirl Bread

2 loaves (16 ounces each) frozen bread dough, thawed according to package directions

2 large cloves garlic, pressed

1 jar (8 ounces) SONOMA® Marinated Tomatoes, drained and blotted with paper towels

3 tablespoons grated Parmesan cheese

2 tablespoons dried basil leaves

Cornmeal for baking sheets

1 egg, beaten

Preheat oven to 400°F. On lightly floured surface, roll and pat one loaf of dough into 12×7-inch rectangle. Gently sprinkle half of garlic over dough. Distribute half of tomatoes evenly over dough, leaving ½-inch border. Sprinkle with half of cheese and basil. Starting from one long edge, roll dough up tightly, jelly-roll style. Carefully pinch seam to seal. Repeat procedure with second loaf. Sprinkle baking sheets with cornmeal. Place loaves on baking sheets, seam sides down. Brush with egg. *Do not let rise.* Bake immediately 25 to 30 minutes or until loaves are browned and sound hollow when tapped.

Remove to racks to cool before slicing. If desired, loaves can be wrapped well and frozen up to 1 month.

Makes 2 loaves (24 slices)

Tip: The flavorful oil from Marinated Tomatoes can be used for sautéing or for vinaigrettes.

Taco Bread

1 loaf frozen bread dough, thawed

1½ cups (6 ounces) shredded Cheddar cheese

1 package (1.0 ounce) LAWRY'S® Taco Spices & Seasonings

3 tablespoons butter or margarine, melted

On baking sheet, stretch dough into 14×8-inch rectangle. Sprinkle with cheese and Taco Seasoning Mix; drizzle with margarine. Roll in jelly-roll fashion (lengthwise), place seam side down on baking sheet. Bake, uncovered, in 350°F oven 20 to 25 minutes until golden brown. *Makes 6 servings*

Serving Suggestions: Slice bread when cooled and serve as a spicy addition to hearty soups.

Garlic Monkey Bread

2 packages (10 ounces each)
   refrigerated buttermilk biscuit
   dough
6 tablespoons unsalted butter or
   margarine, melted
1½ tablespoons chopped parsley
1 tablespoon finely chopped onion
¾ teaspoon LAWRY'S® Garlic Powder
   with Parsley
½ teaspoon LAWRY'S® Seasoned Salt

Separate biscuits. In small bowl, combine remaining ingredients. Dip each biscuit into butter mixture to coat. In Bundt pan or 1½ quart casserole, place one layer of dipped biscuits in bottom, slightly overlapping to fit. Arrange remaining biscuits in a zig-zag fashion, some towards the center and some towards the outside edge. Pour any remaining butter over biscuits. Bake, uncovered, in 375°F oven 15 to 20 minutes. Invert to remove. Serve warm.   *Makes 10 servings*

Serving Suggestion: Perfect last minute bread idea with homemade soup or salad.

Hint: If top biscuits brown too fast, cover with foil and continue baking.

Spicy Cornbread

1 pound BOB EVANS® Original
   Recipe Roll Sausage
3 green onions with tops, chopped
1½ cups biscuit mix
1 cup cornmeal
1 cup grated longhorn cheese
⅔ cup milk
½ cup thick and chunky picante sauce
1 egg, slightly beaten
2 teaspoons hot pepper sauce, or to
   taste
1 jalapeño pepper, seeded and
   chopped (optional)

Preheat oven to 400°F. Crumble sausage into large skillet. Add onions. Cook over medium heat until sausage is browned, stirring occasionally. Drain off any drippings. Place sausage mixture in large bowl; add remaining ingredients, mixing well with wooden spoon. Spread mixture evenly into greased 11×7-inch baking dish. Bake 20 minutes. Cool on wire rack 20 minutes before cutting into squares. Serve warm or at room temperature. Refrigerate leftovers.

Makes 12 servings

Cheese Straws

½ cup (1 stick) butter, softened

⅛ teaspoon salt

   Dash ground red pepper

1 pound sharp Cheddar cheese,
   shredded, at room temperature

2 cups self-rising flour

Heat oven to 350°F. In mixer bowl, beat butter, salt and pepper until creamy. Add cheese; mix well. Gradually add flour, mixing until dough begins to form a ball. Form dough into ball with hands. Fit cookie press with small star plate; fill with dough according to manufacturer's directions. Press dough onto cookie sheets in 3-inch-long strips. Bake 12 minutes, just until lightly browned. Cool completely on wire rack. Store tightly covered. *Makes about 10 dozen*

Savory Pull Apart Biscuits

2 tablespoons butter or margarine

1 tablespoon minced onion

2 tablespoons grated Parmesan
   cheese

½ teaspoon TABASCO® brand
   Pepper Sauce

1 (8-ounce) package refrigerated
   biscuits

Melt butter in small saucepan. Add onion and cook until tender. Stir in cheese and TABASCO® Sauce; remove from heat. Separate biscuits. Dip biscuit tops in butter mixture and arrange biscuits buttered side up in lightly greased 8-inch round cake pan, making sure sides of biscuits touch. Bake 10 to 15 minutes or until golden. Serve warm.

Makes 10 biscuits

Cheese Straws

Sun-Dried Tomato Scones

2 cups buttermilk baking mix

¼ cup (1 ounce) grated Parmesan
    cheese

1½ teaspoons dried basil

⅔ cup reduced-fat (2%) milk

½ cup chopped drained oil-packed
    sun-dried tomatoes

¼ cup chopped green onions

1. Preheat oven to 450°F. Combine baking mix, cheese and basil in medium bowl.

2. Stir in milk, tomatoes and onions. Mix just until dry ingredients are moistened. Drop by heaping teaspoonfuls onto greased baking sheet.

3. Bake 8 to 10 minutes or until light golden brown. Remove baking sheet to cooling rack; let stand 5 minutes. Remove scones and serve warm or at room temperature.   *Makes 1½ dozen scones*

Prep and Cook Time: 20 minutes

Wisconsin Cheese Pull-Apart Bread

3 packages (about 3 dozen) frozen
    bread dough dinner rolls, thawed
    to room temperature

⅓ cup butter, melted

1 cup freshly grated Wisconsin
    Parmesan cheese

1 cup shredded Wisconsin Provolone
    cheese

Roll each dinner roll in butter, then in Parmesan cheese to coat. Arrange half the rolls in well-greased 12-cup fluted tube pan. Sprinkle with Provolone cheese. Top with remaining rolls. Sprinkle with any remaining Parmesan cheese. Let rise about 1 hour or until doubled in bulk.

Preheat oven to 375°F. Bake 35 to 45 minutes or until golden brown. Use table knife to loosen edges of bread. Remove from pan. Serve warm.

Makes 12 servings

Hint: Cover edges of bread with foil during last 10 to 15 minutes of baking if crust becomes too dark.

Favorite recipe from **Wisconsin Milk Marketing Board**

Sun-Dried Tomato Scones

Cheddar Pepper Muffins

2 cups all-purpose flour

1 tablespoon sugar

1 tablespoon baking powder

1 teaspoon black pepper

½ teaspoon salt

1¼ cups milk

¼ cup vegetable oil

1 egg

1 cup (4 ounces) shredded sharp Cheddar cheese, divided

Preheat oven to 400°F. Generously grease or paper-line 12 (2½-inch) muffin cups. Combine flour, sugar, baking powder, pepper and salt in large bowl. Combine milk, oil and egg in small bowl until blended. Stir into flour mixture just until moistened. Fold in ¾ cup cheese. Spoon into muffin cups. Sprinkle with remaining cheese. Bake 15 to 20 minutes or until light golden brown. Cool in pan on wire rack 5 minutes. Remove from pan; serve warm.   *Makes 12 muffins*

Focaccia

1 (1-pound) loaf frozen bread dough

1½ tablespoons olive oil

½ cup finely shredded mozzarella cheese

1 teaspoon dried rosemary

1 teaspoon LAWRY'S® Garlic Powder with Parsley

½ teaspoon dried oregano, crushed

Preheat oven to 375°F. On a lightly floured surface roll thawed loaf into a 13×9-inch rectangle. If dough shrinks back after rolling, let the dough rest for a few minutes then continue rolling to correct size. Transfer dough to a greased 13×9-inch baking pan. Brush with olive oil. Let rise about 30 to 60 minutes. Press down dough with finger tips to make dimples in dough. Sprinkle with cheese and herbs. Bake 15 to 20 minutes or until golden brown. Remove from pan to cool on wire rack.   *Makes 8 servings*

Serving Suggestion: Slice in strips or squares for serving.

Cheddar Pepper Muffins

Touchdown Cheese Scones

    2 cups all-purpose flour
2½ teaspoons baking powder
    ½ teaspoon baking soda
    ¼ teaspoon salt
    2 tablespoons cold butter or
        margarine, cut in pieces
    1 cup shredded mild Cheddar cheese
    ⅔ cup buttermilk
    2 large eggs, divided
    ½ teaspoon TABASCO® brand
        Pepper Sauce

Preheat oven to 350°F. Sift together flour, baking powder, baking soda and salt in large bowl. Cut in butter until mixture resembles cornmeal. Stir in cheese. Blend buttermilk, 1 egg and TABASCO® Sauce together in small bowl. Make a well in center of dry ingredients; add buttermilk mixture. Stir quickly and lightly with fork to form sticky dough. Turn dough out on lightly floured board. Knead 10 times. Divide dough in half; pat each half into circle about ½ inch thick. Cut each circle into 4 wedges. Combine remaining egg and 1 tablespoon water. Brush each wedge with egg mixture. Arrange on greased baking sheet. Bake 13 to 15 minutes or until golden.   *Makes 8 scones*

Fiesta Cornbread

1 box (15 ounces) cornbread mix
1 cup milk
1 egg
1 can (8¾ ounces) whole kernel corn,
    drained
1 can (4 ounces) diced green chiles
1 jar (2 ounces) diced pimiento,
    drained
1 teaspoon LAWRY'S® Seasoned Salt

In large bowl, combine all ingredients; mix well. Pour into greased 8×8×2-inch baking dish. Bake, uncovered, in 425°F oven 25 to 30 minutes.

Makes 6 to 8 servings

Serving Suggestion: Serve warm with butter.

Snappy Southwest Corn Muffins

1 package (8 ounces) corn muffin mix

1 tablespoon chili powder*

½ cup milk

1 egg

1 cup drained canned corn kernels *or* 1 (7-ounce) can whole kernel corn with red and green peppers

1 cup (4 ounces) cubed JARLSBERG cheese

1 can (4 ounces) chopped chili peppers

½ cup (2 ounces) chopped pitted black olives

½ cup (2 ounces) chopped walnuts

*Use 1 to 2 teaspoons chili powder for a milder flavor.

Grease or paper-line 12-cup muffin pan. Preheat oven to 400°F. Combine muffin mix and chili powder in large bowl. Add milk and egg; stir just to moisten. Stir in corn, cheese, chili peppers, olives and walnuts.

Fill each muffin cup with about ½ cup mixture, dividing batter evenly.** Bake 25 to 30 minutes or until golden brown.

Makes 12 muffins

**Or divide batter evenly among 10 muffin cups for more rounded, "domed" muffins.

Hint: Before baking, sprinkle muffins with additional walnuts.

Note: Recipe can easily be doubled.

Cook's Tip: *Use nonstick vegetable cooking spray to easily grease muffin cups. Never grease muffin cups that won't be used—the grease will burn.*

Peanut Butter Surprise Cookies
(page 88)

Busy-Day Cookies

❧ ❧ ❧

Homemade cookies are irresistible—the all-American favorite. Whether you like cookies that are crunchy or chewy, big or small, nutty or gooey, you'll find your favorite in this scrumptious recipe collection. Be prepared for bake sales, after-school snacks, office treats, lunch-box favorites, coffee-break delights or just fill up the cookie jar with this assortment of easy-to-make cookies.

Whip up a batch of Easy Lemon Cookies (page 94) or Fudgy Oatmeal Butterscotch Cookies (page 86) and you'll be a winner at every occasion.

Sandwich Cookies

1 package (20 ounces) refrigerated cookie dough, any flavor

All-purpose flour (optional)

Any combination of colored frostings, peanut butter or assorted ice creams for filling

Colored sprinkles, chocolate-covered raisins, miniature candy-coated chocolate pieces and other assorted small candies for decoration

1. Preheat oven to 350°F. Grease cookie sheets.

2. Remove dough from wrapper according to package directions. Cut dough into 4 equal sections. Reserve 1 section; refrigerate remaining 3 sections.

3. Roll reserved dough to ¼-inch thickness. Sprinkle with flour to minimize sticking, if necessary.

4. Cut out cookies using ¾-inch round or fluted cookie cutter. Transfer cookies to prepared cookie sheets, placing about 2 inches apart. Repeat steps with remaining dough.

5. Bake 8 to 11 minutes or until edges are lightly browned. Remove to wire racks; cool completely.

6. To make sandwich, spread about 1 tablespoon desired filling on flat side of 1 cookie to within ¼ inch of edge. Top with second cookie, pressing gently. Roll side of sandwich in desired decorations. Repeat with remaining cookies.

Makes 20 to 24 sandwich cookies

Cook's Tip: *Be creative—make sandwich cookies using 2 or more flavors of refrigerated cookie dough. Mix and match to come up with your favorite combination.*

Sandwich Cookies

Flourless Peanut Butter Cookies

1 cup peanut butter

1 cup packed light brown sugar

1 egg

24 milk chocolate candy stars or other solid milk chocolate candy

Preheat oven to 350°F. Combine peanut butter, sugar and egg in medium bowl; beat until blended and smooth.

Shape dough into 24 balls about 1½ inches in diameter. Place 2 inches apart on ungreased cookie sheets. Press one chocolate star on top of each cookie. Bake 10 to 12 minutes or until set. Transfer to wire racks to cool completely.

Makes about 2 dozen cookies

> **Cook's Tip**: *Lining the cookie sheets with parchment paper is an alternative to greasing. It eliminates clean-up, bakes the cookies more evenly and allows them to cool right on the paper instead of on wire racks.*

Chocolate-Dipped Almond Crescents

1 cup butter, softened

1 cup powdered sugar

2 egg yolks

2½ cups all-purpose flour

1½ teaspoons almond extract

1 cup (6 ounces) semisweet chocolate chips

Preheat oven to 375°F. Line cookie sheets with parchment paper or leave ungreased. Cream butter, sugar and egg yolks in large bowl. Beat in flour and almond extract until well mixed. Shape dough into 1-inch balls. (If dough is too soft to handle, cover and refrigerate until firm.) Roll balls into 2-inch-long ropes, tapering both ends. Curve ropes into crescent shapes. Place 2 inches apart on cookie sheets. Bake 8 to 10 minutes or until set, but not browned. Remove to wire racks to cool. Melt chocolate chips in top of double boiler over hot, not boiling, water. Dip one end of each crescent in melted chocolate. Place on waxed paper; cool until chocolate is set.

Makes about 5 dozen cookies

Flourless Peanut Butter Cookies

Hidden Treasure Macaroons

¾ cup cold milk

1 teaspoon vanilla

1 package (4-serving size) JELL-O®
   Vanilla Flavor Instant Pudding
   & Pie Filling

1 package (14 ounces) BAKER'S®
   ANGEL FLAKE® Coconut

¼ cup all-purpose flour
   BAKER'S® Semi-Sweet Chocolate
   Chunks

Heat oven to 350°F.

Pour milk and vanilla into medium bowl.
Add pudding mix. Beat with wire whisk
1 minute or until smooth. Add coconut
and flour. Stir to combine completely.
Mixture will be stiff. With hands, roll
cookie dough into balls, about 1 inch in
diameter. Insert chocolate chunk into
center of each ball, closing up the end to
cover chocolate. Place balls 1 inch apart
on lightly greased and floured cookie
sheets.

Bake 15 to 20 minutes or until edges of
cookies are golden brown. Immediately
remove from cookie sheets. Cool on wire
racks.   *Makes about 3 dozen*

Black and White Hidden Treasures:
Prepare Macaroons as directed above,
substituting JELL-O® Chocolate Flavor
Instant Pudding & Pie Filling for vanilla
flavor and BAKER'S® Premium White
Chocolate Chunks for semi-sweet
chocolate chunks.

Nutty Banana Treasures: Prepare
Macaroons as directed above substituting
JELL-O® Banana Cream Flavor Instant
Pudding & Pie filling for vanilla flavor
and pecans or walnuts for chocolate
chunks.

Thumbprint Macaroons: Prepare
Macaroons and form into balls as directed
above. Place 1 inch apart on greased and
floured cookie sheets. Press each ball with
thumb to create a depression in the center
of dough. Place chocolate chunk in the
center of each cookie. Bake as directed
above.

Prep Time: 10 minutes
Bake Time: 20 minutes

Butterscotch Spice Cookies

1 package DUNCAN HINES® Moist
Deluxe® Spice Cake Mix

2 eggs

½ cup vegetable oil

1 teaspoon vanilla extract

1 cup butterscotch chips

1. Preheat oven to 375°F.

2. Combine cake mix, eggs, oil and vanilla extract in large bowl. Beat at low speed with electric mixer until blended. Stir in butterscotch chips. Drop by rounded teaspoonfuls 2 inches apart onto ungreased baking sheets. Bake at 375°F 8 to 10 minutes or until set. Cool 2 minutes on baking sheets. Remove to cooling racks. Cool completely. Store in airtight container.

Makes 3 dozen cookies

Cook's Tip: *For chewy cookies, bake for 8 minutes. Cookies will be slightly puffed when removed from the oven and will settle while cooling.*

Thumbprints

1 package (20 ounces) refrigerated
sugar or chocolate cookie dough

All-purpose flour (optional)

¾ cup plus 1 tablespoon fruit
preserves, any flavor

1. Grease cookie sheets. Remove dough from wrapper according to package directions. Sprinkle with flour to minimize sticking, if necessary.

2. Cut dough into 26 (1-inch) slices. Roll slices into balls, sprinkling with additional flour, if necessary. Place balls 2 inches apart on prepared cookie sheets. Press deep indention in center of each ball with thumb. Freeze dough 20 minutes.

3. Preheat oven to 350°F. Bake cookies 12 to 13 minutes or until edges are light golden brown (cookies will have started to puff up and loose their shape). Quickly press down indentation using tip of teaspoon.

4. Return to oven 2 to 3 minutes or until cookies are golden brown and set. Cool cookies completely on cookie sheets. Fill each indentation with about 1½ teaspoons preserves. *Makes 26 cookies*

Hint: Fill cookies with peanut butter or melted semisweet chocolate chips.

Crispy's Irresistible Peanut Butter Marbles

1 package (18 ounces) refrigerated peanut butter cookie dough

2 cups "M&M's"® Milk Chocolate Mini Baking Bits, divided

1 cup crisp rice cereal, divided (optional)

1 package (18 ounces) refrigerated sugar cookie dough

¼ cup unsweetened cocoa powder

In large bowl combine peanut butter dough, 1 cup "M&M's"® Milk Chocolate Mini Baking Bits and ½ cup cereal, if desired. Remove dough to small bowl; set aside. In large bowl combine sugar dough and cocoa powder until well blended. Stir in remaining 1 cup "M&M's"® Milk Chocolate Mini Baking Bits and remaining ½ cup cereal, if desired. Remove half the dough to small bowl; set aside. Combine half the peanut butter dough with half the chocolate dough by folding together just enough to marble. Shape marbled dough into 8×2-inch log. Wrap log in plastic wrap. Repeat with remaining doughs. Refrigerate logs 2 hours. To bake, preheat oven to 350°F. Cut dough into ¼-inch-thick slices. Place about 2 inches apart on ungreased cookie sheets. Bake 12 to

14 minutes. Cool 1 minute on cookie sheets; cool completely on wire racks. Store in tightly covered container.

Makes 5 dozen cookies

Spicy Oatmeal Raisin Cookies

1 package DUNCAN HINES® Moist Deluxe® Spice Cake Mix

4 egg whites

1 cup uncooked quick-cooking oats (not instant or old-fashioned)

½ cup vegetable oil

½ cup raisins

Preheat oven to 350°F. Grease cookie sheets.

Combine cake mix, egg whites, oats and oil in large mixing bowl. Beat at low speed with electric mixer until blended. Stir in raisins. Drop by rounded teaspoonfuls onto prepared cookie sheets.

Bake 7 to 9 minutes or until lightly browned. Cool 1 minute on cookie sheets. Remove to cooling racks; cool completely.

Makes about 4 dozen cookies

Crispy's Irresistible Peanut Butter Marbles

Coconut Clouds

2⅔ cups flaked coconut, divided
1 package DUNCAN HINES® Moist Deluxe® Classic Yellow Cake Mix
1 egg
½ cup vegetable oil
¼ cup water
1 teaspoon almond extract

1. Preheat oven to 350°F. Reserve 1⅓ cups coconut in medium bowl; set aside.

2. Combine cake mix, egg, oil, water and almond extract in large bowl. Beat at low speed with electric mixer. Stir in remaining 1⅓ cups reserved coconut. Drop rounded teaspoonful dough into reserved coconut. Roll to cover lightly. Place on ungreased baking sheet. Repeat with remaining dough, placing balls 2 inches apart. Bake at 350°F 10 to 12 minutes or until light golden brown. Cool 1 minute on baking sheets. Remove to cooling racks. Cool completely. Store in airtight container.

Makes 3½ dozen cookies

Cook's Note: To save time when forming dough into balls, use a 1-inch spring-operated cookie scoop. Spring-operated cookie scoops are available at kitchen specialty shops.

Fudgy Oatmeal Butterscotch Cookies

1 package (18.25 ounces) devil's food cake mix
1½ cups quick-cooking or old-fashioned oats, uncooked
¾ cup (1½ sticks) butter, melted
2 large eggs
1 tablespoon vegetable oil
1 teaspoon vanilla extract
1¼ cups "M&M's"® Chocolate Mini Baking Bits
1 cup butterscotch chips

Preheat oven to 350°F. In large bowl combine cake mix, oats, butter, eggs, oil and vanilla until well blended. Stir in "M&M's"® Chocolate Mini Baking Bits and butterscotch chips. Drop by heaping tablespoonfuls about 2 inches apart onto ungreased cookie sheets. Bake 10 to 12 minutes. Cool 1 minute on cookie sheets; cool completely on wire racks. Store in tightly covered container.

Makes about 3 dozen cookies

Coconut Clouds

Peanut Butter Surprise Cookies

24 miniature peanut butter cups

1 can (14 ounces) sweetened
    condensed milk (not evaporated
    milk)

¾ cup creamy peanut butter

¼ Butter Flavor CRISCO® Stick or
    ¼ cup Butter Flavor CRISCO®
    all-vegetable shortening

1 egg

1 teaspoon vanilla

2 cups regular all-purpose baking
    mix

1. Remove wrappers from peanut butter cups. Cut candy into quarters.

2. Combine condensed milk, peanut butter, ¼ cup shortening, egg and vanilla in large bowl. Beat at medium speed of electric mixer until smooth. Add baking mix. Beat until well blended. Stir in candy pieces with spoon. Cover. Refrigerate 1 hour.

3. Heat oven to 350°F. Place sheets of foil on countertop for cooling cookies.

4. Drop dough by slightly rounded teaspoonfuls 2 inches apart onto ungreased baking sheet. Shape into balls with spoon.

5. Bake at 350°F for 7 to 9 minutes or until light brown around edges and center is just set. *Do not overbake.* Cool 2 minutes on baking sheet. Remove cookies to foil to cool completely.

    Makes about 4 dozen cookies

Variation: Shape dough into 1¼-inch balls. Place 2 inches apart onto ungreased baking sheet. Dip fork in flour; flatten dough slightly in crisscross pattern.

Cook's Tip: *The best cookie sheets to use are those with little or no sides. They allow the heat to circulate easily during baking and promote even browning.*

Banana Chocolate Chip Cookies

2 extra-ripe, medium DOLE®
    Bananas, peeled
1 package (17.5 ounces) chocolate
    chip cookie mix
½ teaspoon ground cinnamon
1 egg, lightly beaten
1 teaspoon vanilla extract
1 cup toasted wheat germ

• Mash bananas with fork. Measure 1 cup.

• Combine cookie mix and cinnamon. Stir in contents of enclosed flavoring packet, mashed bananas, egg and vanilla until well blended. Stir in wheat germ.

• Drop batter by heaping tablespoonfuls 2 inches apart onto cookie sheets coated with cooking spray. Shape cookies with back of spoon. Bake in 375°F oven 10 to 12 minutes until lightly browned. Cool on wire racks. *Makes 18 cookies*

Nutty Lemon Crescents

1 package (18 ounces) refrigerated
    sugar cookie dough
1 cup chopped pecans, toasted*
1 tablespoon grated lemon peel
1½ cups powdered sugar, divided

*To toast pecans, spread in single layer on baking sheet. Bake in preheated 350°F oven 8 to 10 minutes or until golden brown, stirring frequently.

1. Preheat oven to 375°F. Remove dough from wrapper according to package directions.

2. Combine dough, pecans and lemon peel in large bowl. Stir until thoroughly blended. Shape level tablespoonfuls of dough into crescent shapes. Place 2 inches apart on ungreased cookie sheets. Bake 8 to 9 minutes or until set and very lightly browned. Cool 2 minutes on cookie sheets. Remove to wire racks.

3. Place 1 cup powdered sugar in shallow bowl. Roll warm cookies in powdered sugar. Cool completely. Sift remaining ½ cup powdered sugar over cookies just before serving.

Makes about 4 dozen cookies

Grand Old Flag Cookie

1 package (18 ounces) refrigerated
    sugar cookie dough

1 container (16 ounces) vanilla
    frosting

    Blue food color

50 white chocolate chips

3 cherry- or strawberry-flavored
    chewy fruit snack rolls, divided

2 pretzel rods

Supplies

1 (15×10-inch) cake board, covered,
    or large platter

1. Preheat oven to 350°F. Grease 13×9-inch baking pan with nonstick cooking spray. Place dough in prepared pan; press evenly onto bottom of pan. Bake 15 to 18 minutes or until lightly browned. Cool in pan on wire rack 15 minutes. Remove cookie from pan to rack; cool completely.

2. Place cookie on prepared cake board. Tint ½ cup frosting blue. Spread blue frosting in 4-inch square in top left corner of cookie as background for stars. Frost remaining cookie with remaining white frosting. Arrange chips for stars, alternating 5 rows of 6 stars each with 4 rows of 5 stars each.

3. Cut fruit snack rolls into 3 (9-inch) strips and 3 (13-inch) strips; place on cookie as stripes. Wrap pretzel rods with remaining fruit roll lengths; place next to cookie for flag pole.

Makes 10 to 12 servings

Peanut Butter Shortbreads

½ cup unsalted butter, softened

½ cup granulated sugar

¼ cup creamy peanut butter

2 cups all-purpose flour

Preheat oven to 300°F. In bowl, combine all ingredients with your fingers until mixture resembles coarse meal. Press the mixture into an ungreased 8-inch round pan. With a fork, prick decorative wedges in the dough. Bake for about 1 hour or until very lightly browned. Cut into wedges while warm.

Makes 16 wedge-shaped cookies

Favorite recipe from **Peanut Advisory Board**

Grand Old Flag Cookie

Chocolate Hazelnut Cookie Drops

1 cup (2 sticks) butter or margarine, softened

1 cup firmly packed light brown sugar

2 large eggs

1¾ cups all-purpose flour

1 package (4-serving size) chocolate-flavor instant pudding mix

½ teaspoon baking soda

1¾ cups "M&M's"® Semi-Sweet Chocolate Mini Baking Bits

1 cup coarsely chopped toasted hazelnuts or filberts*

*To toast hazelnuts, spread in single layer on baking sheet. Bake at 350°F for 7 to 10 minutes or until light golden, stirring occasionally. Remove hazelnuts from pan and cool completely before chopping.

Preheat oven to 350°F. In large bowl cream butter and sugar until light and fluffy; beat in eggs. In small bowl combine flour, pudding mix and baking soda; blend into creamed mixture. Stir in "M&M's"® Semi-Sweet Chocolate Mini Baking Bits and nuts. Drop by teaspoonfuls about 2 inches apart onto ungreased cookie sheets. Bake 8 to 10 minutes or until set. *Do not overbake.* Cool completely on wire racks. Store in tightly covered container.

Makes about 5 dozen cookies

Polka Dot Macaroons

1 (14-ounce) bag (5 cups) shredded coconut

1 (14-ounce) can sweetened condensed milk

½ cup all-purpose flour

1¾ cups "M&M's"® Chocolate Mini Baking Bits

Preheat oven to 350°F. Grease cookie sheets; set aside. In large bowl combine coconut, condensed milk and flour until well blended. Stir in "M&M's"® Chocolate Mini Baking Bits. Drop by rounded tablespoonfuls about 2 inches apart onto prepared cookie sheets. Bake 8 to 10 minutes or until edges are golden. Cool completely on wire racks. Store in tightly covered container.

Makes about 5 dozen cookies

Left to right: Chocolate Hazelnut Cookie Drops and Polka Dot Macaroons

Easy Lemon Cookies

1 package DUNCAN HINES® Moist
Deluxe® Lemon Cake Mix

2 eggs

½ cup vegetable oil

1 teaspoon grated lemon peel

Pecan halves, for garnish

1. Preheat oven to 350°F.

2. Combine cake mix, eggs, oil and lemon
peel in large bowl. Stir until thoroughly
blended. Drop by rounded teaspoonfuls
2 inches apart onto ungreased cookie
sheets. Press pecan half in center of each
cookie. Bake at 350°F for 9 to 11 minutes
or until edges are light golden brown.
Cool 1 minute on cookie sheets. Remove
to wire racks. Cool completely. Store in
airtight container.

Makes 4 dozen cookies

Hint: You may substitute whole almonds
or walnut halves for the pecan halves.

Oriental Chews

1 package (6 ounces) chow mein
noodles

1 cup flaked coconut

1 cup (6 ounces) semisweet chocolate
chips

1 cup (6 ounces) butterscotch-
flavored chips

1 package (3 ounces) slivered
almonds

Preheat oven to 350°F. Place noodles and
coconut on cookie sheet in single layer.
Bake 10 minutes or until crisp. Melt
chocolate and butterscotch chips in top of
double boiler over hot, not boiling, water.
Remove from heat; stir in almonds,
coconut and noodles. Drop mixture by
teaspoonfuls onto waxed paper. Cool
until set.   *Makes about 60 chews*

Easy Lemon Cookies

Peanut Butter and Chocolate Spirals

1 package (20 ounces) refrigerated
  sugar cookie dough

1 package (20 ounces) refrigerated
  peanut butter cookie dough

¼ cup unsweetened cocoa powder

⅓ cup peanut butter-flavored chips,
  chopped

¼ cup all-purpose flour

⅓ cup miniature chocolate chips

1. Remove each dough from wrapper according to package directions.

2. Place sugar cookie dough and cocoa in large bowl; mix with fork to blend. Stir in peanut butter chips.

3. Place peanut butter cookie dough and flour in another large bowl; mix with fork to blend. Stir in chocolate chips. Divide each dough in half; cover and refrigerate 1 hour.

4. Roll each dough on floured surface to 12×6-inch rectangle. Layer each half of peanut butter dough onto each half of chocolate dough. Roll up doughs, starting at long end to form 2 (12-inch) rolls. Wrap in plastic wrap; refrigerate 1 hour.

5. Preheat oven to 375°F. Cut dough into ½-inch-thick slices. Place cookies 2 inches apart on ungreased cookie sheets.

6. Bake 10 to 12 minutes or until lightly browned. Remove to wire racks; cool completely. *Makes 4 dozen cookies*

Cook's Tip: *Promote even baking and browning by placing only one cookie sheet at a time in the center of the oven. If you use two sheets at a time, rotate the cookie sheets from front to back halfway through the baking time.*

*Peanut Butter and
Chocolate Spirals*

Snickerdoodles

3 tablespoons sugar

1 teaspoon ground cinnamon

1 package DUNCAN HINES® Moist Deluxe® Classic Yellow Cake Mix

2 eggs

¼ cup vegetable oil

1. Preheat oven to 375°F. Grease cookie sheets. Place sheets of foil on countertop for cooling cookies.

2. Combine sugar and cinnamon in small bowl.

3. Combine cake mix, eggs and oil in large bowl. Stir until well blended. Shape dough into 1-inch balls. Roll in cinnamon-sugar mixture. Place balls 2 inches apart on cookie sheets. Flatten balls with bottom of glass.

4. Bake at 375°F for 8 to 9 minutes or until set. Cool one minute on cookie sheets. Remove to foil to cool completely.

Makes about 3 dozen cookies

Heath Bits Peanut Butter Cookies

½ cup shortening

¾ cup REESE'S® Creamy Peanut Butter

1¼ cups packed light brown sugar

3 tablespoons milk

1 tablespoon vanilla extract

1 egg

1½ cups all-purpose flour

¾ teaspoon baking soda

¾ teaspoon salt

1⅓ cups (8-ounce package) HEATH® BITS, divided

1. Heat oven to 375°F.

2. Beat shortening, peanut butter, brown sugar, milk and vanilla in large bowl until well blended. Add egg; beat just until blended. Combine flour, baking soda and salt; gradually beat into peanut butter mixture. Stir in 1 cup Heath Bits; reserve remainder for topping.

3. Drop by heaping teaspoons 2 inches apart onto ungreased cookie sheet; top each with reserved Heath Bits. Bake 7 to 8 minutes or until set. *Do not overbake.* Cool 2 minutes. Remove to wire rack. Cool completely.

Makes 3 dozen cookies

Quick Chocolate Softies

1 package (about 18 ounces) devil's food cake mix

⅓ cup water

¼ cup butter, softened

1 egg

1 cup white chocolate chips

½ cup coarsely chopped walnuts

Preheat oven to 350°F. Grease cookie sheets. Combine cake mix, water, butter and egg in large bowl. Beat with electric mixer at low speed until moistened. Increase speed to medium; beat 1 minute. (Dough will be thick.) Stir in white chocolate chips and nuts; mix until well blended. Drop dough by heaping teaspoonfuls 2 inches apart onto prepared cookie sheets.

Bake 10 to 12 minutes or until set. Let cookies stand on cookie sheets 1 minute. Remove cookies to wire racks; cool completely.

Makes about 4 dozen cookies

Banana Peanut Jumbles

2 ripe, medium DOLE® Bananas

½ cup packed brown sugar

½ cup peanut butter

½ cup roasted peanuts

1⅓ cups buttermilk baking mix

1 tablespoon water

• **Mash** bananas; measure 1 cup.

• **Combine** bananas, brown sugar, peanut butter and peanuts. Add baking mix and water. Stir until well blended.

• **Drop** batter by heaping tablespoonfuls onto cookie sheets coated with cooking spray.

• **Bake** at 350°F 20 to 25 minutes or until golden. Cool on rack.

Makes 18 cookies

Prep Time: 15 minutes
Bake Time: 25 minutes

Orange Pecan Cookies

1 package (about 17 ounces) sugar cookie mix

½ cup butter, melted

1 egg, slightly beaten

1 teaspoon grated orange peel

½ cup chopped pecans

½ cup powdered sugar

1½ teaspoons orange juice

1. Preheat oven to 375°F.

2. Combine cookie mix, butter, egg, and orange peel in large bowl. Stir with spoon until well blended. Stir in pecans.

3. Drop dough by rounded teaspoonfuls onto *ungreased* cookie sheets about 2 inches apart. Bake for 7 to 8 minutes or until set. Cool 1 minute on cookie sheets. Remove to wire racks; cool completely.

4. Combine powdered sugar and orange juice in small bowl; stir until well blended. Drizzle over top of cooled cookies. Allow glaze to set before storing between layers of waxed paper in airtight container.

Makes about 3 dozen cookies

Fruit Pizza

1 (20-ounce) package refrigerated sugar cookie dough

1 (8-ounce) package cream cheese, softened

1 cup powdered sugar

Assorted fresh fruit (strawberries, bananas, kiwi fruit, blueberries, mandarin oranges, etc.)

½ cup SMUCKER'S® Apricot Preserves or Sweet Orange Marmalade

1 tablespoon water

Cut dough into 1-inch slices and place on ungreased cookie sheet or pizza pan. Bake 17 to 19 minutes or until light golden brown around edges. Cool.

Combine cream cheese and sugar; mix well. Spread over cookies. Decorate with sliced fruit. (Dip banana slices in lemon juice to prevent browning.) Combine preserves and water; mix well. Drizzle over fruit topping. Serve immediately or refrigerate until serving time.

Makes 9 servings

Orange Pecan Cookies

Chocolate Mint Ravioli Cookies

1 package (15 ounces) refrigerated pie crusts

1 bar (7 ounces) cookies 'n' mint chocolate candy

1 egg

1 tablespoon water

Powdered sugar

1. Preheat oven to 400°F. Unfold 1 pie crust on lightly floured surface. Roll into 13-inch circle. Using 2½-inch cutters, cut pastry into 24 circles, rerolling scraps if necessary. Repeat with remaining pie crust.

2. Separate candy bar into pieces marked on bar. Cut each chocolate piece in half. Beat egg and water together in small bowl with fork. Brush half of pastry circles lightly with egg mixture. Place 1 piece of chocolate in center of each circle (there will be some candy bar left over). Top with remaining pastry circles. Seal edges with tines of fork.

3. Place on *ungreased* baking sheets. Brush with egg mixture.

4. Bake 8 to 10 minutes or until golden brown. Remove from cookie sheets; cool completely on wire racks. Dust with powdered sugar.

Makes 2 dozen cookies

Hint: Mix it up! Substitute your favorite candy bar for the cookies 'n' mint chocolate candy for a completely different taste.

Prep and Cook Time: 30 minutes

Cook's Tip: *Most cookies should be removed from cookie sheets immediately after baking and placed in a single layer on wire racks to cool. Fragile cookies may need to cool slightly on the cookie sheets before being moved.*

Chocolate Mint Ravioli Cookies

Date-Nut Macaroons

1 (8-ounce) package pitted dates, chopped

1½ cups flaked coconut

1 cup PLANTERS® Pecan Halves, chopped

¾ cup sweetened condensed milk (not evaporated milk)

½ teaspoon vanilla extract

Preheat oven to 350°F.

Combine dates, coconut and nuts in medium bowl; blend in sweetened condensed milk and vanilla. Drop by rounded tablespoonfuls onto greased and floured cookie sheets. Bake 10 to 12 minutes or until light golden brown. Carefully remove from cookie sheets; cool completely on wire racks. Store in airtight container.

Makes about 2 dozen cookies

Quick Peanut Butter Chocolate Chip Cookies

1 package DUNCAN HINES® Moist Deluxe® Classic Yellow Cake Mix

½ cup creamy peanut butter

½ cup butter or margarine, softened

2 eggs

1 cup milk chocolate chips

1. Preheat oven to 350°F. Grease cookie sheets.

2. Combine cake mix, peanut butter, butter and eggs in large bowl. Mix at low speed with electric mixer until blended. Stir in chocolate chips.

3. Drop by rounded teaspoonfuls onto prepared cookie sheets. Bake 9 to 11 minutes or until lightly browned. Cool 2 minutes on cookie sheets. Remove to cooling racks.

Makes about 4 dozen cookies

Hint: Crunchy peanut butter may be substituted for regular peanut butter.

Date-Nut Macaroons

Chocolate Chip 'n Oatmeal Cookies

1 package (18.25 or 18.5 ounces) yellow cake mix

1 cup quick-cooking rolled oats, uncooked

¾ cup butter or margarine, softened

2 eggs

1 cup HERSHEY'S Semi-Sweet Chocolate Chips

1. Heat oven to 350°F.

2. Combine cake mix, oats, butter and eggs in large bowl; mix well. Stir in chocolate chips. Drop by rounded teaspoons onto ungreased cookie sheets.

3. Bake 10 to 12 minutes or until very lightly browned. Cool slightly; remove from cookie sheets to wire racks. Cool completely.

Makes about 4 dozen cookies

Shortbread Cookies

1½ cups (3 sticks) butter or margarine, softened

1 package (8 ounces) PHILADELPHIA® Cream Cheese, softened

½ cup granulated sugar

3 cups flour

Powdered sugar

Mix butter, cream cheese and granulated sugar until well blended. Mix in flour.

Shape dough into 1-inch balls; place on ungreased cookie sheets.

Bake at 400°F for 10 to 13 minutes or until light golden brown and set; cool on wire racks. Sprinkle with powdered sugar.

Makes about 6 dozen cookies

Holiday Cookies: Tint dough with a few drops of food coloring before shaping to add a festive touch.

Prep Time: 15 minutes
Bake Time: 13 minutes

Chocolate Chip 'n Oatmeal Cookies

Fudgy Walnut Cookie Wedges

1 package (20 ounces) refrigerated cookie dough, any flavor

2 cups (12-ounce package) HERSHEY'S Semi-Sweet Chocolate Chips

2 tablespoons butter or margarine

1 can (14 ounces) sweetened condensed milk (not evaporated milk)

1 teaspoon vanilla extract

½ cup chopped walnuts

1. Heat oven to 350°F.

2. Divide cookie dough into thirds. With floured hands, press dough onto bottoms of 3 aluminum foil-lined 9-inch round cake pans or press into 9-inch circles on ungreased cookie sheets.

3. Bake 10 to 20 minutes or until golden. Cool. Melt chips and butter with sweetened condensed milk in heavy saucepan over medium heat. Cook and stir until thickened, about 5 minutes. Remove from heat; add vanilla.

4. Spread over cookie circles. Top with walnuts. Chill. Cut into wedges. Store loosely covered at room temperature.

Makes about 36 wedges

Elephant Ears

1 package (17¼ ounces) frozen puff pastry, thawed according to package directions

1 egg, beaten

¼ cup sugar, divided

2 squares (1 ounce each) semisweet chocolate

Preheat oven to 375°F. Grease cookie sheets; sprinkle lightly with water. Roll one sheet of pastry to 12×10-inch rectangle. Brush with egg; sprinkle with 1 tablespoon sugar. Tightly roll up 10-inch sides, meeting in center. Brush center with egg and seal rolls tightly together; turn over. Cut into ⅜-inch-thick slices. Place slices on prepared cookie sheets. Sprinkle with 1 tablespoon sugar. Repeat with remaining pastry, egg and sugar. Bake 16 to 18 minutes until golden brown. Remove to wire racks; cool completely.

Melt chocolate in small saucepan over low heat, stirring constantly. Remove from heat. Spread bottoms of cookies with chocolate. Place on wire rack, chocolate side up. Let stand until chocolate is set. Store between layers of waxed paper in airtight containers.

Makes about 4 dozen cookies

Almond Raspberry Macaroons

2 cups BLUE DIAMOND® Blanched Almond Paste

1 cup granulated sugar

6 large egg whites

Powdered sugar

Seedless raspberry jam, stirred until smooth

Beat almond paste and granulated sugar until mixture resembles coarse cornmeal. Beat in egg whites, a little at a time, until thoroughly combined. Place heaping teaspoonfuls onto cookie sheet lined with waxed paper or parchment paper. Coat finger with powdered sugar and make an indentation in the middle of each cookie. (Coat finger with powdered sugar each time.) Bake at 350°F for 15 to 20 minutes or until lightly browned. Remove from oven and fill each indentation with about ¼ teaspoon raspberry jam. Cool. If using waxed paper, carefully peel paper off cookies when cooled.

Makes about 30 cookies

Peanut Butter Chocolate Chippers

1 cup creamy or chunky peanut butter

1 cup firmly packed light brown sugar

1 large egg

¾ cup milk chocolate chips

Granulated sugar

1. Preheat oven to 350°F.

2. Combine peanut butter, brown sugar and egg in medium bowl; mix until well blended. Add chips; mix well.

3. Roll heaping tablespoonfuls of dough into 1½-inch balls. Place balls 2 inches apart on ungreased cookie sheets.

4. Dip table fork into granulated sugar; press criss-cross fashion onto each ball, flattening to ½-inch thickness.

5. Bake 12 minutes or until set. Let cookies stand on cookie sheets 2 minutes. Remove cookies with spatula to wire racks; cool completely.

Makes about 2 dozen cookies

Note: This simple recipe is unusual because it doesn't contain any flour—but it still makes great cookies!

Chocolate Macadamia Chippers

1 package (18 ounces) refrigerated chocolate chip cookie dough

3 tablespoons unsweetened cocoa powder

½ cup coarsely chopped macadamia nuts

Preheat oven to 375°F. Remove dough from wrapper according to package directions.

Place dough in medium bowl; stir in cocoa until well blended. (Dough may be kneaded lightly, if desired.) Stir in nuts. Drop by heaping tablespoons 2 inches apart onto ungreased cookie sheets.

Bake 9 to 11 minutes or until almost set. Transfer to wire racks to cool completely.

Makes 2 dozen cookies

Simpler Than Sin Peanut Chocolate Cookies

1 cup PETER PAN® Extra Crunchy Peanut Butter

1 cup sugar

1 egg, at room temperature and beaten

2 teaspoons vanilla

1 (6-ounce) dark or milk chocolate candy bar, broken into squares

Preheat oven to 350°F. In medium bowl, combine Peter Pan® Peanut Butter, sugar, egg and vanilla; mix well. Roll dough into 1-inch balls. Place 2 inches apart on ungreased cookie sheet. Bake 12 minutes. Remove from oven and place chocolate square in center of each cookie. Bake an additional 5 to 7 minutes or until cookies are lightly golden around edges. Cool 5 minutes. Remove to wire rack. Cool.

Makes 21 to 24 cookies

Note: This simple recipe is unusual because it doesn't contain any flour—but it still makes great cookies!

Preparation Time: 10 minutes
Bake Time: 19 minutes

Chocolate Macadamia Chippers

Mexican Wedding Cookies

1 cup pecan pieces or halves
1 cup butter, softened
2 cups powdered sugar, divided
2 cups all-purpose flour, divided
2 teaspoons vanilla
⅛ teaspoon salt

1. Place pecans in food processor. Process using on/off pulsing action until pecans are ground, but not pasty.

2. Beat butter and ½ cup powdered sugar in large bowl with electric mixer at medium speed until light and fluffy. Gradually add 1 cup flour, vanilla and salt. Beat at low speed until well blended. Stir in remaining 1 cup flour and ground nuts with spoon. Shape dough into ball; wrap in plastic wrap and refrigerate 1 hour or until firm.

3. Preheat oven to 350°F. Shape tablespoons of dough into 1-inch balls. Place 1 inch apart on ungreased cookie sheets.

4. Bake 12 to 15 minutes or until pale golden brown. Let cookies stand on cookie sheets 2 minutes.

5. Meanwhile, place 1 cup powdered sugar in 13×9-inch glass dish. Transfer hot cookies to powdered sugar. Roll cookies in powdered sugar, coating well. Let cookies cool in sugar.

6. Sift remaining ½ cup powdered sugar over sugar-coated cookies before serving. Store tightly covered at room temperature or freeze up to 1 month.

Makes about 4 dozen cookies

Cook's Tip: Unbaked cookie dough can be refrigerated for up to two weeks or frozen up to six weeks. Label the dough with baking information for convenience.

Double Chocolate Oat Cookies

1 package (12 ounces) semisweet
    chocolate pieces, divided (about
    2 cups
½ cup (1 stick) margarine or butter,
    softened
½ cup granulated sugar
1 egg
¼ teaspoon vanilla
¾ cup all-purpose flour
¾ cup QUAKER® Oats (quick or old
    fashioned, uncooked)
1 teaspoon baking powder
¼ teaspoon baking soda
¼ teaspoon salt (optional)

Preheat oven to 375°F. Melt 1 cup
chocolate pieces in small saucepan; set
aside. Beat margarine and sugar until
fluffy; add melted chocolate, egg and
vanilla. Add combined flour, oats, baking
powder, baking soda and salt; mix well.
Stir in remaining chocolate pieces. Drop
by rounded tablespoonfuls onto
ungreased cookie sheets. Bake 8 to 10
minutes. Cool 1 minute on cookie sheets;
removed to wire rack.

Makes about 3 dozen cookies

Walnut Meringues

3 egg whites
  Pinch of salt
¾ cup sugar
⅓ cup finely chopped walnuts

Preheat oven to 350°F. Line baking sheet
with parchment pater. Place egg whites
and salt in large bowl. Beat until soft
peaks form. Gradually add sugar, beating
until stiff peaks form. Gently fold in
walnuts. Drop mounds about 1 inch in
diameter 1 inch apart onto prepared
baking sheet. Bake 20 minutes or until
lightly browned and dry to the touch. Let
cool completely before removing from
baking sheet. Store in airtight container.

Makes 48 cookies

Coconut Raspberry Bars
(page 118)

Cookie Bar Magic

❧ ❧ ❧

No time to bake dozens of cookies? Simply mix the batter, spread it in a pan, bake and enjoy! From sinfully rich chocolate and caramel bars to nut-studded fruit bars, these fabulous sweets are sure to become your all-time favorites. Start with a variety of prepared mixes, add a few ingredients and presto! You'll discover just how easy it is to create rich, sensational surprises.

Have some fun and tempt your taste buds with Blueberry Cheesecake Bars (page 148), Chocolate Caramel Nut Bars (page 120) or Creamy Lemon Bars (page 136).

Easy Cookie Bars

½ cup (1 stick) butter *or* margarine, melted

1½ cups HONEY MAID® Graham Cracker Crumbs

1⅓ cups (3½ ounces) BAKER'S® ANGEL FLAKE® Coconut

1 cup BAKER'S® Semi-Sweet Chocolate Chunks

1 cup chopped nuts

1 can (14 ounces) sweetened condensed milk

HEAT oven to 350°F. Line 13×9-inch baking pan with foil; grease foil.

MIX butter and graham cracker crumbs in medium bowl. Press into prepared pan. Sprinkle with coconut, chocolate chunks and nuts. Pour condensed milk over top.

BAKE 25 to 30 minutes or until golden brown. Cool in pan on wire rack. Lift out of pan onto cutting board.

Makes 3 dozen

Tip: For 13×9-inch glass baking dish, bake at 325°F.

Prep Time: 15 minutes
Bake Time: 30 minutes

Almond Toffee Bars

¾ cup butter or margarine, softened

¾ cup packed brown sugar

1½ cups all-purpose flour

½ teaspoon almond extract

½ teaspoon vanilla extract

¼ teaspoon salt

1 package (6 ounces) semi-sweet real chocolate pieces

¾ cup BLUE DIAMOND® Chopped Natural Almonds, toasted

Preheat oven to 350°F. Cream butter and sugar; blend in flour. Add extracts and salt, mixing well. Spread in bottom of ungreased 13×9-inch baking pan. Bake in 350°F oven for 15 to 20 minutes or until deep golden brown. Remove from oven; sprinkle with chocolate. When chocolate has melted, spread evenly; sprinkle with almonds. Cut into bars; cool.

Makes about 40 bars

Easy Cookie Bars

Coconut Raspberry Bars

2 cups graham cracker crumbs

½ cup butter, melted

1⅓ cups (3.5-ounce can) flaked coconut

1 can (14 ounces) sweetened condensed milk

1 cup red raspberry jam or preserves

½ cup chopped pecans

½ cup semisweet chocolate chips

½ cup white chocolate chips

1. Preheat oven to 350°F.

2. Combine graham cracker crumbs and butter in medium bowl. Press on bottom of 13×9-inch *ungreased* baking pan to make crust. Sprinkle with coconut; pour sweetened condensed milk evenly over coconut.

3. Bake 20 to 25 minutes or until lightly browned. Cool completely in pan on wire rack.

4. Spread jam over coconut layer; sprinkle with pecans. Chill for 3 to 4 hours.

5. Place semisweet chocolate chips in small resealable plastic bag; seal bag. Microwave at HIGH (100%) 1 minute. Turn bag over; heat at HIGH 1 to 2 minutes or until chocolate is melted. Knead bag until chocolate is smooth.

Cut off very tiny corner of bag; drizzle chocolate onto jam layer. Melt white chocolate chips as directed for chocolate chips. Drizzle over top of chocolate layer to make lacy effect; chill until chocolate is set. Cut into bars.

Makes 3 to 3½ dozen bars

Hershey's Chocolate Chip Blondies

6 tablespoons butter or margarine, softened

¾ cup packed light brown sugar

1 egg

1 tablespoon milk

1 teaspoon vanilla extract

1 cup all-purpose flour

½ teaspoon baking soda

⅛ teaspoon salt

2 cups (12-ounce package) HERSHEY'S Semi-Sweet Chocolate Chips

½ cup coarsely chopped nuts (optional)

1. Heat oven to 350°F. Grease 9-inch square baking pan.

2. Beat butter and brown sugar in large bowl until fluffy. Add egg, milk and

vanilla; beat well. Stir together flour, baking soda and salt; add to butter mixture. Stir in chocolate chips and nuts, if desired; spread in prepared pan.

3. Bake 20 to 25 minutes or until lightly browned. Cool completely; cut into bars.

Makes about 1½ dozen bars

Pumpkin Snack Bars

Cake

    1 package (2-layer size) spice cake mix
    1 can (16 ounces) pumpkin
    ¾ cup MIRACLE WHIP® *or* MIRACLE WHIP® LIGHT Dressing
    3 eggs

Frosting

    3½ cups powdered sugar
    ½ cup (1 stick) butter *or* margarine, softened
    2 tablespoons milk
    1 teaspoon vanilla

Cake

BLEND cake mix, pumpkin, dressing and eggs with electric mixer on medium speed until well blended. Pour into greased 15×10-inch baking pan.

BAKE at 350°F for 18 to 20 minutes or until toothpick inserted in center comes out clean. Cool completely on wire rack.

Frosting

BLEND all ingredients with electric mixer on low speed until moistened. Beat on high speed until light and fluffy. Spread over cake. Cut into bars.

Makes about 3 dozen bars

Note: Bars can be baked in greased 13×9-inch baking pan. Bake at 350°F for 32 to 35 minutes or until toothpick inserted in center comes out clean. Cool and frost as directed.

Prep Time: 20 minutes
Bake Time: 20 minutes

Chocolate Caramel Nut Bars

1 package (18¼ ounces) devil's food cake mix

¾ cup butter, melted

½ cup milk, divided

60 vanilla caramels

1 cup cashews, coarsely chopped

1 cup semisweet chocolate chips

Preheat oven to 350°F. Grease 13×9-inch baking pan. Combine cake mix, butter and ¼ cup milk in medium bowl; mix well. Press half of batter into bottom of prepared pan.

Bake 7 to 8 minutes or until batter just begins to form crust. Remove from oven.

Meanwhile, combine caramels and remaining ¼ cup milk in heavy medium saucepan. Cook over low heat, stirring often, about 5 minutes or until caramels are melted and mixture is smooth.

Pour melted caramel mixture over partially baked crust. Combine cashews and chocolate chips in small bowl; sprinkle over caramel mixture.

Drop spoonfuls of remaining batter evenly over nut mixture. Return pan to oven; bake 18 to 20 minutes more or until top layer springs back when lightly touched. (Caramel center will be soft.) Let cool on wire rack before cutting into squares or bars.   *Makes about 48 bars*

Cook's Tip: *Bars can be frozen; let thaw 20 to 25 minutes before serving.*

Chocolate Caramel Nut Bars

Dish: **Bar Cookies**

Recipe
Serves:

Chocolate - Caramel - Nut Bars

1 package (18¼ ounces) devils food cake mix
¾ cup butter or margarine, melted
½ cup milk, divided
60 vanilla caramels
1 cup cashew pieces, coarsely chopped
1 cup semisweet chocolate chips

PREHEAT oven to 350° F. Grease 13×9 inch ba
Combine cake mix, butter and ¼ cup milk in m

Peachy Oatmeal Bars

Crumb Mixture

1½ cups all-purpose flour

1 cup uncooked old-fashioned oats

¾ cup butter, melted

½ cup sugar

2 teaspoons almond extract

½ teaspoon baking soda

¼ teaspoon salt

Filling

¾ cup peach preserves

⅓ cup flaked coconut

Preheat oven to 350°F. Grease 9-inch square baking pan.

Combine flour, oats, butter, sugar, almond extract, baking soda and salt in large bowl. Beat with electric mixer at low speed 1 to 2 minutes until mixture is crumbly. Reserve ¾ cup crumb mixture; press remaining crumb mixture onto bottom of prepared baking pan.

Spread peach preserves to within ½ inch of edge of crumb mixture; sprinkle reserved crumb mixture and coconut over top. Bake 22 to 27 minutes or until edges are lightly browned. Cool completely. Cut into bars.

Makes 2 to 2½ dozen bars

Strawberry Streusel Bars

Crumb Mixture

2 cups all-purpose flour

1 cup sugar

1 cup butter, softened

¾ cup pecans, coarsely chopped

1 egg

Filling

1 jar (10 ounces) strawberry preserves

Preheat oven to 350°F. Grease 9-inch square baking pan. Set aside.

For crumb mixture, combine flour, sugar, butter, pecans and egg in large mixer bowl. Beat at low speed of electric mixer, scraping bowl often, until mixture is crumbly, 2 to 3 minutes. Reserve 1 cup crumb mixture; press remaining crumb mixture onto bottom of prepared baking pan. Spread preserves to within ½ inch of edge of unbaked crumb mixture. Crumble remaining crumb mixture over preserves. Bake 42 to 50 minutes or until lightly browned. Cool completely. Cut into bars.

Makes about 24 bars

Top to Bottom:
Peachy Oatmeal Bars and
Strawberry Streusel Bars

Mini Kisses Coconut Macaroon Bars

3¾ cups (10-ounce package) MOUNDS® Sweetened Coconut Flakes

¾ cup sugar

¼ cup all-purpose flour

¼ teaspoon salt

3 egg whites

1 whole egg, slightly beaten

1 teaspoon almond extract

1 cup HERSHEY'S MINI KISSES™ Milk Chocolate Baking Pieces

1. Heat oven to 350°F. Lightly grease 9-inch square baking pan.

2. Stir together coconut, sugar, flour and salt in large bowl. Add egg whites, whole egg and almond extract; stir until well blended. Stir in Mini Kisses™. Spread mixture into prepared pan, covering all chocolate pieces with coconut mixture.

3. Bake 35 minutes or until lightly browned. Cool completely in pan on wire rack. Cover with foil; allow to stand at room temperature about 8 hours or overnight. Cut into bars.

Makes about 24 bars

Variation: Omit Mini Kisses™ in batter. Immediately after removing pan from oven, place desired number of chocolate pieces on top, pressing down lightly. Cool completely. Cut into bars.

Prep Time: 15 minutes
Bake Time: 35 minutes
Cool Time: 9 hours

Cook's Tip: Most bar cookies should cool in the pan on a wire rack until barely warm before cutting into bars or squares. Try cutting bar cookies into triangles or diamonds for a festive new shape.

Mini Kisses Coconut Macaroon Bars

Razzle-Dazzle Apple Streusel Bars

Crust and Streusel

> 2 cups QUAKER® Oats (quick or old fashioned, uncooked)
>
> 2½ cups all-purpose flour
>
> 1¼ cups sugar
>
> 2 teaspoons baking powder
>
> 1 cup (2 sticks) margarine or butter, melted

Filling

> 3 cups peeled, thinly sliced apples (about 3 medium)
>
> 2 tablespoons all-purpose flour
>
> 1 (12 ounce) jar (1 cup) raspberry or apricot preserves

Heat oven to 375°F. For crust and streusel, combine oats, flour, sugar and baking powder; mix well. Add margarine, mixing until moistened. Reserve 2 cups; set aside. Press remaining oat mixture onto bottom of 13×9-inch baking pan. Bake 15 minutes.

For filling, combine apples and flour. Stir in preserves. Spread onto crust to within ½ inch of edge. Sprinkle with reserved oat mixture, pressing lightly. Bake 30 to 35 minutes or until light golden brown. Cool completely; cut into bars. Store tightly covered.　　*Makes 2 dozen bars*

Chocolate Peanutty Crumble Bars

> ½ cup butter or margarine
>
> 1 cup all-purpose flour
>
> ¾ cup instant oats, uncooked
>
> ⅓ cup firmly packed brown sugar
>
> ½ teaspoon baking soda
>
> ½ teaspoon vanilla extract
>
> 4 SNICKERS® Bars (2.07 ounces each), cut into 8 slices each

Preheat oven to 350°F. Grease bottom of an 8-inch square pan. Melt butter in large saucepan. Remove from heat and stir in flour, oats, brown sugar, baking soda and vanilla. Blend until crumbly. Press ⅔ of the mixture into prepared pan. Arrange SNICKERS® Bar slices in pan, about ½ inch from the edge of pan. Finely crumble the remaining mixture over the sliced SNICKERS® Bars. Bake for 25 minutes or until edges are golden brown. Cool in pan on cooling rack. Cut into bars or squares to serve.

Makes 24 bars

Banana Gingerbread Bars

1 package (14.5 ounces) gingerbread
   cake mix

½ cup lukewarm water

1 ripe, medium DOLE® Banana,
   mashed (about ½ cup)

1 egg

1 small DOLE® Banana, peeled and
   chopped

½ cup DOLE® Seedless Raisins

½ cup slivered almonds

1½ cups powdered sugar

   Juice from 1 lemon

• Preheat oven to 350°F.

• In large mixer bowl, combine
gingerbread mix, water, banana purée and
egg. Beat on low speed of electric mixer
1 minute.

• Stir in chopped banana, raisins and
almonds.

• Spread batter in greased 13×9-inch
baking pan. Bake 20 to 25 minutes or
until springs back when lightly touched.

• In medium bowl, mix powdered sugar
and 3 tablespoons lemon juice to make
thin glaze. Spread over warm gingerbread.
Cool before cutting into bars.

Makes about 32 bars

Apricot Crumb Squares

1 package (about 18 ounces) light
   yellow cake mix

1 teaspoon ground cinnamon

½ teaspoon ground nutmeg

6 tablespoons cold margarine, cut
   into pieces

¾ cup uncooked multigrain oatmeal
   cereal or old-fashioned oats

1 whole egg

2 egg whites

1 tablespoon water

1 jar (10 ounces) apricot fruit spread

2 tablespoons firmly packed light
   brown sugar

Preheat oven to 350°F. Combine cake
mix, cinnamon and nutmeg in bowl. Cut
in margarine with pastry blender until
coarse crumbs form. Stir in cereal.
Reserve 1 cup mixture. Mix egg, egg
whites and water into remaining mixture.

Spread batter evenly in ungreased
13×9-inch baking pan; top with fruit
spread. Sprinkle reserved 1 cup cereal
mixture over fruit; top with brown sugar.

Bake 35 to 40 minutes or until top is
golden brown. Cool in pan on wire rack;
cut into squares. *Makes 15 squares*

Easy Turtle Squares

1 package (about 18 ounces) chocolate cake mix

½ cup butter, melted

¼ cup milk

1 cup (6-ounce package) semisweet chocolate chips

1 cup chopped pecans, divided

1 jar (12 ounces) caramel ice cream topping

1. Preheat oven to 350°F. Spray 13×9-inch pan with nonstick cooking spray.

2. Combine cake mix, butter and milk in large bowl. Press half the cake mixture into greased 13×9-inch baking pan.

3. Bake 7 to 8 minutes or until batter begins to form crust. Remove from oven. Sprinkle chips and ½ cup pecans over crust. Drizzle caramel topping over chips and pecans. Drop spoonfuls of remaining batter over caramel mixture; sprinkle with remaining ½ cup pecans.

4. Return to oven; bake 18 to 20 minutes longer or until top layer springs back when lightly touched. (Caramel center will be soft.) Cool completely on wire rack. Cut into squares. *Makes 24 bars*

Chewy Red Raspberry Bars

1 cup firmly packed light brown sugar

½ cup butter or margarine, room temperature

½ teaspoon almond extract

1 cup all-purpose flour

1 cup quick-cooking or old-fashioned oats

1 teaspoon baking powder

½ cup SMUCKER'S® Red Raspberry Preserves

Combine brown sugar and butter; beat until fluffy. Beat in almond extract. Mix in flour, oats and baking powder until crumbly. Reserve ¼ cup mixture; pat remaining mixture into bottom of greased 8-inch square baking pan. Dot preserves over crumb mixture in pan; sprinkle with reserved crumb mixture.

Bake at 350°F for 30 to 40 minutes or until brown. Cool on wire rack. Cut into bars. *Makes 12 bars*

Easy Turtle Squares

Orange Coconut Cream Bars

1 (18¼-ounce) package yellow cake mix

1 cup quick-cooking or old-fashioned oats, uncooked

¾ cup chopped nuts

½ cup butter or margarine, melted

1 large egg

1 (14-ounce) can sweetened condensed milk

2 teaspoons grated orange zest

1 cup shredded coconut

1 cup "M&M's"® Semi-Sweet Chocolate Mini Baking Bits

Preheat oven to 375°F. Lightly grease 13×9-inch baking pan; set aside. In large bowl combine cake mix, oats, nuts, butter and egg until ingredients are thoroughly moistened and mixture resembles coarse crumbs. Reserve 1 cup mixture. Firmly press remaining mixture onto bottom of prepared pan; bake 10 minutes. In separate bowl combine condensed milk and orange zest; spread over baked base. Combine reserved crumb mixture, coconut and "M&M's"® Semi-Sweet Chocolate Mini Baking Bits; sprinkle evenly over condensed milk mixture and press in lightly. Continue baking 20 to 25 minutes or until golden brown. Cool completely. Cut into bars. Store in tightly covered container. *Makes 26 bars*

S'More Cookie Bars

¾ cup (1½ sticks) IMPERIAL® Spread, melted

3 cups graham cracker crumbs

1 package (6 ounces) semi-sweet chocolate chips (1 cup)

1 cup butterscotch chips

1 cup mini marshmallows

1 can (14 ounces) sweetened condensed milk

Preheat oven to 350°F.

In 13×9-inch baking dish, combine Imperial spread with crumbs; press to form even layer. Evenly sprinkle with chocolate chips, then butterscotch chips, then marshmallows. Pour condensed milk evenly over mixture.

Bake 25 minutes or until bubbly. On wire rack, let cool completely. To serve, cut into squares. *Makes 2 dozen bars*

Orange Coconut Cream Bars

Chocolate Caramel Bars

2 cups all-purpose flour

1½ cups packed brown sugar, divided

1¼ cups butter, softened, divided

1 cup chopped pecans

1 cup (6 ounces) milk chocolate chips

Preheat oven to 350°F. Blend flour with 1 cup sugar and ½ cup butter in large bowl until crumbly. Press firmly on bottom of a 13×9-inch pan; sprinkle pecans evenly over the top. Combine remaining ½ cup sugar and ¾ cup butter in small saucepan. Cook over medium heat, stirring constantly, until mixture comes to a boil. Boil 1 minute, stirring constantly, until butter and sugar blend into a caramel sauce. Pour sauce evenly over pecans in pan. Bake 18 to 20 minutes or until caramel layer bubbles evenly all over. Remove from oven; sprinkle chocolate chips over the top. Let stand a few minutes until chips melt, then spread evenly over bars. Cool until chocolate is set. Cut into 2×1-inch bars.

Makes about 5 dozen bars

Buttery Black Raspberry Bars

1 cup butter or margarine

1 cup sugar

2 egg yolks

2 cups all-purpose flour

1 cup chopped walnuts

½ cup SMUCKER'S® Seedless Black Raspberry Jam

Beat butter until soft and creamy. Gradually add sugar, beating until mixture is light and fluffy. Add egg yolks; blend well. Gradually add flour; mix thoroughly. Fold in walnuts.

Spoon half of batter into greased 8-inch square pan; spread evenly. Top with jam; cover with remaining batter.

Bake at 325°F for 1 hour or until lightly browned. Cool and cut into 2×1-inch bars. *Makes 32 bars*

Mystical Layered Bars

⅓ cup butter

1 cup graham cracker crumbs

½ cup uncooked old-fashioned or quick oats

1 can (14 ounces) sweetened condensed milk

1 cup flaked coconut

¾ cup semisweet chocolate chips

¾ cup raisins

1 cup coarsely chopped pecans

Preheat oven to 350°F. Melt butter in 13×9-inch baking pan. Remove from oven.

Sprinkle graham cracker crumbs and oats evenly over butter; press with fork. Drizzle condensed milk over oats. Layer coconut, chocolate chips, raisins and pecans over milk.

Bake 25 to 30 minutes or until lightly browned. Cool in pan on wire rack 5 minutes; cut into 2×1½-inch bars. Cool completely in pan on wire rack. Store tightly covered at room temperature or freeze up to 3 months.

Makes 3 dozen bars

Oatmeal Brownie Gems

2¾ cups quick-cooking or old-fashioned oats, uncooked

1 cup all-purpose flour

1 cup firmly packed light brown sugar

1 cup coarsely chopped walnuts

1 teaspoon baking soda

1 cup butter or margarine, melted

1¾ cups "M&M's"® Semi-Sweet Chocolate Mini Baking Bits

1 (19- to 21-ounce) package fudge brownie mix, prepared according to package directions for fudge-like brownies

Preheat oven to 350°F. In large bowl combine oats, flour, sugar, nuts and baking soda; add butter until mixture forms coarse crumbs. Toss in "M&M's"® Semi-Sweet Chocolate Mini Baking Bits until evenly distributed. Reserve 3 cups mixture. Pat remaining mixture onto bottom of 15×10-inch pan to form crust. Pour prepared brownie mix over crust, carefully spreading into thin layer. Sprinkle reserved crumb mixture over top of brownie mixture; pat down. Bake 25 to 30 minutes or until toothpick inserted in center comes out with moist crumbs. Cool. Cut into bars. *Makes 48 bars*

Marshmallow Krispie Bars

1 package (21 ounces) DUNCAN HINES® Family-Style Chewy Fudge Brownie Mix

1 package (10½ ounces) miniature marshmallows

1½ cups semi-sweet chocolate chips

1 cup creamy peanut butter

1 tablespoon butter or margarine

1½ cups crisp rice cereal

1. Preheat oven to 350°F. Grease bottom of 13×9-inch pan.

2. Prepare and bake brownies following package directions for cake-like recipe. Remove from oven. Sprinkle marshmallows on hot brownies. Return to oven. Bake for 3 minutes longer.

3. Place chocolate chips, peanut butter and butter in medium saucepan. Cook over low heat, stirring constantly, until chips are melted. Add rice cereal; mix well. Spread mixture over marshmallow layer. Refrigerate until chilled. Cut into bars.   *Makes about 2 dozen bars*

Tip: For a special presentation, cut cookies into diamond shapes.

Chewy Bar Cookies

½ cup margarine, softened

1 cup firmly packed light brown sugar

2 eggs

3 (1¼-ounce) packages Instant CREAM OF WHEAT® Cereal Baked Apple-Cinnamon Flavor

⅔ cup all-purpose flour

2 teaspoons baking powder

1 cup PLANTERS® Walnuts, finely chopped

Preheat oven to 350°F. Beat margarine and brown sugar in large bowl with electric mixer at medium speed until creamy. Beat in eggs until light and fluffy. Stir in cereal, flour and baking powder. Mix in walnuts. Spread batter in greased 15½×10½-inch baking pan.

Bake 20 to 25 minutes or until golden brown. Cool completely in pan on wire rack. Cut into bars.

Makes about 48 bars

Marshmallow Krispie Bars

Creamy Lemon Bars

1 package (2-layer size) lemon cake mix

3 large eggs, divided

½ cup oil

2 packages (8 ounces each) PHILADELPHIA® Cream Cheese, softened

1 container (8 ounces) BREAKSTONE'S® or KNUDSEN® Sour Cream

½ cup granulated sugar

1 teaspoon grated lemon peel

1 tablespoon lemon juice

Powdered sugar

MIX cake mix, 1 egg and oil. Press mixture onto bottom and up sides of lightly greased 15×10-inch baking pan. Bake at 350°F for 10 minutes.

BEAT cream cheese with electric mixer on medium speed until smooth. Add remaining 2 eggs, sour cream, granulated sugar, peel and juice; mix until blended. Pour batter into crust.

BAKE at 350°F for 30 to 35 minutes or until filling is just set in center and edges are light golden brown. Cool. Sprinkle with powdered sugar. Cut into bars. Store leftover bars in refrigerator.

Makes 2 dozen

Prep: 15 minutes
Bake: 35 minutes

Cook's Tip: *If both lemon peel and juice are needed, grate the lemon before juicing. Always wash the lemon before using the peel.*

Creamy Lemon Bars

Minty Shortbread Squares

1½ cups (3 sticks) butter, softened

1½ cups powdered sugar

2 teaspoons mint extract, divided

3 cups all-purpose flour

½ cup unsweetened cocoa powder

1¾ cups "M&M's"® Chocolate Mini Baking Bits, divided

1 (16-ounce) container prepared white frosting

Several drops green food coloring

Preheat oven to 325°F. Lightly grease 15×10-inch baking pan; set aside. In large bowl cream butter and sugar until light and fluffy; add 1 teaspoon mint extract. In medium bowl combine flour and cocoa powder; blend into creamed mixture. Stir in 1 cup "M&M's"® Chocolate Mini Baking Bits. Dough will be stiff. Press dough into prepared baking pan with lightly floured fingers. Bake 16 to 18 minutes. Cool completely. Combine frosting, remaining 1 teaspoon mint extract and green food coloring. Spread frosting over shortbread; sprinkle with remaining ¾ cup "M&M's"® Chocolate Mini Baking Bits. Cut into squares. Store in tightly covered container.

Makes 36 squares

Variation: Use 1 (19- to 21-ounce) package fudge brownie mix, prepared according to package directions for chewy brownies, adding 1 teaspoon mint extract to liquid ingredients. Stir in 1 cup "M&M's"® Chocolate Mini Baking Bits. Spread dough in lightly greased 13×9-inch baking pan. Bake in preheated oven according to package directions. Cool completely. Prepare frosting and decorate as directed above. Store in tightly covered container. Makes 24 squares.

Minty Shortbread Squares

Peanut Butter "Makes Everything Better" Bars

1¼ cups "M&M's"® Milk Chocolate Mini Baking Bits, divided

1 package (18 ounces) refrigerated sugar cookie dough

½ cup creamy peanut butter

¼ cup all-purpose flour

¼ cup powdered sugar

1 square (1 ounce) milk chocolate

Preheat oven to 350°F. Lightly grease 8×8-inch baking pan; set aside. In medium bowl stir 1 cup "M&M's"® Milk Chocolate Mini Baking Bits into dough. In small bowl beat peanut butter, flour and powdered sugar until well combined. Reserve ½ of cookie dough. Press remaining dough into prepared pan; layer with peanut butter mixture. Top with reserved dough. Bake 20 to 25 minutes or until golden brown. Remove pan to wire rack; cool completely. Place chocolate square in small microwave-safe bowl. Microwave at HIGH 20 seconds; stir. Repeat as necessary until chocolate is completely melted, stirring at 10-second intervals. Drizzle melted chocolate over bars and sprinkle with remaining ¼ cup "M&M's"® Milk Chocolate Mini Baking

Bits. Cut into bars. Store in tightly covered container. *Makes 16 bars*

Walnut Apple Dumpling Bars

6 tablespoons (¾ stick) butter or margarine

1 cup packed light brown sugar

1 cup all-purpose flour

1 teaspoon baking powder

1½ teaspoons ground cinnamon

2 eggs

1½ cups coarsely chopped California walnuts

1 Granny Smith or Pippin apple, coarsely grated* (about 1 cup lightly packed)

Powdered sugar

*It is not necessary to peel or core apple. Use hand-held grater, turning apple as you go, until only core remains.

Preheat oven to 350°F.

Melt butter in 3-quart saucepan. Add sugar. Stir until sugar is melted and mixture begins to bubble; cool. In small bowl combine flour, baking powder and cinnamon; mix to blend thoroughly. Beat eggs into butter mixture in saucepan, 1 at a time, then add flour mixture. Add walnuts and apple. Turn into buttered and floured 9-inch square baking pan; smooth top. Bake 25 to 35 minutes until pick inserted in center comes out clean and edges begin to pull away from sides of pan. Cool completely on rack. Cut into 3×1-inch bars. Garnish with powdered sugar. *Makes 24 bars*

Favorite recipe from **Walnut Marketing Board**

Spiced Date Bars

½ cup margarine, softened
1 cup packed brown sugar
2 eggs
¾ cup light sour cream
2 cups all-purpose flour
1 teaspoon baking soda
1 teaspoon ground cinnamon
½ teaspoon ground nutmeg
1 package (8 or 10 ounces) DOLE® Chopped Dates or Pitted Dates, chopped
Powdered sugar (optional)

• Beat margarine and brown sugar until light and fluffy. Beat in eggs, one at a time. Stir in sour cream.

• Combine dry ingredients. Beat into sour cream mixture; stir in dates. Spread batter evenly into greased 13×9-inch baking pan.

• Bake at 350°F 25 to 30 minutes or until toothpick inserted in center comes out clean. Cool completely in pan on wire rack. Cut into bars. Dust with powdered sugar. *Makes 24 bars*

Prep Time: 15 minutes
Bake Time: 30 minutes

Power Bars

¾ cup butter or margarine

2 cups firmly packed brown sugar

2 cups all-purpose flour

2 cups old-fashioned or quick-cooking oats, uncooked

2 teaspoons baking soda

1 (21-ounce) can cherry pie filling

2 tablespoons granulated sugar

1 tablespoon cornstarch

½ teaspoon almond extract

Beat butter and brown sugar in medium bowl with electric mixer at medium speed until light and fluffy. Combine flour, oats and baking soda. Add flour mixture to sugar mixture; mix on low speed until crumbly.

Spread two-thirds of oat mixture into bottom of ungreased 13×9-inch baking pan. Press down to form crust.

Process cherry filling in food processor or blender until smooth. Pour into medium saucepan. Combine granulated sugar and cornstarch; stir into cherry filling. Cook, stirring constantly, over low heat until mixture is thick and bubbly. Stir in almond extract. Pour cherry mixture over oat layer; spread evenly. Top with remaining oat mixture.

Bake in preheated 325°F oven 45 minutes or until golden brown. Cool before cutting.

Makes 32 (2-inch) bars

Favorite recipe from **Cherry Marketing Institute**

Toffee Bars

½ cup butter, softened

½ cup packed light brown sugar

1 egg yolk

1 teaspoon vanilla

1 cup all-purpose flour

1 cup (6 ounces) milk chocolate chips

½ cup chopped walnuts or pecans

Preheat oven to 350°F. Lightly grease a 13×9-inch pan. Cream butter and sugar in large bowl. Blend in egg yolk and vanilla. Stir in flour until well blended. Press on bottom of prepared pan. Bake 15 minutes or until golden. Remove from oven; sprinkle chocolate chips over the top. Let stand a few minutes until chips melt, then spread evenly over bars. Sprinkle nuts over chocolate. Score into 2×1½-inch bars while still warm. Cool completely in pan on wire rack before cutting and removing from pan.

Makes about 3 dozen bars

Power Bars

Chocolate Dream Bars

½ cup butter, softened

1½ cups packed light brown sugar, divided

1 egg yolk

1 cup plus 2 tablespoons all-purpose flour, divided

2 eggs

1 cup (6 ounces) semisweet chocolate chips

½ cup chopped toasted walnuts

Preheat oven to 375°F. Grease 13×9-inch baking pan. Beat butter with ½ cup brown sugar and egg yolk in large bowl until light and well blended. (There should be no brown sugar lumps.) Stir in 1 cup flour until well blended. Press dough onto bottom of prepared pan. Bake 12 to 15 minutes or until golden. Meanwhile, beat remaining 1 cup sugar, 2 tablespoons flour and whole eggs in same bowl until light and frothy. Spread mixture over hot baked crust. Return to oven; bake about 15 minutes or until topping is set. Remove from oven; sprinkle chocolate chips over top. Let stand until chips melt, then spread evenly over bars. Sprinkle walnuts over chocolate. Cool in pan on wire rack. Cut into bars. *Makes about 4 dozen bars*

Orange Chess Bars

Crust

1 package DUNCAN HINES® Moist Deluxe® Orange Supreme Cake Mix

½ cup vegetable oil

⅓ cup chopped pecans

Topping

1 pound confectioners' sugar (3½ to 4 cups)

1 (8-ounce) package cream cheese, softened

2 eggs

2 teaspoons grated orange peel

1. Preheat oven to 350°F. Grease 13×9-inch baking pan.

2. For crust, combine cake mix, oil and pecans in large bowl. Stir until blended (mixture will be crumbly). Press in bottom of prepared pan.

3. For topping, combine confectioners' sugar and cream cheese in large bowl. Beat at low speed with electric mixer until blended. Add eggs and orange peel. Beat at low speed until blended. Pour over crust. Bake 30 to 35 minutes or until topping is set. Cool. Refrigerate until ready to serve. *Makes about 24 bars*

Heath® Bits Bars

2 packages (8 ounces each) HEATH®
   BITS, divided
1 cup (2 sticks) butter, softened
1 cup packed light brown sugar
1 egg yolk
1 teaspoon vanilla extract
2 cups all-purpose flour
½ cup finely chopped pecans

1. Heat oven to 350°F. Set aside ¾ cups Heath Bits.

2. Beat butter in large bowl until creamy; add brown sugar, egg yolk and vanilla; beat until blended. Using spoon, mix in flour, remaining Heath Bits and pecans. Press into ungreased 15½×10½-inch jelly-roll pan.

3. Bake 18 to 20 minutes or until browned. Remove from oven; immediately sprinkle reserved ¾ cup Heath Bits over top. Cool slightly. Cut into bars while warm. Cool completely.

Makes about 4 dozen bars

Chocolate Pecan Pie Bars

Crust

1½ cups all-purpose flour
 ½ cup (1 stick) butter, softened
 ¼ cup firmly packed brown sugar

Filling

 3 eggs
¾ cup dark or light corn syrup
¾ cup granulated sugar
2 tablespoons (¼ stick) butter, melted
1 teaspoon vanilla extract
1½ cups coarsely chopped pecans
2 cups (12-ounce package) NESTLÉ®
   TOLL HOUSE® Semi-Sweet
   Chocolate Morsels

For Crust

BEAT flour, butter and brown sugar in small mixer bowl until crumbly. Press into greased 13×9-inch baking pan. Bake in preheated 350°F. oven for 12 to 15 minutes until lightly browned.

For Filling

BEAT eggs, corn syrup, granulated sugar, melted butter and vanilla in bowl with wire whisk. Stir in pecans and morsels. Pour over baked crust. Bake in preheated 350°F. oven for 25 to 30 minutes until set. Cool. *Makes 3 dozen bars*

Mini Kisses Praline Bars

2 cups all-purpose flour

1⅓ cups packed light brown sugar, divided

½ cup (1 stick) plus ⅔ cup butter, divided

1 cup coarsely chopped pecans

1¾ cups (10-ounce package) HERSHEY'S MINI KISSES™ Chocolate Baking Pieces

1. Heat oven to 350°F.

2. Stir together flour and 1 cup brown sugar in large bowl; cut in ½ cup butter with pastry blender until fine crumbs form. Press mixture into 13×9-inch baking pan; sprinkle with pecans.

3. Place remaining ⅔ cup butter and remaining ⅓ cup brown sugar in small saucepan; cook over medium heat, stirring constantly, until mixture boils. Continue boiling, stirring constantly, 30 seconds, until sugar dissolves; drizzle evenly over pecans and crust.

4. Bake 18 to 22 minutes until topping is bubbly and golden; remove from oven. Immediately sprinkle Mini Kisses™ over top. Cool completely in pan on wire rack. Cut into bars.   *Makes about 36 bars*

Note: Bloom, the gray film that sometimes appears on chocolate and chocolate chips, occurs when chocolate is exposed to varying temperatures or has been stored in damp conditions. Bloom does not affect the taste or quality of the chocolate.

Cook's Tip: Store cookies in airtight containers, such as screw-top jars or resealable plastic food storage bags. Bar cookies may be stored tightly covered in the baking pan.

Mini Kisses Praline Bars

Blueberry Cheesecake Bars

1 package DUNCAN HINES®
   Bakery-Style Blueberry Streusel
   Muffin Mix

¼ cup cold butter or margarine

⅓ cup finely chopped pecans

1 (8-ounce) package cream cheese,
   softened

½ cup sugar

1 egg

3 tablespoons lemon juice

1 teaspoon grated lemon peel

1. Preheat oven to 350°F. Grease 9-inch square pan.

2. Rinse blueberries from Mix with cold water and drain.

3. Place muffin mix in medium bowl; cut in butter with pastry blender or two knives. Stir in pecans. Press into bottom of prepared pan. Bake 15 minutes or until set.

4. Combine cream cheese and sugar in medium bowl. Beat until smooth. Add egg, lemon juice and lemon peel. Beat well. Spread over baked crust. Sprinkle with blueberries. Sprinkle topping packet from Mix over blueberries. Return to oven. Bake 35 to 40 minutes or until

filling is set. Cool completely. Refrigerate until ready to serve. Cut into bars.

Makes about 16 bars

White Chocolate & Almond Brownies

12 ounces white chocolate, broken
   into pieces

1 cup unsalted butter

3 eggs

¾ cup all-purpose flour

1 teaspoon vanilla

½ cup slivered almonds

Preheat oven to 325°F. Grease and flour 9-inch square pan. Melt white chocolate and butter in large saucepan over low heat, stirring constantly. (Do not be concerned if the white chocolate separates.) Remove from heat when chocolate is just melted. With electric mixer, beat in eggs until mixture is smooth. Beat in flour and vanilla. Spread batter evenly in prepared pan. Sprinkle almonds evenly over top. Bake 30 to 35 minutes or just until set in center. Cool completely in pan on wire rack. Cut into squares.   *Makes 16 brownies*

Blueberry Cheesecake Bars

"Everything but the Kitchen Sink" Bar Cookies

1 package (18 ounces) refrigerated chocolate chip cookie dough

1 jar (7 ounces) marshmallow creme

½ cup creamy peanut butter

1½ cups toasted corn cereal

½ cup miniature candy-coated chocolate pieces

1. Preheat oven to 350°F. Grease 13×9-inch baking pan. Remove dough from wrapper according to package directions.

2. Press dough into prepared baking pan. Bake 13 minutes.

3. Remove baking pan from oven. Drop teaspoonfuls of marshmallow creme and peanut butter over hot cookie base.

4. Bake 1 minute. Carefully spread marshmallow creme and peanut butter over cookie base.

5. Sprinkle cereal and chocolate pieces over melted marshmallow and peanut butter mixture.

6. Bake 7 minutes. Cool completely on wire rack. Cut into 2-inch bars.

Makes 3 dozen bars

Butterscotch Pan Cookies

1 package DUNCAN HINES® Moist Deluxe® French Vanilla Cake Mix

2 eggs

1 cup butter or margarine, melted

¾ cup firmly packed light brown sugar

1 teaspoon vanilla extract

1 package (12 ounces) butterscotch flavored chips

1½ cups chopped pecans

1. Preheat oven to 375°F. Grease 15½×10½×1-inch jelly-roll pan.

2. Combine cake mix, eggs, melted butter, brown sugar and vanilla extract in large bowl. Beat at low speed with electric mixer until smooth and creamy. Stir in butterscotch chips and pecans. Spread in pan. Bake at 375°F for 20 to 25 minutes or until golden brown. Cool completely. Cut into bars.

Makes 48 bars

Tip: You can substitute chocolate or peanut butter flavored chips for the butterscotch flavored chips.

"Everything but the Kitchen Sink" Bar Cookies

Sweet Walnut Maple Bars

Crust

> 1 package DUNCAN HINES® Moist Deluxe® Classic Yellow Cake Mix, divided
>
> ⅓ cup butter or margarine, melted
>
> 1 egg

Topping

> 1⅓ cups MRS. BUTTERWORTH'S® Maple Syrup
>
> 3 eggs
>
> ⅓ cup firmly packed light brown sugar
>
> ½ teaspoon maple flavoring or vanilla extract
>
> 1 cup chopped walnuts

1. Preheat oven to 350°F. Grease 13×9-inch pan.

2. For crust, reserve ⅔ cup cake mix; set aside. Combine remaining cake mix, melted butter and egg in large bowl. Stir until thoroughly blended. (Mixture will be crumbly.) Press into pan. Bake at 350°F for 15 to 20 minutes or until light golden brown.

3. For topping, combine reserved cake mix, maple syrup, eggs, brown sugar and maple flavoring in large bowl. Beat at low speed with electric mixer for 3 minutes. Pour over crust. Sprinkle with walnuts. Bake at 350°F for 30 to 35 minutes or until filling is set. Cool completely. Cut into bars. Store leftover cookie bars in refrigerator.   *Makes 24 bars*

Chocolate Peanut Butter Bars

> 2 cups creamy peanut butter
>
> 1 cup sugar
>
> 2 eggs
>
> 1 package (8 squares) BAKER'S® Semi-Sweet Baking Chocolate, melted, divided
>
> 1 cup chopped peanuts

HEAT oven to 350°F. Line 13×9-inch baking pan with foil.

BEAT peanut butter, sugar and eggs in large bowl with electric mixer on medium speed until light and fluffy. Reserve 1 cup; set aside.

STIR ½ of the melted chocolate into mixture in bowl. Press into prepared pan. Spread reserved peanut butter mixture over top.

BAKE 30 minutes or until edges are lightly browned. Spread remaining melted chocolate evenly over top. Sprinkle with peanuts. Cool in pan on wire rack. Lift out of pan onto cutting board.

Makes 3 dozen

Storage Know-How: Store in tightly covered container up to 1 week.

Prep Time: 15 minutes
Bake Time: 30 minutes

Fruit and Oat Squares

1 cup all-purpose flour
1 cup uncooked quick oats
¾ cup packed light brown sugar
½ teaspoon baking soda
¼ teaspoon salt
¼ teaspoon ground cinnamon
⅓ cup margarine or butter, melted
¾ cup apricot, cherry or other fruit flavor preserves

1. Preheat oven to 350°F. Spray 9-inch square baking pan with nonstick cooking spray; set aside.

2. Combine flour, oats, brown sugar, baking soda, salt and cinnamon in medium bowl; mix well. Add margarine; stir with fork until mixture is crumbly. Reserve ¾ cup crumb mixture for

topping. Press remaining crumb mixture evenly onto bottom of prepared pan. Bake 5 to 7 minutes or until lightly browned. Spread preserves onto crust; sprinkle with reserved crumb mixture.

3. Bake 20 to 25 minutes or until golden brown. Cool completely in pan on wire rack. Cut into 16 squares.

Makes 16 servings

Tip: Store individually wrapped Fruit and Oat Squares at room temperature up to 3 days or freeze up to 1 month.

Chocolate Cherry Torte
(page 166)

Chocolate Indulgences

❧ ❧ ❧

Chocolate is delightful, divine, heavenly, sinful and simple. Start with any type of chocolate and create an indulgence. From casual to elegant, we've collected a chocolate lover's assortment of luscious bars, chewy cookies, fudgy cakes, decadent pies, and rich and gooey brownies.

Satisfy your cravings with Chocolate Pecan Pie (page 188), Ultimate Brownies (page 168) or Chocolate Dream Torte (page 162). It must be chocolate—and, it must be easy.

Chocolate Nut Bars

1¾ cups graham cracker crumbs

½ cup (1 stick) butter or margarine, melted

1 (14-ounce) can EAGLE® BRAND Sweetened Condensed Milk (NOT evaporated milk)

2 cups (12 ounces) semi-sweet chocolate chips, divided

1 teaspoon vanilla extract

1 cup chopped nuts

1. Preheat oven to 375°F. Combine crumbs and butter; press firmly on bottom of 13×9-inch baking pan. Bake 8 minutes. Reduce oven temperature to 350°F.

2. In small saucepan, melt Eagle Brand with 1 cup chocolate chips and vanilla. Spread chocolate mixture over prepared crust. Top with remaining 1 cup chocolate chips, then nuts; press down firmly.

3. Bake 25 to 30 minutes. Cool. Chill if desired. Cut into bars. Store loosely covered at room temperature.

Makes 24 to 36 bars

Prep Time: 10 minutes
Bake Time: 33 to 38 minutes

Scrumptious Minted Brownies

1 (21-ounce) package DUNCAN HINES® Family-Style Chewy Fudge Brownie Mix

⅓ cup water

⅓ cup vegetable oil

1 egg

48 chocolate crème de menthe candy wafers, divided

1. Preheat oven to 350°F. Grease bottom of 13×9-inch pan.

2. Combine brownie mix, water, oil and egg in large bowl. Stir with spoon until well blended, about 50 strokes. Spread in prepared pan. Bake at 350°F for 25 minutes or until set. Place 30 candy wafers evenly over hot brownies. Let stand for 1 minute to melt. Spread candy wafers to frost brownies. Score frosting into 36 bars by running tip of knife through melted candy. (Do not cut through brownies.) Cut remaining 18 candy wafers in half lengthwise; place halves on each scored bar. Cool completely. Cut into bars.

Makes 36 brownies

Chocolate Nut Bars

Cappuccino Bon Bons

1 (21-ounce) package DUNCAN
   HINES® Family-Style Chewy
   Fudge Brownie Mix
2 eggs
⅓ cup water
⅓ cup vegetable oil
1½ tablespoons instant coffee
1 teaspoon ground cinnamon
   Whipped topping
   Cinnamon

1. Preheat oven to 350°F. Place 2-inch foil cupcake liners on cookie sheet.

2. Combine brownie mix, eggs, water, oil, instant coffee and cinnamon. Stir with spoon until well blended, about 50 strokes. Fill each cupcake liner with 1 measuring tablespoon batter. Bake 12 to 15 minutes or until wooden toothpick inserted in center comes out clean. Cool completely. Garnish with whipped topping and a dash of cinnamon. Refrigerate until ready to serve.

Makes about 40 bon bons

Tip: To make larger Bon Bons, use twelve 2½-inch foil cupcake liners and fill with ¼ cup batter. Bake 28 to 30 minutes.

Banana Rum Brownies

1 box (about 21 ounces) brownie mix
¼ cup chocolate milk or regular milk
1 tablespoon rum extract
3 DOLE® Bananas, cubed
½ cup toasted chopped pecans

• Prepare brownie mix as directed on package in large bowl; set aside.

• Heat milk and extract in medium saucepan until hot. Add bananas and stir for 1 minute to heat through.

• Pour banana mixture and nuts into brownie mix and stir. Pour into lightly greased 9-inch square pan.

• Bake at 350°F 35 to 40 minutes or until toothpick inserted in center comes out clean. Sprinkle with powdered sugar, if desired. Cut into bars.

Makes 16 servings

Prep Time: 15 minutes
Bake Time: 40 minutes

Cappuccino Bon Bons

Decadent Pie

¾ cup packed brown sugar

¾ cup light or dark corn syrup

4 squares BAKER'S® Semi-Sweet
  Baking Chocolate

6 tablespoons butter or margarine

3 eggs

1⅓ cups BAKER'S® ANGEL FLAKE®
  Coconut

1 cup chopped pecans

1 unbaked deep dish pie crust (9 inch)

1 tub (8 ounces) COOL WHIP®
  Whipped Topping, thawed

2 tablespoons bourbon whiskey
  (optional)

HEAT oven to 350°F.

MICROWAVE brown sugar and corn syrup in large microwavable bowl on HIGH 3 minutes or until boiling. Stir in chocolate and butter until chocolate is completely melted. Cool slightly.

STIR in eggs, one at a time, beating well after each addition. Stir in coconut and pecans. Pour into crust.

BAKE 1 hour or until pie is set. Cool on wire rack. Mix whipped topping and bourbon. Serve with pie.

Makes 8 servings

Top of Stove: Cook and stir brown sugar and corn syrup in heavy 3-quart saucepan on medium heat until boiling. Remove from heat. Add chocolate and butter; stir until chocolate is completely melted. Cool slightly. Continue as directed.

Prep Time: 15 minutes
Bake Time: 1 hour

Double Chocolate Peanut Cookies Made with Snickers® Bars

¾ cup margarine, softened

⅓ cup granulated sugar

⅓ cup firmly packed light brown
  sugar

1 large egg

1 teaspoon vanilla extract

1½ cups all-purpose flour

2 tablespoons cocoa powder

¾ teaspoon baking soda

¼ teaspoon salt

4 SNICKERS® Bars (2.07 ounces
  each), coarsely chopped

Preheat oven to 350°F. In large mixing bowl, cream margarine and sugars. Add egg and vanilla; beat until light and fluffy. Combine flour, cocoa powder, baking soda and salt; gradually blend into creamed mixture. Stir in chopped SNICKERS® Bars until evenly blended. Drop by heaping tablespoonfuls about 2 inches apart onto ungreased cookie sheets. Bake 9 to 13 minutes. Cool 1 minute on cookie sheets; remove to wire cooling racks. Store in tightly covered container.

Makes about 3 dozen cookies

Cook's Tip: *Chocolate chips and chocolate squares hold their shapes when melted in a microwave oven and can easily scorch if you wait for them to look melted. Stir chocolate often to determine if it is melted.*

Brownie Peanut Butter Cupcakes

18 REYNOLDS® Foil Baking Cups

⅓ **cup creamy peanut butter**

¼ **cup light cream cheese**

2 **tablespoons sugar**

1 **egg**

1 **package (about 19 ounces) fudge brownie mix**

½ **cup candy coated peanut butter candies**

PREHEAT oven to 350°F. Place Reynolds Foil Baking Cups in muffin pans or on cookie sheet; set aside. Beat peanut butter, cream cheese, sugar and egg in bowl with electric mixer; set aside.

PREPARE brownie mix following package directions; set aside. Place 1 heaping teaspoon of peanut butter mixture in center of each baking cup. With spoon or small ice cream scoop, fill baking cups half full with brownie batter. Sprinkle each brownie cupcake with peanut butter candies.

BAKE 25 minutes; do not overbake. Cool.

Makes 18 brownie cupcakes

Chocolate Dream Torte

1 package DUNCAN HINES® Moist
Deluxe® Dark Chocolate Fudge
Cake Mix

1 (6-ounce) package semisweet
chocolate chips, melted

1 (8-ounce) container frozen nondairy whipped topping, thawed,
divided

1 container DUNCAN HINES®
Creamy Home-Style Milk
Chocolate Frosting

3 tablespoons finely chopped dry
roasted pistachios

1. Preheat oven to 350°F. Grease and flour
two 9-inch round cake pans.

2. Prepare, bake and cool cake as directed
on package for basic recipe.

3. For chocolate hearts garnish, spread
melted chocolate to ⅛-inch thickness on
waxed paper-lined baking sheet. Cut
shapes with heart cookie cutter when
chocolate begins to set. Refrigerate until
firm. Push out heart shapes. Set aside.

4. To assemble, split each cake layer in
half horizontally. Place one split cake
layer on serving plate. Spread one-third
of whipped topping on top. Repeat with
remaining layers and whipped topping,
leaving top plain. Frost sides and top with
frosting. Sprinkle pistachios on top.
Position chocolate hearts by pushing
points down into cake. Refrigerate until
ready to serve.

Makes 12 to 16 servings

Chocolate Strawberry Dream Torte:
Omit semisweet chocolate chips and
chopped pistachios. Proceed as directed
through step 2. Fold 1½ cups chopped
fresh strawberries into whipped topping
in large bowl. Assemble as directed, filling
torte with strawberry mixture and
frosting with Milk Chocolate frosting.
Garnish cake with strawberry fans and
mint leaves, if desired.

Chocolate Dream Torte

Chocolate Chunk Cookie Pie

½ package (15 ounces) refrigerated pie crust

¾ cup (1½ sticks) butter *or* margarine, softened

½ cup granulated sugar

½ cup firmly packed brown sugar

2 eggs

1 teaspoon vanilla

½ cup flour

1 cup BAKER'S® Semi-Sweet Chocolate Chunks

1 cup chopped nuts (optional)

HEAT oven to 325°F. Prepare pie crust as directed on package, using 9-inch pie plate.

BEAT butter and sugars in large bowl with electric mixer on medium speed until light and fluffy. Add eggs and vanilla; beat well. Beat in flour on low speed. Stir in chocolate chunks and nuts. Spread in prepared crust.

BAKE 65 to 70 minutes or until toothpick inserted into center comes out clean. Cool completely on wire rack.

Makes 8 servings

Prep Time: 20 minutes
Bake Time: 70 minutes

Quick Rocky Road Cake

1 package DUNCAN HINES® Moist Deluxe® Devil's Food Cake Mix

1 container DUNCAN HINES® Creamy Home-Style Classic Vanilla Frosting

½ cup creamy peanut butter

⅓ cup semi-sweet chocolate chips

⅓ cup salted cocktail peanuts

1. Preheat oven to 350°F. Grease and flour 13×9-inch pan.

2. Prepare, bake and cool cake following package directions for basic recipe.

3. Combine Vanilla frosting and peanut butter in medium bowl. Frost top of cake. Sprinkle with chocolate chips and peanuts.
Makes 12 to 16 servings

Tip: For an easy treat for kids, follow package directions for making cupcakes. Frost and decorate as directed above.

Chocolate Chunk Cookie Pie

Chocolate Cherry Torte

1 package DUNCAN HINES® Moist Deluxe® Devil's Food Cake Mix

1 can (21 ounces) cherry pie filling

¼ teaspoon almond extract

1 container (8 ounces) frozen whipped topping, thawed and divided

¼ cup toasted sliced almonds, for garnish (see Tip)

1. Preheat oven to 350°F. Grease and flour two 9-inch round cake pans.

2. Prepare, bake and cool cake following package directions for basic recipe. Combine cherry pie filling and almond extract in small bowl. Stir until blended.

3. To assemble, place one cake layer on serving plate. Spread with 1 cup whipped topping, then half the cherry pie filling mixture. Top with second cake layer. Spread remaining pie filling to within 1½ inches of cake edge. Decorate cake edge with remaining whipped topping. Garnish with sliced almonds.

Makes 12 to 16 servings

Tip: To toast almonds, spread in a single layer on baking sheet. Bake at 325°F 4 to 6 minutes or until fragrant and golden.

Decadent Brownie Pie

1 (9-inch) unbaked pastry shell

1 cup (6 ounces) semi-sweet chocolate chips

¼ cup (½ stick) butter or margarine

1 (14-ounce) can EAGLE® BRAND Sweetened Condensed Milk (NOT evaporated milk)

½ cup biscuit baking mix

2 eggs

1 teaspoon vanilla extract

1 cup chopped nuts

Vanilla ice cream

1. Preheat oven to 375°F. Bake pastry shell 10 minutes; remove from oven. Reduce oven temperature to 325°F.

2. In saucepan over low heat, melt chips with butter.

3. In mixing bowl, beat chocolate mixture with Eagle Brand, biscuit mix, eggs and vanilla until smooth. Add nuts. Pour into pastry shell.

4. Bake 35 to 40 minutes or until center is set. Serve warm or at room temperature with ice cream. *Makes 1 (9-inch) pie*

Prep Time: 25 minutes
Bake Time: 45 to 50 minutes

Easy Chocolate Macaroons

2 squares BAKER'S® Unsweetened Baking Chocolate

1 can (15 ounces) sweetened condensed milk

2 squares BAKER'S® Premium White Baking Chocolate, chopped

2 cups BAKER'S® ANGEL FLAKE® Coconut

1 cup chopped pecans

HEAT oven to 350°F.

MICROWAVE unsweetened chocolate and condensed milk in large microwavable bowl on HIGH 2 minutes or until chocolate is almost melted. Stir until chocolate is completely melted.

STIR in chopped white chocolate, coconut and pecans. Drop by heaping teaspoonfuls onto greased cookie sheets.

BAKE 10 to 12 minutes or until tops are set. Immediately remove to wire racks and cool completely. *Makes 2 dozen*

Storage Know-How: Store in tightly covered container up to 1 week.

Prep Time: 15 minutes
Bake Time: 10 to 12 minutes

Chocolate Pie

1¼ cups sugar

½ cup reduced-fat biscuit mix

3 tablespoons unsweetened cocoa powder, sifted

2 tablespoons margarine, melted

1 whole egg

3 egg whites

1½ teaspoons vanilla

1. Preheat oven to 350°F. Spray 9-inch pie pan with nonstick cooking spray. Set aside.

2. Combine sugar, biscuit mix and cocoa in large bowl; mix well. Add margarine, egg, egg whites and vanilla; mix well. Pour mixture into prepared pan.

3. Bake 40 minutes or until knife inserted in center comes out clean. Garnish with powdered sugar, if desired.

Makes 8 servings

> **Cook's Tip:** *Cocoa powder is sold plain for baking, or mixed with other ingredients such as milk powder and sugar, commonly known as hot chocolate mix. Cocoa mixes should not be substituted for cocoa powder in recipes.*

Ultimate Brownies

½ cup MIRACLE WHIP® *or*
　MIRACLE WHIP LIGHT
　Dressing

2 eggs, beaten

¼ cup cold water

1 package (21.5 ounces) fudge
　brownie mix

3 milk chocolate bars (7 ounces each),
　divided

　PLANTERS® Walnut halves
　(optional)

MIX dressing, eggs and water until well blended. Stir in brownie mix, mixing just until moistened. Coarsely chop two chocolate bars; stir into brownie mixture.

POUR into greased 13×9-inch baking pan. Chop remaining chocolate bar.

BAKE at 350°F for 30 to 35 minutes or until edges begin to pull away from sides of pan. Immediately top with remaining chopped chocolate bar. Let stand about 5 minutes or until melted; spread evenly over brownies. Garnish with walnut halves, if desired. Cool. Cut into squares.
Makes about 24 brownies

Great Substitute: Omit walnut halves. Stir in 1 cup PLANTERS® Chopped Pecans or Walnuts or raisins when adding chopped chocolate bars to brownie mixture.

Prep Time: 10 minutes
Bake Time: 35 minutes plus standing

Cook's Tip: *Cool brownies completely before cutting into squares. This helps prevent them from breaking.*

Ultimate Brownies

Cappuccino Cupcakes

1 package (about 18 ounces) dark chocolate cake mix

1⅓ cups strong brewed or instant coffee at room temperature

3 large eggs

⅓ cup vegetable oil or melted butter

1 container (16 ounces) prepared vanilla frosting

2 tablespoons coffee liqueur, divided

Grated chocolate*

Chocolate-covered coffee beans (optional)

Additional coffee liqueur (optional)

*Grate half of a 3 or 4 ounce milk, dark chocolate or espresso chocolate candy bar on the large holes of a standing grater.

1. Preheat oven to 350°F. Line 24 regular-size (2½-inch) muffin cups with paper muffin cup liners.

2. Beat cake mix, coffee, eggs and oil with electric mixer at low speed 30 seconds. Beat at medium speed 2 minutes.

3. Spoon batter into prepared muffin cups filling ⅔ full. Bake 18 to 20 minutes or until toothpick inserted into centers comes out clean. Cool in pans on wire racks 10 minutes. Remove cupcakes to racks; cool completely. (At this point, cupcakes may be frozen up to 3 months. Thaw at room temperature before frosting.)

4. Combine frosting and 2 tablespoons liqueur in small bowl; mix well. Before frosting, poke about 10 holes in cupcake with toothpick. Pour 1 to 2 teaspoons liqueur over top of each cupcake, if desired. Frost and sprinkle with chocolate. Garnish with chocolate-covered coffee beans, if desired.

Makes 24 cupcakes

Cappuccino Cupcakes

Brownie Cake Delight

1 package reduced-fat fudge brownie mix

⅓ cup strawberry all-fruit spread

2 cups thawed frozen reduced-fat nondairy whipped topping

¼ teaspoon almond extract

2 cups strawberries, stems removed, halved

¼ cup chocolate sauce

1. Prepare brownies according to package directions, substituting 11×7-inch baking pan. Cool completely in pan.

2. Whisk fruit spread in small bowl until smooth.

3. Combine whipped topping and almond extract in medium bowl.

4. Cut brownie horizontally in half. Place half of brownie on serving dish. Spread with fruit spread and 1 cup whipped topping. Place second half of brownie, cut side down, over bottom layer. Spread with remaining whipped topping. Arrange strawberries on whipped topping. Drizzle chocolate sauce over cake before serving. Garnish with fresh mint, if desired.

Makes 16 servings

Mint Chocolate Macaroons

1½ cups (10-ounce package) NESTLÉ® TOLL HOUSE® Mint-Chocolate Morsels

3 egg whites

¼ cup granulated sugar

2¼ cups (7-ounce package) flaked or shredded coconut

MELT morsels in small, *heavy-duty* saucepan over *lowest possible* heat. When morsels begin to melt, remove from heat; stir. Return to heat for a few seconds at a time, stirring until smooth; cool to room temperature.

BEAT egg whites in large mixer bowl until foamy. Gradually add sugar; beat until stiff peaks form. Fold in melted chocolate and coconut. Drop by rounded tablespoons onto foil- or parchment paper-lined baking sheets.

BAKE in preheated 350°F. oven for 15 to 18 minutes. Cool on baking sheets for 5 minutes; remove to wire racks to cool completely.

Makes about 2½ dozen cookies

Brownie Cake Delight

Cream Cheese Brownies

4 squares BAKER'S® Unsweetened Baking Chocolate

¾ cup (1½ sticks) butter or margarine

2½ cups sugar, divided

5 eggs, divided

1¼ cups flour, divided

1 package (8 ounces) PHILADELPHIA® Cream Cheese, softened

HEAT oven to 350°F. Line 13×9-inch baking pan with foil; grease foil.

MICROWAVE chocolate and butter in large microwavable bowl on HIGH 2 minutes or until butter is melted. Stir until chocolate is completely melted.

STIR 2 cups of the sugar into chocolate mixture until well blended. Mix in 4 of the eggs. Stir in 1 cup of the flour until well blended. Spread in prepared pan. Beat cream cheese, remaining ½ cup sugar, 1 egg and ¼ cup flour in same bowl with wire whisk until well blended. Spoon mixture over brownie batter. Swirl batters with knife to marbleize.

BAKE 40 minutes or until toothpick inserted into center comes out with fudgy crumbs. *Do not overbake.* Cool in pan on wire rack. Lift out of pan onto cutting board.   *Makes 2 dozen brownies*

Prep Time: 15 minutes
Bake Time: 40 minutes

Kahlúa® Black Forest Cake

1 package (18.25 ounces) chocolate fudge cake mix with pudding

3 eggs

¾ cup water

½ cup KAHLÚA® Liqueur

⅓ cup vegetable oil

1 can (16 ounces) vanilla or chocolate frosting

1 can (21 ounces) cherry filling and topping

Chocolate sprinkles or chocolate shavings for garnish (optional)

Preheat oven to 350°F. Grease and flour 2 (9-inch) cake pans; set aside. In large mixer bowl, prepare cake mix according to package directions, using eggs, water, Kahlúa® and oil. Pour batter into prepared pans. Bake 25 to 35 minutes or until toothpick inserted into center comes out clean. Cool cake in pans 10 minutes; turn layers out onto wire racks to cool completely.

Place one cake layer bottom side up on serving plate. Spread thick layer of frosting in circle, 1½ inches around outer edge of cake. Spoon half of cherry filling into center of cake layer to frosting edge. Top with second cake layer, bottom side down. Repeat with frosting and remaining cherry filling. Spread remaining frosting around side of cake. Decorate with chocolate sprinkles or shavings, if desired.

Makes 1 (9-inch) cake

Fudge Brownie Pie

1 package (19 to 21 ounces) fudge brownie mix

1 cup cold milk

1 package (4-serving size) JELL-O® Chocolate Flavor Instant Pudding & Pie Filling

1 tub (8 ounces) COOL WHIP® Whipped Topping, thawed

PREPARE brownie mix as directed on package. Bake in greased 9-inch pie plate 40 minutes or until done according to doneness test on brownie package. Cool completely on wire rack.

SCOOP out center of brownie, using spoon, leaving 1-inch crust around edge and thin layer of brownie on bottom; reserve brownie scraps.

POUR milk into medium bowl. Add pudding mix. Beat with wire whisk until blended. Gently stir in half of the whipped topping and all but ¼ cup reserved brownie scraps. Spoon into center of crust. Top with remaining whipped topping and reserved ¼ cup brownie scraps.

REFRIGERATE 3 hours or until ready to serve. *Makes 8 servings*

Prep Time: 20 minutes

Festive Fudge Blossoms

¼ cup butter, softened

1 box (about 18 ounces) chocolate fudge cake mix

1 egg, slightly beaten

2 tablespoons water

¾ to 1 cup finely chopped walnuts

48 chocolate star candies

1. Preheat oven to 350°F. Cut butter into cake mix in large bowl until mixture resembles coarse crumbs. Stir in egg and water until well blended.

2. Shape dough into ½-inch balls; roll in walnuts, pressing nuts gently into dough. Place about 2 inches apart on ungreased baking sheets.

3. Bake cookies 12 minutes or until puffed and nearly set. Place chocolate star in center of each cookie; bake 1 minute. Cool 2 minutes on baking sheets. Remove cookies from baking sheets to wire racks to cool completely.

Makes 4 dozen cookies

Prep and Bake Time: 30 minutes

Hershey's Syrup Snacking Brownies

½ cup (1 stick) butter or margarine, softened

1 cup sugar

1½ cups (16-ounce can) HERSHEY'S Syrup

4 eggs

1¼ cups all-purpose flour

1 cup HERSHEY'S Semi-Sweet Chocolate Chips

1. Heat oven to 350°F. Grease 13×9×2-inch baking pan.

2. Beat butter and sugar in large bowl. Add syrup, eggs and flour; beat well. Stir in chocolate chips. Pour batter into prepared pan.

3. Bake 30 to 35 minutes or until brownies begin to pull away from sides of pan. Cool completely in pan on wire rack. Cut into bars.

Makes about 36 brownies

Festive Fudge Blossoms

Buckeye Cookie Bars

1 (18¼-ounce) package chocolate cake mix

¼ cup vegetable oil

1 egg

1 cup chopped peanuts

1 (14-ounce) can EAGLE® BRAND Sweetened Condensed Milk (NOT evaporated milk)

½ cup peanut butter

1. Preheat oven to 350°F.

2. In large mixing bowl, combine cake mix, oil and egg; beat at medium speed until crumbly. Stir in peanuts. Reserve 1½ cups crumb mixture; press remaining crumb mixture firmly on bottom of greased 13×9-inch baking pan.

3. In medium bowl, beat Eagle Brand with peanut butter until smooth; spread over prepared crust. Sprinkle with reserved crumb mixture.

4. Bake 25 to 30 minutes or until set. Cool. Cut into bars. Store loosely covered at room temperature.

Makes 24 to 36 bars

Prep Time: 20 minutes
Bake Time: 25 to 30 minutes

Candy Bar Brownies

1 (21-ounce) package DUNCAN HINES® Family-Style Chewy Fudge Brownie Mix

4 bars (5.3 ounces each) milk chocolate candy bars

⅓ cup mini candy-coated milk chocolate pieces

1. Preheat oven to 350°F. Grease bottom of 13×9-inch pan.

2. Prepare and bake brownies following package directions for basic recipe chewy brownies. Break chocolate candy bars along scored lines. Place pieces immediately on hot brownies. Cover pan with aluminum foil for 3 to 5 minutes or until chocolate is shiny and soft. Spread gently to cover surface of brownies. Sprinkle with candy-coated chocolate pieces. Cool completely. Cut into bars.

Makes 18 brownies

Tip: For another delicious candy topping, try sprinkling melted chocolate with ½ cup chopped chocolate-covered toffee chips.

Double Fudge Marble Cake

1 package DUNCAN HINES® Moist Deluxe® Fudge Marble Cake Mix

1 container DUNCAN HINES® Creamy Home-Style Milk Chocolate Frosting

¼ cup hot fudge topping

1. Preheat oven to 350°F. Grease and flour 13×9-inch pan.

2. Prepare, bake and cool cake following package directions for basic recipe.

3. Frost top of cooled cake with Milk Chocolate frosting. Place hot fudge topping in small microwave-safe bowl. Microwave at HIGH (100% power) 30 seconds or until thin. Drop hot fudge by spoonfuls on top of cake in 18 places. Pull tip of knife once through each hot fudge dollop to form heart shapes.

Makes 12 to 16 servings

Tip: Hot fudge topping may also be marbled in frosting by using flat blade of knife to swirl slightly.

Chewy Chocolate Macaroons

5⅓ cups MOUNDS® Sweetened Coconut Flakes

½ cup HERSHEY'S® Cocoa

1 can (14 ounces) sweetened condensed milk (not evaporated milk)

2 teaspoons vanilla extract

About 24 red candied cherries, halved (optional)

1. Heat oven to 350°F. Generously grease cookie sheet.

2. Stir together coconut and cocoa in large bowl; stir in sweetened condensed milk and vanilla until well blended. Drop by rounded teaspoons onto prepared cookie sheet. Press cherry half into center of each cookie, if desired.

3. Bake 8 to 10 minutes or until almost set. Immediately remove from cookie sheet to wire rack. Cool completely. Store loosely covered at room temperature.

Makes about 4 dozen cookies

Prep Time: 15 minutes
Bake Time: 8 minutes
Cool Time: 1 hour

Philadelphia® Cheesecake Brownies

1 package (19.8 ounces) brownie mix (do not use mix that includes syrup pouch)
1 package (8 ounces) PHILADELPHIA® Cream Cheese, softened
⅓ cup sugar
1 egg
½ teaspoon vanilla

PREPARE brownie mix as directed on package. Pour into greased 13×9-inch baking pan.

BEAT cream cheese with electric mixer on medium speed until smooth. Mix in sugar until blended. Add egg and vanilla; mix just until blended. Pour cream cheese mixture over brownie batter; cut through batter with knife several times for marble effect.

BAKE at 350°F for 35 to 40 minutes or until cream cheese mixture is lightly browned. Cool. Cut into squares.

Makes 2 dozen

Prep Time: 20 minutes
Bake Time: 40 minutes

Chocolate Walnut Meringues

3 egg whites
  Pinch of salt
¾ cup sugar
½ cup good-quality Dutch-processed cocoa
⅓ cup finely chopped California walnuts

Preheat oven to 350°F. Place egg whites and salt in large mixing bowl. Beat with electric mixer or wire whisk until soft peaks form. Gradually add sugar, beating until stiff peaks form. Sift cocoa over peaks and fold into egg white mixture with walnuts. Spoon mounds about 1 inch in diameter and about 1 inch apart onto parchment-lined baking sheets. Bake 20 minutes or until dry to the touch. Let cool completely before removing from baking sheets. Store in airtight container.

Makes 48 cookies

Favorite recipe from **Walnut Marketing Board**

Philadelphia® Cheesecake Brownies

Sinfully Simple Chocolate Cake

1 package (about 18 ounces)
    chocolate cake mix plus
    ingredients to prepare mix
1 cup whipping cream, chilled
⅓ cup chocolate syrup
    Fresh fruit for garnish (optional)

Prepare cake mix according to package directions for two 8- or 9-inch layers. Cool layers completely.

Beat whipping cream with electric mixer at high speed until it begins to thicken. Gradually add chocolate syrup; continue beating until soft peaks form.

To assemble, place one cake layer on serving plate; spread half of whipped cream mixture over top. Set second cake layer on top; spread remaining whipped cream mixture over top. Garnish, if desired. Store in refrigerator.

Makes 12 servings

Fudgy Peanut Butter Cake

1 (18.25-ounce) box chocolate fudge
    cake mix
1½ cups plus ⅔ cup water, divided
2 eggs
1 (16-ounce) package chocolate fudge
    frosting mix
1¼ cups SMUCKER'S® Chunky
    Natural Peanut Butter or
    LAURA SCUDDER'S® Nutty
    Old-Fashioned Peanut Butter

Grease and flour 10-inch tube pan. In large bowl, blend cake mix, 1½ cups water and eggs until moistened; mix as directed on cake package. Pour batter into pan.

In medium bowl, combine frosting mix, peanut butter and ⅔ cup water; blend until smooth. Spoon over batter in pan.

Bake in preheated 350°F oven 35 to 45 minutes or until top springs back when touched lightly in center. Cool upright in pan 1 hour; remove from pan. Cool completely.   *Makes 12 to 15 servings*

Sinfully Simple Chocolate Cake

Chocolate Cappuccino Cupcakes

24 REYNOLDS® Baking Cups

1 package (about 18 ounces) chocolate cake mix

¼ cup instant coffee, divided

2 teaspoons hot water

1 container (16 ounces) ready-to-spread cream cheese frosting

½ cup semi-sweet chocolate morsels

2 teaspoons vegetable oil

PREHEAT oven to 350°F. Place Reynolds Baking Cups in muffin pans; set aside. Prepare cake mix following package directions for 24 cupcakes, adding 2 tablespoons instant coffee before mixing. Spoon batter into baking cups. Bake as directed. Cool.

DISSOLVE remaining instant coffee in hot water. Stir frosting into coffee mixture until smooth. Frost cupcakes.

MICROWAVE chocolate morsels and oil on HIGH power in a small microwave-safe dish, 1 to 1½ minutes, stirring once, until chocolate is melted.

DRIZZLE melted chocolate over frosted cupcakes. Let stand until chocolate sets.

Makes 24 cupcakes

Mississippi Mud Bars

¾ cup packed brown sugar

½ cup butter, softened

1 egg

1 teaspoon vanilla

½ teaspoon baking soda

¼ teaspoon salt

1 cup plus 2 tablespoons all-purpose flour

1 cup (6 ounces) semisweet chocolate chips, divided

1 cup (6 ounces) white chocolate chips, divided

½ cup chopped walnuts or pecans

Preheat oven to 375°F. Line 9×9-inch pan with foil; grease foil. Beat sugar and butter in large bowl until blended. Beat in egg and vanilla until light. Blend in baking soda and salt. Add flour, mixing until well blended. Stir in ¾ cup each semisweet and white chocolate chips and nuts. Spread dough in prepared pan. Bake 23 to 25 minutes or until center feels firm. (Do not overbake.) Remove from oven; sprinkle remaining ¼ cup each semisweet and white chocolate chips over top. Let stand until chips melt; spread over bars. Cool on wire rack until chocolate is set. Cut into bars. *Makes 3 dozen bars*

Molten Mocha Cakes

1 package **BAKER'S®** Semi-Sweet
    Baking Chocolate

1 cup (2 sticks) butter

2 cups powdered sugar

½ cup **GENERAL FOODS
    INTERNATIONAL COFFEES®**,
    any flavor

5 eggs

4 egg yolks

¾ cup flour

    Powdered sugar (optional)

    Raspberries (optional)

HEAT oven to 425°F. Butter eight ¾-cup custard cups or soufflé dishes. Place on cookie sheet.

MICROWAVE chocolate and butter in large microwavable bowl on HIGH 2 minutes or until butter is melted. Stir with wire whisk until chocolate is completely melted. Stir in sugar and flavored instant coffee until well blended. Whisk in eggs and egg yolks. Stir in flour. Divide batter among custard cups.

BAKE 14 to 15 minutes or until sides are firm but centers are soft. Let stand 1 minute, then run small knife around cakes to loosen. Invert cakes onto dessert dishes. Sprinkle with powdered sugar and garnish with raspberries, if desired.

Makes 8 cakes

Make-Ahead: Bake as directed above. Cool slightly, then cover custard cups with plastic wrap. Refrigerate up to 2 days. Place custard cups on cookie sheet. Reheat in 425°F oven for 12 to 13 minutes.

Prep Time: 15 minutes
Bake Time: 15 minutes

> ***Cook's Tip:*** *All chocolate should be melted slowly over low heat because it scorches easily. Consistency of melted chocolate varies. Unsweetened chocolate becomes runny; semisweet and white chocolate hold their shape until stirred.*

Mini Turtle Cupcakes

1 package (21.5 ounces) brownie mix
plus ingredients to prepare mix

½ cup chopped pecans

1 cup prepared or homemade dark
chocolate frosting

½ cup chopped pecans, toasted

12 caramels, unwrapped

1 to 2 tablespoons whipping cream

1. Heat oven to 350°F. Line 54 mini
(1½-inch) muffin cups with paper muffin
cup liners.

2. Prepare brownie batter as directed on
package. Stir in chopped pecans.

3. Spoon batter into prepared muffin cups
filling ⅔ full. Bake 18 minutes or until
toothpick inserted into centers comes out
clean. Cool in pans on wire racks
5 minutes. Remove cupcakes to racks;
cool completely. (At this point, cupcakes
may be frozen up to 3 months. Thaw at
room temperature before frosting.)

4. Spread frosting over cooled cupcakes;
top with pecans.

5. Combine caramels and 1 tablespoon
cream in small saucepan. Cook over low
heat until caramels are melted and mixture
is smooth, stirring constantly. Add
additional 1 tablespoon cream if needed.
Drizzle caramel decoratively over
cupcakes. Store at room temperature up
to 24 hours or cover and refrigerate for up
to 3 days before serving.

Makes 54 mini cupcakes

Mini Turtle Cupcakes

Chocolate Pecan Pie

½ package (15 ounces) refrigerated pie crust

1 package (8 squares) BAKER'S® Semi-Sweet Baking Chocolate, divided

2 tablespoons butter or margarine

3 eggs, slightly beaten

1 cup corn syrup

¼ cup firmly packed light brown sugar

1 teaspoon vanilla

1½ cups pecan halves or walnut pieces

HEAT oven to 350°F. Prepare pie crust as directed on package, using 9-inch pie plate. Coarsely chop 4 squares of the chocolate; set aside.

MICROWAVE remaining 4 squares of chocolate and butter in large microwavable bowl on HIGH 2 minutes or until butter is melted. Stir until chocolate is completely melted.

BRUSH bottom of pie crust with small amount of beaten eggs. Stir remaining eggs, corn syrup, sugar and vanilla into chocolate mixture until well blended. Stir in pecans and chopped chocolate. Pour into crust.

BAKE 55 minutes or until knife inserted 2 inches from edge comes out clean. Cool completely on wire rack.

Makes 8 servings

Note: A frozen deep-dish pie crust (9-inch) can be substituted for the refrigerated pie crust.

Prep Time: 15 minutes
Bake Time: 55 minutes

Cook's Tip: Make sure the oven is ready before baking a pie. Put the oven rack in the center of the oven. Preheat the oven and use an oven thermometer to insure an accurate temperature.

Chocolate Pecan Pie

Brownie with Ice Cream and Warm Mocha Pecan Sauce

1 package (15½ ounces) brownie mix
½ cup dark brown sugar
2 teaspoons instant coffee granules
½ cup unsweetened cocoa powder
¼ teaspoon ground cinnamon
¼ teaspoon ground nutmeg
3 tablespoons butter
1 teaspoon vanilla
⅓ cup pecan pieces
1 pint vanilla or coffee ice cream

1. Prepare brownie mix according to package directions for 9×9-inch baking pan.

2. Combine brown sugar, ½ cup warm water and coffee granules in small saucepan. Cook and stir over medium heat until sugar is dissolved. Add cocoa powder, cinnamon and nutmeg. Simmer, stirring until smooth. Add butter and vanilla; stir until butter is melted. Stir in pecans.

3. Top 1 brownie with 1 scoop ice cream. Drizzle with 2 tablespoons mocha pecan sauce.   *Makes 6 to 9 servings*

Devil's Food Fudge Cookies

1 package DUNCAN HINES® Moist Deluxe® Devil's Food Cake Mix
2 eggs
½ cup vegetable oil
1 cup semisweet chocolate chips
½ cup chopped walnuts

1. Preheat oven to 350°F. Grease baking sheets.

2. Combine cake mix, eggs and oil in large bowl. Stir until thoroughly blended. Stir in chocolate chips and walnuts. (Mixture will be stiff.) Shape dough into 36 (1¼-inch) balls. Place 2 inches apart on prepared baking sheets.

3. Bake at 350°F for 10 to 11 minutes. (Cookies will look moist.) *Do not overbake.* Cool 2 minutes on baking sheets. Remove to cooling racks. Cool completely. Store in airtight container.
      Makes 3 dozen cookies

Tip: For a delicious flavor treat, substitute peanut butter chips for the chocolate chips and chopped peanuts for the chopped walnuts.

Brownie with Ice Cream and Warm Mocha Pecan Sauce

Chocolate Toffee Crunch Fantasy

1 package DUNCAN HINES® Moist Deluxe® Devil's Food Cake Mix

12 bars (1.4 ounces each) chocolate covered toffee bars, divided

3 cups whipping cream, chilled

1. Preheat oven to 350°F. Grease and flour 10-inch tube pan.

2. Prepare, bake and cool cake following package directions. Split cake horizontally into three layers; set aside. Chop 11 candy bars into pea-size pieces (see Tip). Whip cream until stiff peaks form. Fold candy pieces into whipped cream.

3. To assemble, place one split cake layer on serving plate. Spread 1½ cups whipped cream mixture on top. Repeat with remaining layers and whipped cream mixture. Frost sides and top with remaining filling. Chop remaining candy bar coarsely. Sprinkle over top. Refrigerate until ready to serve. *Makes 12 servings*

Tip: To quickly chop toffee candy bars, place a few bars in food processor fitted with steel blade. Pulse several times until pea-size pieces form. Repeat with remaining candy bars.

Chewy Chocolate Cookies

1 package (2-layer size) chocolate cake mix

2 eggs

1 cup MIRACLE WHIP® or MIRACLE WHIP® LIGHT Dressing

1 cup BAKER'S® Semi-Sweet Chocolate Chunks

½ cup chopped PLANTERS® Walnuts

• MIX cake mix, eggs and dressing in large bowl with electric mixer on medium speed until blended. Stir in remaining ingredients.

• DROP by rounded teaspoonfuls onto greased cookie sheets.

• BAKE at 350°F for 10 to 12 minutes or until edges are lightly browned.
Makes 4 dozen cookies

Prep Time: 10 minutes
Bake Time: 12 minutes

Chocolate Pots de Crème

1½ cups whipping (heavy) cream

4 squares BAKER'S® Semi-Sweet
    Baking Chocolate

3 egg yolks

2 tablespoons sugar

    Boiling water

HEAT oven to 325°F. Place four ¾-cup custard cups in 8- or 9-inch square baking pan.

HEAT cream and chocolate in medium saucepan on medium heat until just simmering, stirring constantly. Beat egg yolks and sugar in large bowl with wire whisk until well blended. Gradually whisk in hot cream mixture. Divide mixture among custard cups. Place pan in oven. Pour boiling water into pan to come halfway up sides of custard cups.

BAKE 25 to 30 minutes or until just set around edges but still soft in center. Remove cups from pan of water.

REFRIGERATE 4 hours or until ready to serve. *Makes 4 servings*

Prep Time: 20 minutes
Bake Time: 30 minutes
Refrigeration Time: 4 hours

Chocolate Peanut Butter Chip Cookies

8 (1-ounce) squares semi-sweet
    chocolate

3 tablespoons butter or margarine

1 (14-ounce) can EAGLE® BRAND
    Sweetened Condensed Milk
    (NOT evaporated milk)

2 cups biscuit baking mix

1 teaspoon vanilla extract

1 cup (6 ounces) peanut butter-
    flavored chips

1. Preheat oven to 350°F. In large saucepan, over low heat, melt chocolate and butter with Eagle Brand; remove from heat. Add biscuit mix and vanilla; with mixer, beat until smooth and well blended.

2. Let mixture cool to room temperature. Stir in chips. Shape into 1¼-inch balls. Place 2 inches apart on ungreased baking sheets. Bake 6 to 8 minutes or until tops are lightly crusty. Cool. Store tightly covered at room temperature.

Makes about 4 dozen

Prep Time: 15 minutes
Bake Time: 6 to 8 minutes

Philadelphia® 3-Step® Mint Cheesecakes (page 207)

Simple & Sinful Cheesecakes

❧ ❧ ❧ ❧

Dazzle family and friends with a rich and luscious cheesecake. No other dessert is quite as extravagant as an incredibly smooth and creamy cheesecake. Demonstrate your baking prowess with any of these temptations.

Prepare a classic like Philadelphia® 3-STEP® Cheesecake (page 212) or choose a delicious flavor like Chocolate Raspberry Cheesecake (page 214)—just mix and pop in the oven. While the cheesecake bakes, you'll have time to relax. The result is an impressive dessert that will always be the center of attention.

Philadelphia® 3-Step® Caramel Pecan Cheesecake

2 packages (8 ounces each)
    PHILADELPHIA® Cream
    Cheese, softened

½ cup sugar

½ teaspoon vanilla

2 eggs

20 KRAFT® Caramels

2 tablespoons milk

½ cup chopped PLANTERS® Pecans

1 HONEY MAID® Graham Pie
    Crust (6 ounces)

MIX cream cheese, sugar and vanilla with electric mixer on medium speed until well blended. Add eggs; mix until blended. Melt caramels with milk on low heat, stirring frequently until smooth. Stir in pecans.

POUR caramel mixture into crust. Pour cream cheese batter over caramel mixture.

BAKE at 350°F for 40 minutes or until center is almost set. Cool. Refrigerate 3 hours or overnight. Garnish as desired.

Makes 8 servings

How To Easily Slice Cheesecake: Let cheesecake stand at room temperature for at least 30 minutes before slicing to allow caramel layer to soften.

Prep Time: 10 minutes
Bake Time: 40 minutes

> **Cook's Tip:** *Bring cream cheese to room temperature to make it easier to blend with other ingredients to create a smooth mixture.*

Baker's® One Bowl Chocolate Swirl Cheesecake

4 squares BAKER'S® Semi-Sweet Baking Chocolate

2 packages (8 ounces each) PHILADELPHIA® Cream Cheese, softened, divided

½ cup sugar, divided

2 eggs

½ teaspoon vanilla

1 prepared chocolate flavor or graham cracker crumb crust (6 ounces or 9 inches)

HEAT oven to 350°F.

MICROWAVE chocolate in large microwavable bowl on HIGH 1½ to 2 minutes or until chocolate is almost melted, stirring halfway through heating time. Stir until chocolate is completely melted.

WHISK 1 package of the cream cheese, ¼ cup of the sugar and 1 egg into the melted chocolate with wire whisk until well blended. Pour into crust. Whisk remaining cream cheese, sugar, egg and vanilla in same bowl until well blended. Spoon plain batter over chocolate batter. Swirl with knife to marbleize.

BAKE 40 minutes or until center is almost set. Cool. Refrigerate 3 hours or overnight. Let stand at room temperature 20 minutes before serving.

Makes 8 servings

Prep Time: 10 minutes plus refrigerating
Bake Time: 40 minutes

Mini Cheesecakes

1½ cups graham cracker or chocolate wafer crumbs

¼ cup sugar

¼ cup (½ stick) butter or margarine, melted

3 (8-ounce) packages cream cheese, softened

1 (14-ounce) can EAGLE® BRAND Sweetened Condensed Milk (NOT evaporated milk)

3 eggs

2 teaspoons vanilla extract

1. Preheat oven to 300°F. Combine graham cracker crumbs, sugar and butter; press equal portions onto bottoms of 24 lightly greased or paper-lined muffin cups.

2. In large mixing bowl, beat cream cheese until fluffy. Gradually beat in Eagle Brand until smooth. Add eggs and vanilla; mix well. Spoon equal amounts of mixture (about 3 tablespoons) into prepared cups. Bake 20 minutes or until cakes spring back when lightly touched. Cool.* Chill.

Makes 2 dozen

*If greased muffin cups are used, cool baked cheesecakes. Freeze 15 minutes; remove with narrow spatula. Proceed as above.

Chocolate Mini Cheesecakes: Melt 1 cup (6 ounces) semi-sweet chocolate chips; mix into batter. Proceed as above. Bake 20 to 25 minutes.

Prep Time: 20 minutes
Bake Time: 20 minutes

Chocolate Swirl Cheesecake

2 packages (8 ounces each)
   PHILADELPHIA® Cream
   Cheese, softened, divided

½ cup sugar, divided

2 eggs

4 squares BAKER'S® Semi-Sweet
   Baking Chocolate, melted,
   slightly cooled

1 OREO® Pie Crust (6 ounces or
   9 inch)

½ teaspoon vanilla

HEAT oven to 350°F.

BEAT 1 package of the cream cheese, ¼ cup of the sugar and 1 egg in large bowl with electric mixer on medium speed until well blended. Stir in melted chocolate. Pour into crust. Beat remaining cream cheese, ¼ cup sugar, egg and vanilla until well blended. Spoon over chocolate batter; swirl with knife to marbleize.

BAKE 40 minutes or until center is almost set. Cool completely on wire rack.

REFRIGERATE 3 hours or overnight.

Makes 8 servings

To soften cream cheese in the microwave: Place 1 completely unwrapped 8-ounce package of cream cheese in microwavable bowl. Microwave on HIGH for 15 seconds. Add 15 seconds for each additional package of cream cheese.

Prep Time: 10 minutes
Bake Time: 40 minutes
Refrigeration Time: 3 hours

Strawberry Cheesecake

3 packages (8 ounces each) cream cheese, softened

¾ cup strawberry fruit spread

3 teaspoons vanilla, divided

¼ teaspoon salt

4 eggs

1 cup sour cream*

Fresh sliced strawberries (optional)

*Do not use reduced-fat sour cream.

1. Preheat oven to 325°F. Spray 9-inch springform pan with nonstick cooking spray.

2. Place cream cheese in large bowl; beat with electric mixer at medium speed until creamy. Add fruit spread, 1 teaspoon vanilla and salt; blend well Add eggs, one at a time, beating well after each addition.

3. Pour into prepared springform pan. Bake 50 minutes.

4. Combine sour cream and remaining 2 teaspoons vanilla; mix well. Carefully spoon over warm cheesecake. Return to oven; continue baking 10 minutes or just until set. Turn oven off; leave cheesecake in oven, with door closed, 30 minutes.

5. Transfer cheesecake to wire rack; loosen edge from rim of pan. Cool completely before removing rim. Cover; chill at least 6 hours or overnight.

6. Garnish cheesecake with strawberries just before serving.   *Makes 10 servings*

Strawberry Cheesecake

Philadelphia® 3-Step® White Chocolate Raspberry Swirl Cheesecake

2 packages (8 ounces each)
    PHILADELPHIA® Cream
    Cheese, softened

½ cup sugar

½ teaspoon vanilla

2 eggs

3 squares (1 ounce each) BAKER'S®
    Premium White Baking
    Chocolate, melted

1 OREO® Pie Crust (6 ounces)

3 tablespoons red raspberry preserves

MIX cream cheese, sugar and vanilla with electric mixer on medium speed until well blended. Add eggs; mix until blended. Stir in white chocolate.

POUR into crust. Microwave preserves in microwavable bowl on HIGH 15 seconds or until melted. Dot top of cheesecake with small spoonfuls of preserves. Cut through top of batter with knife several times to marbleize.

BAKE at 350°F for 35 to 40 minutes or until center is almost set. Cool. Refrigerate 3 hours or overnight. Store in refrigerator.

Makes 8 servings

Great Substitute: To lower the fat, prepare as directed, substituting PHILADELPHIA® Neufchatel Cheese, ⅓ Less Fat than Cream Cheese for cream cheese.

Prep Time: 10 minutes plus refrigerating
Bake Time: 40 minutes

Cook's Tip: At the end of baking time the cheesecake center may be slightly soft. It will firm as the cheesecake cools.

*Philadelphia® 3-Step®
White Chocolate Raspberry
Swirl Cheesecake*

Easy Chocolate Lover's Cheesepie

3 packages (8 ounces each) cream cheese, softened

¾ cup sugar

3 eggs

1 teaspoon vanilla extract

2 cups (12-ounce package) HERSHEY'S MINI CHIPS™ Semi-Sweet Chocolate, divided

1 extra serving-size packaged graham cracker crumb crust (9 ounces)

2 tablespoons whipping cream

1. Heat oven to 450°F.

2. Beat cream cheese and sugar in large bowl with mixer until well blended. Add eggs and vanilla; beat well. Stir in 1⅔ cups small chocolate chips; pour into crust.

3. Bake 10 minutes. Without opening oven door, reduce temperature to 250°F; continue baking 30 minutes or just until set. Remove from oven to wire rack. Cool completely. Cover; refrigerate until thoroughly chilled.

4. Place remaining ⅓ cup chips and whipping cream in small microwave-safe bowl. Microwave at HIGH (100%) 20 to 30 seconds or just until chips are melted and mixture is smooth when stirred. Cool slightly; spread over top of cheesepie. Refrigerate 15 minutes or until topping is set. Cover; refrigerate leftover cheesepie.

Makes 10 servings

Prep Time: 15 minutes
Bake Time: 40 minutes
Cool Time: 1 hour

Easy Chocolate Lover's Cheesepie

Pecan Eggnog Cheesecake

¾ cup PLANTERS® Pecan Halves, toasted, divided

2 (8-ounce) packages PHILADELPHIA® Cream Cheese, softened

½ cup sugar

2 eggs

⅓ cup BREAKSTONE'S® or KNUDSEN® Sour Cream

1 teaspoon rum extract

¾ teaspoon ground nutmeg, divided

1 (9-inch) HONEY MAID® Honey Graham Pie Crust

COOL WHIP® Whipped Topping, thawed, for garnish

1. Reserve 8 pecan halves for garnish; finely chop remaining pecans.

2. Beat cream cheese, sugar, eggs, sour cream, rum extract and ½ teaspoon nutmeg in medium bowl with electric mixer until creamy; stir in chopped pecans. Spread into prepared crust.

3. Bake at 350°F for 40 to 45 minutes or until filling is set. Cool completely; refrigerate 3 to 4 hours.

4. Garnish cheesecake with whipped topping, pecan halves and remaining nutmeg.   *Makes 8 servings*

Preparation Time: 20 minutes
Cook Time: 40 minutes
Cooling Time: 1 hour
Chill Time: 3 hours
Total Time: 5 hours

Cook's Tip: *Cheesecakes are the perfect dessert because they can be prepared ahead of time. For easier cutting and creamier texture, leave the cooled cheesecake in its pan, cover tightly and refrigerate overnight.*

Philadelphia® *3-Step*® *Mini Cheesecakes*

2 packages (8 ounces each)
    PHILADELPHIA® Cream
    Cheese, softened
½ cup sugar
½ teaspoon vanilla
2 eggs
12 NILLA® Wafers
    Fresh fruit

BEAT cream cheese, sugar and vanilla with electric mixer on medium speed until well blended. Add eggs, 1 at a time, mixing on low speed after each addition just until blended.

PLACE 1 wafer on bottom of each of 12 paper-lined muffin cups. Pour batter evenly into prepared cups.

BAKE at 350°F for 20 minutes or until centers are almost set. Cool. Refrigerate 3 hours or overnight. Top with fresh fruit just before serving.   *Makes 12 servings*

Great Substitute: Substitute OREO® Chocolate Sandwich Cookies for NILLA® Wafers.

Cheesecake Squares: Omit wafers. Line 8-inch square baking pan with foil. Mix 1½ cups HONEY MAID® Graham Cracker Crumbs or OREO® Chocolate Cookie Crumbs with ¼ (½ stick) butter, melted; press onto bottom of prepared pan. Prepare cheesecake batter as directed. Pour over crust. Bake and cool as directed. Cut into squares. Makes 16 servings.

Prep Time: 10 minutes
Bake Time: 20 minutes

Apple-Pecan Cheesecake

2 packages (8 ounces each) cream cheese, softened

⅔ cup sugar, divided

2 eggs

½ teaspoon vanilla

1 (9-inch) prepared graham cracker pie crust

½ teaspoon cinnamon

4 cups Golden Delicious apples, peeled, cored and thinly sliced (about 2½ pounds apples)

½ cup chopped pecans

1. Preheat oven to 350°F.

2. Beat cream cheese and ⅓ cup sugar in large bowl with electric mixer at medium speed until well blended. Add eggs, 1 at a time, beating well after each addition. Blend in vanilla; pour into crust.

3. Combine remaining ⅓ cup sugar and cinnamon in large bowl. Add apples; toss gently to coat. Spoon or arrange apple mixture over cream cheese mixture. Sprinkle with pecans.

4. Bake 1 hour and 10 minutes or until set. Cool completely. Store in refrigerator.

Makes one 9-inch cheesecake

Philadelphia® 3-Step® Amaretto Berry Cheesecake

2 packages (8 ounces each) PHILADELPHIA® Cream Cheese, softened

½ cup sugar

½ teaspoon vanilla

2 eggs

3 tablespoons almond-flavored liqueur

1 ready-to-use graham cracker crumb crust (6 ounces or 9 inch)

2 cups blueberries, raspberries and sliced strawberries

MIX cream cheese, sugar and vanilla with electric mixer on medium speed until well blended. Add eggs; mix until blended. Stir in liqueur.

POUR into crust.

BAKE at 350°F for 35 to 40 minutes or until center is almost set. Cool. Refrigerate 3 hours or overnight. Top with fruit just before serving. *Makes 8 servings*

Prep Time: 10 minutes plus refrigerating
Bake Time: 40 minutes

Apple-Pecan Cheesecake

Toffee Bits Cheesecake Cups

About 16 to 18 vanilla wafer
    cookies
3 packages (8 ounces each) cream
    cheese, softened
¾ cup sugar
3 eggs
1 teaspoon vanilla extract
1¼ cups SKOR® English Toffee Bits or
    HEATH® BITS 'O BRICKLE™,
    divided

1. Heat oven to 350°F. Line 2½-inch muffin cups with paper bake cups; place vanilla wafer on bottom of each cup.

2. Beat cream cheese and sugar in large bowl on low speed of mixer until smooth. Beat in eggs and vanilla just until blended. Do not overbeat. Set aside ¼ cup toffee bits. Gently stir remaining 1 cup bits into batter; pour into prepared cups to ¼ inch from top.

3. Bake 20 to 25 minutes or until almost set. Remove from oven. Immediately sprinkle about ½ teaspoon toffee bits onto each cup. Cool completely in pan on wire rack. Remove from pan. Cover; refrigerate about 3 hours. Store in refrigerator.

Makes about 16 to 18 cups

Rich Heath Bits Cheesecake

Vanilla Wafer Crust (recipe page
    211)
3 packages (8 ounces each) cream
    cheese, softened
1 cup sugar
3 eggs
1 container (8 ounces) sour cream
½ teaspoon vanilla extract
1⅓ cups (8-ounce package) HEATH
    BITS®, divided

1. Prepare crust. Heat oven to 350°F.

2. Beat cream cheese and sugar in large bowl on medium speed of mixer until well blended. Add eggs, one at a time, beating well after each addition. Add sour cream and vanilla; beat on low speed until blended.

3. Pour half of cheese mixture into crust. Reserve ¼ cup BITS for topping; sprinkle remaining BITS over cheese mixture in pan. Spoon on remaining cheese mixture.

4. Bake 1 hour or until filling is set. Cool 15 minutes. Sprinkle reserved BITS over top; with knife, loosen cake from side of pan. Cool completely; remove side of pan.

Cover, refrigerate at least 4 hours before serving. Cover; refrigerate leftover cheesecake. *Makes 12 to 16 servings*

Vanilla Wafer Crust: Combine 1¼ cups vanilla wafer crumbs (about 55 wafers) and 2 tablespoons sugar; stir in ⅓ cup melted butter or margarine. Press onto bottom and 1 inch up side of 9-inch springform pan. Refrigerate about 30 minutes.

White Chocolate Cheesecake

½ cup (1 stick) butter or margarine, softened

¾ cup sugar, divided

1½ teaspoons vanilla, divided

1 cup flour

4 packages (8 ounces each) PHILADELPHIA® Cream Cheese, softened

4 eggs

2 packages (12 squares) BAKER'S® Premium White Baking Chocolate, melted, slightly cooled

HEAT oven to 325°F.

BEAT butter, ¼ cup sugar and ½ teaspoon vanilla in large bowl with electric mixer on medium speed until light and fluffy. Gradually add flour, beating on low speed until blended. Press onto bottom of 9-inch springform pan; prick with fork. Bake 20 minutes or until edges are light brown.

BEAT cream cheese, remaining ½ cup sugar and 1 teaspoon vanilla with electric mixer on medium speed until well blended. Add eggs, 1 at a time, beating on low speed after each addition, just until blended. Beat in melted chocolate. Pour over crust.

BAKE 55 to 60 minutes or until center is almost set. Run small knife or spatula around rim of pan to loosen cake; cool before removing rim of pan.

REFRIGERATE 4 hours or overnight. Garnish with grated chocolate, if desired.
Makes 12 to 16 servings

To soften cream cheese in the microwave: Place 1 completely unwrapped 8-ounce package of cream cheese in a microwavable bowl. Microwave on HIGH for 15 seconds. Add 15 seconds for each additional package of cream cheese.

Prep Time: 30 minutes
Bake Time: 1 hour 20 minutes
Refrigeration Time: 4 hours

Philadelphia® 3-Step® Cheesecake

2 packages (8 ounces each)
  PHILADELPHIA® Cream
  Cheese or PHILADELPHIA®
  Neufchâtel Cheese, ⅓ Less Fat
  than Cream Cheese, softened
½ cup sugar
½ teaspoon vanilla
2 eggs
1 HONEY MAID Graham Cracker
  Pie Crust (6 ounces)

BEAT cream cheese, sugar and vanilla with electric mixer on medium speed until well blended. Add eggs, 1 at a time, mixing on low speed after each addition just until blended.

POUR into crust.

BAKE at 350°F 40 minutes or until center is almost set. Cool. Refrigerate 3 hours or overnight. *Makes 8 servings*

Fruit Topped: Top chilled cheesecake with sliced assorted fresh fruit. Drizzle with 2 tablespoons strawberry or apple jelly, heated, if desired.

Chocolate Chip: Stir ½ cup miniature semi-sweet chocolate chips into batter. Sprinkle with additional ¼ cup chips before baking.

Pumpkin: Beat ½ cup canned pumpkin, ½ teaspoon ground cinnamon and dash *each* ground cloves and nutmeg in with cream cheese.

Lemon: Stir 1 tablespoon fresh lemon juice and ½ teaspoon grated lemon peel into batter.

Chocolate: Stir 4 squares BAKER'S® Semi-Sweet Baking Chocolate, melted, into batter.

Crème de Menthe: Stir 4 teaspoons green crème de menthe into batter. Substitute OREO® Pie Crust for HONEY MAID® Graham Cracker Pie Crust.

Prep Time: 10 minutes
Cook Time: 40 minutes

*Philadelphia® 3-Step®
Cheesecake*

Chocolate Raspberry Cheesecake

2 (3-ounce) packages cream cheese, softened

1 (14-ounce) can sweetened condensed milk

1 egg

3 tablespoons lemon juice

1 teaspoon vanilla

1 cup fresh or frozen raspberries

1 (6-ounce) READY CRUST® Chocolate Pie Crust

Chocolate Glaze (recipe follows)

1. Preheat oven to 350°F. Beat cream cheese in medium bowl with electric mixer at medium speed until fluffy. Gradually beat in sweetened condensed milk until smooth. Add egg, lemon juice and vanilla; mix well. Arrange raspberries on bottom of crust. Slowly pour cream cheese mixture over raspberries.

2. Bake 30 to 35 minutes or until center is almost set. Cool on wire rack.

3. Prepare Chocolate Glaze; spread over cheesecake. Refrigerate 3 hours. Garnish as desired. Refrigerate leftovers.

Makes 8 servings

Chocolate Glaze: Melt 2 (1-ounce) squares semisweet baking chocolate with ¼ cup whipping cream in small saucepan over low heat. Cook and stir until thickened and smooth. Remove from heat.

Prep Time: 15 minutes
Chilling Time: 3 hours

Chocolate Raspberry Cheesecake

Chocolate Chip Cheesecake

2 packages (8 ounces each)
  PHILADELPHIA® Cream
  Cheese, softened

½ cup sugar

½ teaspoon vanilla

2 eggs

¾ cup mini semi-sweet chocolate
  chips, divided

1 ready-to-use graham cracker or
  chocolate-flavored crumb crust
  (6 ounces or 9-inch)

MIX cream cheese, sugar and vanilla at medium speed with electric mixer until well blended. Add eggs; mix until blended. Stir in ½ cup of the chips.

POUR into crust. Sprinkle with remaining ¼ cup chips.

BAKE at 350°F for 40 minutes or until center is almost set. Cool. Refrigerate 3 hours or overnight.

Makes 8 servings

Peanut Butter Chocolate Chip Cheesecake: Beat in ⅓ cup peanut butter with cream cheese.

Banana Chocolate Chip Cheesecake: Beat in ½ cup mashed ripe banana with cream cheese.

Prep Time: 10 minutes plus refrigeration
Bake Time: 40 minutes

Cook's Tip: Cracks in cheesecakes are a common problem but they do not ruin a cheesecake. To serve, cover up cracks with various toppings such as sweetened sour cream, whipped cream, fresh berries, or your favorite jam mixed with liqueur.

Raspberry Swirl Cheesecake

1½ cups fresh or thawed lightly sweetened loose-pack frozen red raspberries

1 (14-ounce) can EAGLE® BRAND Sweetened Condensed Milk (NOT evaporated milk), divided

2 (8-ounce) packages cream cheese, softened

3 eggs

2 (6-ounce) chocolate-flavored crumb pie crusts

Chocolate and white chocolate leaves (recipe follows, optional)

Fresh raspberries (optional)

1. Preheat oven to 350°F. In blender container, blend 1½ cups raspberries until smooth; press through sieve to remove seeds. Stir ⅓ cup Eagle Brand into sieved raspberries; set aside.

2. With mixer, beat cream cheese, eggs and remaining Eagle Brand in large bowl. Spoon into crusts. Drizzle with raspberry mixture. With table knife, gently swirl raspberry mixture through cream cheese mixture.

3. Bake 25 minutes or until center is nearly set when shaken. Cool; chill at least 4 hours. Garnish with chocolate leaves and fresh raspberries, if desired. Store leftovers covered in refrigerator.

Makes 16 servings (2 cheesecakes)

Chocolate Leaves: Place 1 (1-ounce) square semi-sweet chocolate in microwave-safe bowl. Microwave at HIGH (100% power) 1 to 2 minutes, stirring every minute until smooth. With small, clean paintbrush, paint several coats of melted chocolate on the undersides of nontoxic leaves, such as mint, lemon or strawberry. Wipe off any chocolate from top sides of leaves. Place leaves, chocolate sides up, on waxed paper-lined baking sheet or on curved surface, such as rolling pin. Refrigerate leaves until chocolate is firm. To use, carefully peel leaves away from chocolate.

Prep Time: 15 minutes
Bake Time: 25 minutes
Chill Time: 4 hours

Philadelphia® 3-Step® Chocolate Swirl Cheesecake

2 packages (8 ounces each)
PHILADELPHIA® Cream
Cheese, softened

½ cup sugar

½ teaspoon vanilla

2 eggs

1 square BAKER'S® Semi-Sweet
Chocolate, melted, slightly
cooled

1 OREO® Pie Crust (6 ounces)

BEAT cream cheese, sugar and vanilla
with electric mixer on medium speed until
well blended. Add eggs, 1 at a time,
mixing on low speed after each addition
just until blended. Stir melted chocolate
into ¾ cup of the cream cheese batter.

POUR remaining cream cheese batter
into crust. Spoon chocolate batter over
cream cheese batter; cut through batter
with knife several times for marble effect.

BAKE at 350°F for 35 to 40 minutes or
until center is almost set. Cool.
Refrigerate 3 hours or overnight.

Makes 8 servings

Prep Time: 10 minutes
Bake Time: 40 minutes

Blueberry Cheesecake

1 (8-ounce) package cream cheese,
softened

½ cup sugar

2 eggs, beaten

1 (6-ounce) READY CRUST®
Graham Cracker Pie Crust

1 (21-ounce) can blueberry pie filling
Frozen whipped topping, thawed

1. Preheat oven to 325°F. Beat cream
cheese, sugar and eggs in small bowl until
fluffy. Place crust on baking sheet. Pour
mixture into crust.

2. Bake 25 to 30 minutes or until center is
almost set. Cool.

3. Spread blueberry filling on top.
Garnish with whipped topping. Chill
3 hours. Refrigerate leftovers.

Makes 8 servings

Preparation Time: 10 minutes
Baking Time: 25 to 30 minutes
Chilling Time: 3 hours

*Philadelphia® 3-Step®
Chocolate Swirl Cheesecake*

Brownie Bottom Cheesecake

Crust

    1 package (10 to 16 ounces) brownie mix, any variety (8×8 pan size)

Filling

    3 packages (8 ounces each) PHILADELPHIA® Cream Cheese, softened

    ¾ cup sugar

    1 teaspoon vanilla

    ½ cup BREAKSTONE'S® or KNUDSEN® Sour Cream

    3 eggs

Crust

PREPARE and bake brownie mix as directed on package for 8-inch square pan in bottom of well-greased 9-inch springform pan.

Filling

MIX cream cheese, sugar and vanilla with electric mixer on medium speed until well blended. Blend in sour cream. Add eggs, mixing on low speed just until blended. Pour over brownie crust.

BAKE at 325°F for 1 hour to 1 hour and 5 minutes or until center is almost set if using a shiny springform pan. (Bake at 300°F for 1 hour to 1 hour and 5 minutes or until center is almost set if using a dark nonstick springform pan.) Run knife or metal spatula around rim of pan to loosen cake; cool before removing rim of pan. Refrigerate 4 hours or overnight.

Makes 12 servings

Prep Time: 20 minutes plus refrigerating
Bake Time: 1 hour 5 minutes

Brownie Bottom Cheesecake

Philadelphia® 3-Step® Lime Cheesecake

2 packages (8 ounces each) PHILADELPHIA® Cream Cheese, softened

½ cup sugar

2 tablespoons fresh lime juice

1 teaspoon grated lime peel

½ teaspoon vanilla

2 eggs

1 HONEY MAID® Graham Pie Crust (6 ounces)

1. **BEAT** cream cheese, sugar, juice, peel and vanilla with electric mixer on medium speed until well blended. Add eggs, 1 at a time, mixing on low speed after each addition until blended.

2. **POUR** into crust.

3. **BAKE** at 350°F 35 to 40 minutes or until center is almost set. Cool. Refrigerate 3 hours or overnight. Store leftover cheesecake in refrigerator.

Makes 8 servings

How to Make Your Own Crust: Mix 1½ cups HONEY MAID® Graham Cracker Crumbs, 3 tablespoons sugar and ½ cup (1 stick) butter or margarine, melted. Press onto bottom and up side of 9-inch pie plate.

Prep Time: 10 minutes plus refrigerating
Bake Time: 40 minutes

Cook's Tip: Always heat the oven before mixing the cheesecake. Position the oven rack in the center of the oven and preheat the oven. Use an oven thermometer, for an accurate temperature.

Philadelphia® 3-Step® Lime Cheesecake

Amaretto Macaroon Cheesecake

Crust

- 1 package (7 ounces) BAKER'S® ANGEL FLAKE® Coconut, lightly toasted
- ½ cup finely chopped lightly toasted almonds
- 1 can (14 ounces) sweetened condensed milk, divided
- ⅓ cup flour
- ¼ cup (½ stick) butter or margarine, melted

Filling

- 4 packages (8 ounces each) PHILADELPHIA® Cream Cheese, softened
- ¼ cup sugar
- ¼ cup almond-flavored liqueur
- 4 eggs

Crust

MIX coconut, almonds, ½ cup of the sweetened condensed milk, flour and butter; press onto bottom of greased 9-inch springform pan.

Filling

MIX cream cheese, sugar and remaining ¾ cup sweetened condensed milk with electric mixer on medium speed until well blended. Blend in liqueur. Add eggs, mixing on low speed just until blended. Pour over crust.

BAKE at 325°F for 55 to 60 minutes or until center is almost set if using a shiny springform pan. (Bake at 300°F for 55 to 60 minutes or until center is almost set if using a dark nonstick springform pan.) Run knife or metal spatula around rim of pan to loosen cake; cool before removing rim of pan. Refrigerate 4 hours or overnight. *Makes 12 servings*

Prep Time: 25 minutes plus refrigerating
Bake Time: 1 hour

Cheesecake Sensation

¼ cup graham cracker crumbs

4 (8-ounce) packages cream cheese, softened

1¾ cups sugar

4 eggs

2 tablespoons lemon juice

2 tablespoons grated lemon peel

1 teaspoon vanilla

½ cup SMUCKER'S® Natural Apricot Syrup

½ cup SMUCKER'S® Strawberry Preserves

Butter inside of straight-sided casserole or soufflé dish 8 inches wide and 3 inches deep. Do not use a springform pan. Sprinkle with graham cracker crumbs and shake around bottom and side until coated. Set aside.

Combine cream cheese, sugar, eggs, lemon juice, lemon peel and vanilla; beat at low speed and, as ingredients blend, increase speed to high, scraping bowl several times. Continue beating until thoroughly blended and smooth. Pour batter into prepared dish; shake gently to level mixture. Set dish inside slightly wider pan; add boiling water to larger pan to a depth of about ½ inch. Do not let edge of cheesecake dish touch rim of larger pan.

Bake at 325°F for 1½ to 2 hours or until set. Turn off oven; let cake sit in oven 20 minutes longer. Lift cake dish out of larger pan and place on wire rack. Cool about 2 hours or until cake reaches room temperature.

Invert plate over the cheesecake and carefully turn upside down so cake comes out crumb side up. Slowly spoon syrup over cake. Just before serving, spoon preserves in a narrow ring around outer rim of cake.   *Makes 12 to 14 servings*

Chocolate Truffle Cheesecake

Crust

- 1½ cups crushed chocolate sandwich cookies (about 18 cookies)
- 2 tablespoons butter or margarine, melted

Filling

- 3 packages (8 ounces each) PHILADELPHIA® Cream Cheese, softened
- 1 cup sugar
- 1 teaspoon vanilla
- 8 squares BAKER'S® Semi-Sweet Baking Chocolate, melted, slightly cooled
- ¼ cup hazelnut liqueur (optional)
- 3 eggs

Crust

MIX crumbs and butter; press onto bottom of 9-inch springform pan. Bake at 325°F for 10 minutes if using a shiny springform pan. (Bake at 300°F for 10 minutes if using a dark nonstick springform pan.)

Filling

MIX cream cheese, sugar and vanilla with electric mixer on medium speed until well blended. Blend in melted chocolate and liqueur. Add eggs, mixing on low speed just until blended. Pour over crust.

BAKE at 325°F for 55 to 60 minutes or until center is almost set if using a silver springform pan. (Bake at 300°F for 55 to 60 minutes or until center is almost set if using a dark nonstick springform pan.) Run knife or metal spatula around rim of pan to loosen cake; cool before removing rim of pan. Refrigerate 4 hours or overnight. *Makes 12 servings*

Prep Time: 30 minutes plus refrigerating
Bake Time: 1 hour

Chocolate Truffle Cheesecake

Mocha Marble Cheesecake

12 ounces cream cheese, softened

½ cup sugar

1 teaspoon vanilla

2 eggs

½ cup white crème de cacao

1 teaspoon instant coffee granules

1 (6-ounce) READY CRUST® Graham Cracker Pie Crust

1. Preheat oven to 325°F. Beat cream cheese in medium bowl until smooth. Add sugar and vanilla. Add eggs, one at a time, beating until well blended.

2. Reserve ½ cup cream cheese mixture; set aside. Pour remaining mixture into crust. Mix crème de cacao and coffee granules with reserved cream cheese mixture.

3. Place crust on baking sheet. Pour coffee mixture over cheesecake filling. Gently cut through coffee layer with knife to create marbled appearance. Bake 30 to 35 minutes or until just set in center. Cool on wire rack. Chill 3 hours. Refrigerate leftovers. *Makes 8 servings*

Prep Time: 10 minutes
Bake Time: 30 to 35 minutes
Chill Time: 3 hours

Chocolate Cherry Cheesecake

1 (8-ounce) package cream cheese, softened

¾ cup sugar

2 eggs

2 (1-ounce) squares semi-sweet chocolate, melted

1 teaspoon vanilla

1 (6-ounce) READY CRUST® Chocolate Pie Crust

1 (21-ounce) can cherry pie filling

1. Preheat oven to 325°F. Beat cream cheese in medium bowl until fluffy. Add sugar, eggs, chocolate and vanilla; mix well. Place crust on baking sheet. Pour mixture into crust.

2. Bake 35 minutes or until filling springs back when touched lightly. Cool on wire rack.

3. Spread cherry pie filling over top. Chill 3 hours. Refrigerate leftovers.
Makes 8 servings

Prep Time: 15 minutes
Bake Time: 35 minutes
Chill Time: 3 hours

Mocha Marble Cheesecake

Philadelphia® 3-Step® Chocolate Lover's Cheesecake

2 packages (8 ounces each)
  PHILADELPHIA® Cream
  Cheese, softened

½ cup sugar

½ teaspoon vanilla

2 eggs

4 squares BAKER'S® Semi-Sweet
  Chocolate, melted, slightly
  cooled

1 OREO® Pie Crust (6 ounces)

BEAT cream cheese, sugar and vanilla with electric mixer on medium speed until well blended. Add eggs, 1 at a time, mixing on low speed after each addition just until blended. Stir in melted chocolate.

POUR into crust.

BAKE at 350°F for 35 to 40 minutes or until center is almost set. Cool. Refrigerate 3 hours or overnight.

Makes 8 servings

Mocha: Blend 3 tablespoons coffee-flavored liqueur or black coffee into batter.

Prep Time: 10 minutes
Bake Time: 40 minutes

Cook's Tip: For a successful cheesecake, be sure to use the size pan specified in the recipe and blend ingredients in the precise order given in the recipe.

Creamy Chocolate Marble Cheesecake

Cinnamon Graham Crust (recipe follows)

3 packages (8 ounces each) cream cheese, softened

¾ cup sugar

3 eggs

1 cup dairy sour cream

1 teaspoon vanilla extract

1 square (1 ounce) unsweetened chocolate, melted*

*For plain cheesecake, omit melted chocolate. Proceed as directed.

Preheat oven to 450°F. Prepare Cinnamon Graham Crust.

Beat cream cheese in large bowl with electric mixer on medium speed until fluffy. Beat in sugar on medium speed until light and fluffy. Beat in eggs, 1 at a time, on low speed until well blended. Stir in sour cream and vanilla on low speed. Blend melted chocolate into 1 cup batter. Spoon plain and chocolate batters alternately over crust. Cut through batters several times with a knife for marble effect.

Bake 10 minutes. Reduce oven temperature to 250°F. Bake 30 minutes more or until center is just set. Remove pan to wire rack. Carefully loosen edge of cake with narrow knife. Cool completely on wire rack. Refrigerate several hours or overnight.

To serve, place on plate. Carefully remove side of pan.

Makes one 9-inch cheesecake

Cinnamon Graham Crust

1 cup graham cracker crumbs

3 tablespoons sugar

½ teaspoon ground cinnamon

3 tablespoons butter or margarine, melted

Preheat oven to 350°F. Combine crumbs, sugar and cinnamon in small bowl. Stir in melted butter until blended. Press onto bottom of 9-inch springform pan. Bake 10 minutes. Cool on wire rack while preparing filling.

Jeweled Brownie Cheesecake

¾ cup (1½ sticks) butter or margarine

4 squares (1 ounce each) unsweetened baking chocolate

1½ cups sugar

4 large eggs

1 cup all-purpose flour

1¾ cups "M&M's"® Chocolate Mini Baking Bits, divided

½ cup chopped walnuts, optional

1 (8-ounce) package cream cheese, softened

1 teaspoon vanilla extract

Preheat oven to 350°F. Lightly grease 9-inch springform pan; set aside. Place butter and chocolate in large microwave-safe bowl. Microwave at HIGH 1 minute; stir. Microwave at HIGH an additional 30 seconds; stir until chocolate is completely melted. Add sugar and 3 eggs, one at a time, beating well after each addition; blend in flour. Stir in 1¼ cups "M&M's"® Chocolate Mini Baking Bits and nuts, if desired; set aside. In large bowl, beat cream cheese, remaining 1 egg and vanilla. Spread half of the chocolate mixture in prepared pan. Carefully spread cream cheese mixture evenly over chocolate mixture, leaving 1-inch border. Spread remaining chocolate mixture evenly over top, all the way to the edge. Sprinkle with remaining ½ cup "M&M's"® Chocolate Mini Baking Bits. Bake 40 to 45 minutes or until firm to the touch. Cool completely. Store in refrigerator in tightly covered container.

Makes 12 slices

Pumpkin Pie Crunch (page 242)

Simply Delicious Pies

❧ ❧ ❧

Show off your baking skills with a freshly baked pie or a comforting crisp or cobbler. To save time, take advantage of the wide variety of prepared crusts. Then, choose a filling bursting with flavor. Everyone will love juicy seasonal fruit in Apple-Raisin Cobbler Pie (page 244) or Very Cherry Pie (page 236). Or, try traditional favorites like Caramel-Pecan Pie (page 264) or Honey Pumpkin Pie (page 254).

For a simply delicious dessert any time of the year, cobblers, pies and tarts are truly easy as pie.

Very Cherry Pie

4 cups frozen unsweetened tart
    cherries

1 cup dried tart cherries

1 cup sugar

2 tablespoons quick-cooking tapioca

½ teaspoon almond extract

    Pastry for double-crust 9-inch pie

¼ teaspoon ground nutmeg

1 tablespoon butter

Combine frozen cherries, dried cherries,
sugar, tapioca and almond extract in large
mixing bowl; mix well. (It is not necessary
to thaw cherries before using.) Let cherry
mixture stand 15 minutes.

Line 9-inch pie plate with pastry; fill with
cherry mixture. Sprinkle with nutmeg.
Dot with butter. Cover with top crust,
cutting slits for steam to escape. Or, cut
top crust into strips for lattice top and
cherry leaf cutouts.

Bake in preheated 375°F oven about
1 hour or until crust is golden brown and
filling is bubbly. If necessary, cover edge
of crust with foil to prevent overbrowning.

Makes 8 servings

Note: Two (16-ounce) cans unsweetened
tart cherries, well drained, can be
substituted for frozen tart cherries. Dried
cherries are available at gourmet and
specialty food stores and at selected
supermarkets.

Favorite recipe from **Cherry Marketing Institute**

Old-Fashioned Caramel Pie

3 large eggs

1 cup quick-cooking or old-fashioned
    oats

1 cup (12-ounce jar) SMUCKER'S®
    Caramel Topping

½ cup sugar

½ cup milk

¼ cup butter, melted

1 teaspoon vanilla

⅛ teaspoon salt

1 (9-inch) pie shell, baked

In large bowl, beat eggs. Add remaining
ingredients except pie shell; blend well.
Pour into baked pie shell.

Bake at 350°F for 1 hour or until filling
is set. *Makes 6 to 8 servings*

Very Cherry Pie

Rustic Apple Croustade

1⅓ cups all-purpose flour

¼ teaspoon salt

2 tablespoons margarine or butter

2 tablespoons vegetable shortening

4 to 5 tablespoons ice water

⅓ cup packed light brown sugar

1 tablespoon cornstarch

1 teaspoon cinnamon, divided

3 large Jonathan or MacIntosh apples peeled, cored and thinly sliced (4 cups)

1 egg white, beaten

1 tablespoon granulated sugar

1. Combine flour and salt in small bowl. Cut in margarine and shortening with pastry blender or two knives until mixture resembles coarse crumbs. Mix in ice water, 1 tablespoon at a time, until mixture comes together and forms a soft dough. Wrap in plastic wrap; refrigerate 30 minutes.

2. Preheat oven to 375°F. Roll out pastry on floured surface to ⅛-inch thickness. Cut into 12-inch circle. Transfer pastry to nonstick jelly-roll pan.

3. Combine brown sugar, cornstarch and ¾ teaspoon cinnamon in medium bowl; mix well. Add apples; toss well. Spoon apple mixture into center of pastry leaving a 1½-inch border. Fold pastry over apples, folding edges in gently and pressing down lightly. Brush egg white over pastry. Combine remaining ¼ teaspoon cinnamon and granulated sugar in small bowl; sprinkle evenly over tart.

4. Bake 35 to 40 minutes or until apples are tender and crust is golden brown. Let stand 20 minutes before serving. Cut into wedges.   *Makes 8 servings*

> **Cook's Tip:** *Substitute a refrigerated pie crust for homemade pastry. Roll out pie crust as directed in step 2.*

Rustic Apple Croustade

Easy Fruit Tarts

12 wonton skins

  Vegetable cooking spray

2 tablespoons apple jelly or apricot
  fruit spread

1½ cups sliced or cut-up fruit such as
  DOLE® Bananas, Strawberries,
  Raspberries or Red or Green
  Seedless Grapes

1 cup nonfat or low-fat yogurt, any
  flavor

• Press wonton skins into 12 muffin cups
sprayed with vegetable cooking spray,
allowing corners to stand up over edges of
muffin cups.

• Bake at 375°F 5 minutes or until lightly
browned. Carefully remove wonton cups
to wire rack; cool.

• Cook and stir jelly in small saucepan
over low heat until jelly melts.

• Brush bottoms of cooled wonton cups
with melted jelly. Place two fruit slices in
each cup; spoon rounded tablespoon of
yogurt on top of fruit. Garnish with fruit
slice and mint leaves. Serve immediately.

Makes 12 servings

Prep Time: 20 minutes
Bake Time: 5 minutes

Blueberry Crumble Pie

1 (6-ounce) READY CRUST®
  Graham Cracker Pie Crust

1 egg yolk, beaten

1 (21-ounce) can blueberry pie filling

⅓ cup all-purpose flour

⅓ cup quick-cooking oats

¼ cup sugar

3 tablespoons margarine, melted

1. Preheat oven to 375°F. Brush bottom
and side of crust with egg yolk; bake on
baking sheet 5 minutes or until light
brown.

2. Pour blueberry pie filling into crust.
Combine flour, oats and sugar in small
bowl; mix in margarine. Spoon over pie
filling.

3. Bake on baking sheet about 35 minutes
or until filling is bubbly and topping is
browned. Cool on wire rack.

Makes 8 servings

Preparation Time: 15 minutes
Baking Time: 40 minutes

Easy Fruit Tarts

Pumpkin Pie Crunch

1 can (16 ounces) solid pack pumpkin

1 can (12 ounces) evaporated milk

1½ cups sugar

3 eggs

4 teaspoons pumpkin pie spice

½ teaspoon salt

1 package DUNCAN HINES® Moist Deluxe® Classic Yellow Cake Mix

1 cup chopped pecans

1 cup butter or margarine, melted

Whipped topping

1. Preheat oven to 350°F. Grease bottom of 13×9×2-inch pan.

2. Combine pumpkin, evaporated milk, sugar, eggs, pumpkin pie spice and salt in large bowl. Pour into pan. Sprinkle dry cake mix evenly over pumpkin mixture. Top with pecans. Drizzle with melted butter. Bake at 350°F 50 to 55 minutes or until golden. Cool completely. Serve with whipped topping. Refrigerate leftovers.

Makes 16 to 20 servings

Tip: For a richer flavor, try using Duncan Hines® Moist Deluxe® Butter Recipe Golden Cake Mix.

Easy Peach Cobbler

8 cups peeled and sliced peaches, nectarines or apples (½-inch-thick slices)

1 cup granulated sugar

⅔ cup plus 2 tablespoons BISQUICK®, divided

1 tablespoon ground cinnamon

2 tablespoons firmly packed brown sugar

¼ cup (½ stick) I CAN'T BELIEVE IT'S NOT BUTTER!® Spread

2 tablespoons milk

Preheat oven to 400°F.

In large bowl, combine peaches, granulated sugar, 2 tablespoons baking mix and cinnamon. In 11×7-inch baking dish, arrange peach mixture; set aside.

In medium bowl, mix remaining ⅔ cup baking mix with brown sugar. With pastry blender or 2 knives, cut in I Can't Believe It's Not Butter! until mixture is size of small peas. Stir in milk just until moistened. Drop by teaspoonfuls onto peach mixture.

Bake 30 minutes or until peaches are tender and topping is golden. Let stand 5 minutes before serving. Serve warm.

Makes 6 servings

Bourbon Pecan Pie

Pastry for a single-crust 9-inch pie

¼ **cup butter or margarine, softened**

½ **cup sugar**

3 **eggs**

1½ **cups light or dark corn syrup**

2 **tablespoons bourbon**

1 **teaspoon vanilla extract**

1 **cup pecan halves**

Preheat oven to 350°F. Roll out pastry and line 9-inch pie pan; flute edge. Beat butter in large bowl of electric mixer on medium speed until creamy. Add sugar; beat until fluffy. Add eggs, one at a time, beating well after each addition. Add corn syrup, bourbon and vanilla; beat until well blended. Pour filling into pastry shell. Arrange pecan halves on top. Bake on lowest oven rack 50 to 55 minutes or until knife inserted slightly off center comes out clean (filling will be puffy). Place on rack and cool. Serve at room temperature or refrigerate up to 24 hours.

Makes 6 to 8 servings

Tip: Use your favorite recipe for pastry or purchase a 1½-inch-deep, 9-inch frozen pie shell.

Rhubarb Pie

Pastry for 9-inch 2-crust pie

1¼ **cups sugar**

¼ **cup ARGO® or KINGSFORD'S® Corn Starch**

1 **teaspoon grated orange peel (optional)**

¼ **teaspoon salt**

2 **pounds fresh rhubarb, cut into 1-inch pieces (6 cups) *or* 1 bag (20 ounces) frozen cut rhubarb, thawed and drained**

1 **tablespoon margarine or butter**

1. Preheat oven to 425°F. Roll out half of pastry and line 9-inch pie plate.

2. In large bowl combine sugar, corn starch, orange peel and salt. Add rhubarb; toss to coat. Spoon into pie plate; dot with margarine.

3. Roll remaining pastry to 12-inch circle; cover pie with pastry. Trim overhang to 1 inch. Fold pie crust edges together and under bottom crust; pinch edge to flute. Cut several vents in top crust.

4. Bake 45 to 50 minutes or until fruit is tender and juices that bubble up in center are clear and shiny. If edge begins to overbrown, cover with strips of foil. Cool on wire rack. *Makes 6 to 8 servings*

Apple Raisin Pie

2 cans (20 ounces each) apple
   pie filling
1 cup raisins
½ teaspoon ground ginger
1 unbaked 9-inch pie shell
¼ cup all-purpose flour
¼ cup packed brown sugar
2 tablespoons butter, melted
¾ cup walnut pieces

1. Preheat oven to 375°F.

2. Combine pie filling, raisins and
¼ teaspoon ginger in large bowl. Spoon
into pie shell.

3. Combine flour, sugar and remaining
¼ teaspoon ginger in small bowl; stir in
butter until crumbly. Stir in walnuts;
evenly sprinkle over filling.

4. Bake 35 to 45 minutes or until topping
is golden brown.   *Makes 8 servings*

Lemon Buttermilk Pie

1 (9-inch) unbaked pie crust*
1½ cups sugar
½ cup (1 stick) butter, softened
3 eggs
1 cup buttermilk
1 tablespoon cornstarch
1 tablespoon fresh lemon juice
⅛ teaspoon salt

*If using a commercial frozen pie crust, purchase
a deep-dish crust and thaw before using.

Heat oven to 350°F. Prick crust all over
with fork. Bake until light golden brown,
about 8 minutes; cool on wire rack.
Reduce oven temperature to 325°F. In
large bowl, beat sugar and butter until
creamy. Add eggs, one at a time, beating
well after each addition. Add buttermilk,
cornstarch, lemon juice and salt; mix well.
Pour filling into crust. Bake 55 to
60 minutes or just until knife inserted
near center comes out clean. Cool; cover
and chill.   *Makes 8 servings*

*Favorite recipe from **Southeast United Dairy
Industry Association, Inc.***

Apple Raisin Pie

Country Peach Tart

Pastry for single crust 9-inch pie

1 tablespoon all-purpose flour

2½ teaspoons EQUAL® FOR RECIPES *or* 8 packets EQUAL® sweetener *or* ⅓ cup EQUAL® SPOONFUL™

4 cups sliced pitted peeled fresh peaches (about 4 medium) or frozen peaches, thawed

Ground nutmeg

• Roll pastry on floured surface into 12-inch circle; transfer to ungreased cookie sheet. Combine flour and Equal®; sprinkle over peaches and toss. Arrange peaches on pastry, leaving 2-inch border around edge of pastry. Sprinkle peaches lightly with nutmeg. Bring pastry edge toward center, overlapping as necessary.

• Bake tart in preheated 425°F oven until crust is browned and fruit is tender, 25 to 30 minutes.   *Makes 8 servings*

Traditional Cherry Pie

4 cups frozen tart cherries

1⅓ cups granulated sugar

3 tablespoons quick-cooking tapioca or cornstarch

½ teaspoon almond extract

Pastry for double crust 9-inch pie

2 tablespoons butter or margarine

In medium bowl, combine cherries, sugar, tapioca and almond extract; mix well. (It is not necessary to thaw cherries before using.) Let cherry mixture stand 15 minutes.

Line 9-inch pie plate with pastry; fill with cherry mixture. Dot with butter. Cover with top crust, cutting slits for steam to escape.

Bake in preheated oven 400°F 50 to 55 minutes or until crust is golden brown and filling is bubbly.

Makes 6 to 8 servings

Favorite recipe from **Cherry Marketing Institute**

Country Peach Tart

Chocolate Chip Walnut Pie

¾ cup packed light brown sugar

½ cup all-purpose flour

½ teaspoon baking powder

¼ teaspoon ground cinnamon

2 eggs, slightly beaten

1 cup HERSHEY'S Semi-Sweet Chocolate Chips, MINI CHIPS™ or Milk Chocolate Chips

1 cup coarsely chopped walnuts

1 baked (9-inch) pie crust

Spiced Cream (recipe follows)

1. Heat oven to 350°F.

2. Combine brown sugar, flour, baking powder and cinnamon in medium bowl. Add eggs; stir until well blended. Add chocolate chips and walnuts. Pour into baked pie crust.

3. Bake 25 to 30 minutes or until lightly browned and set. Serve slightly warm or at room temperature with Spiced Cream. Refrigerate leftovers.

Makes 1 (9-inch) pie

Spiced Cream: Combine ½ cup chilled whipping cream, 1 tablespoon powdered sugar, ¼ teaspoon vanilla extract, ¼ teaspoon ground cinnamon and dash ground nutmeg in bowl; beat until stiff.

Golden Apple Turnovers

2 cups diced Washington Golden Delicious apples (about 2 apples)

¼ cup raisins

2 tablespoons chopped walnuts

2 teaspoons grated orange peel

⅓ cup granulated sugar

Pastry for 2-crust 9-inch pie

Orange Glaze (recipe follows)

Preheat oven to 400°F. Combine apples, raisins, nuts, 2 teaspoons orange peel and sugar. Roll pastry to ⅛-inch thickness; cut into 10 to 12 (4½-inch) circles. Divide apple mixture evenly among pastry circles. Fold circles in half; seal edges with fork. Cut steam vents into tops of pastry. Bake 25 to 30 minutes or until golden. Drizzle with Orange Glaze while still warm.   *Makes 10 to 12 turnovers*

Orange Glaze: Combine ¾ cup powdered sugar, 1 tablespoon orange juice, ¼ teaspoon grated orange peel and dash salt.

*Favorite recipe from **Washington Apple Commission***

Blueberry Pie

6 cups fresh blueberries *or* 2 packages (16 ounces each) frozen unsweetened blueberries

3 tablespoons lemon juice

6 tablespoons cornstarch

8 teaspoons EQUAL® FOR RECIPES *or* 27 packets EQUAL® sweetener *or* 1 cup plus 2 tablespoons EQUAL® SPOONFUL™

Pastry for double crust 9-inch pie

• Toss blueberries and lemon juice in large bowl. Sprinkle with combined cornstarch and Equal®; toss to coat. Let stand 30 minutes.

• Roll half of pastry on lightly floured surface into circle 1 inch larger than inverted 9-inch pie pan. Ease pastry into pan; trim within 1 inch of edge of pan. Roll remaining pastry to ⅛-inch thickness; cut into 10 to 12 strips, ½-inch-wide.

• Pour blueberry mixture into pastry. Arrange pastry strips over filling and weave into lattice design. Trim ends of lattice strips; fold edge of lower crust over ends of lattice strips. Seal and flute edge.

• Bake in preheated 425°F oven until pastry is browned and filling is bubbly, about 1 hour. Cover edge of crust with aluminum foil if browning too quickly. Cool on wire rack; refrigerate leftovers.

Makes 8 servings

Cook's Tip: *A pie pan or plate is exclusively designed for baking a pie. Both are round, about 1½ inches deep and have a sloping side. They range in diameter from 8 to 12 inches. Nine inches is the most popular. Deep dish pie pans are 2 inches deep. Reduce the oven temperature by 25°F when using a glass pie plate.*

Orange Pecan Pie

3 eggs

½ cup GRANDMA'S® Molasses

½ cup light corn syrup

¼ cup orange juice

1 teaspoon grated orange peel

1 teaspoon vanilla

1½ cups whole pecan halves

1 (9-inch) unbaked pie shell

Whipping cream (optional)

Heat oven to 350°F. In large bowl, beat eggs. Add molasses, corn syrup, orange juice, orange peel and vanilla; beat until well blended. Stir in pecans. Pour into unbaked pie shell. Bake 30 to 45 minutes or until filling sets. Cool on wire rack. Serve with whipping cream, if desired.

Makes 8 servings

Apple Mince Pie

1 (27-ounce) jar NONE SUCH®
  Ready-to-Use Mincemeat
  (Regular or Brandy & Rum)

Pastry for 2-crust pie

3 medium all-purpose apples, cored,
  peeled and thinly sliced

3 tablespoons all-purpose flour

2 tablespoons butter or margarine,
  melted

1 egg yolk plus 2 tablespoons water,
  mixed

1. Place rack in lower half of oven; preheat oven to 425°F. Turn mincemeat into pastry-lined 9-inch pie plate.

2. In large bowl, toss apples with flour and butter; spoon evenly over mincemeat. Cover with top crust; cut slits near center. Seal and flute. Brush egg mixture over crust.

3. Bake 10 minutes. *Reduce oven temperature to 375°F;* bake 25 minutes longer or until golden. Cool. Garnish as desired.   *Makes 1 (9-inch) pie*

Prep Time: 30 minutes
Bake Time: 35 minutes

Orange Pecan Pie

Mixed Berry Tart with Ginger-Raspberry Glaze

1 refrigerated pie crust, at room temperature

¾ cup no-sugar-added seedless raspberry fruit spread

½ teaspoon grated fresh ginger *or* ¼ teaspoon ground ginger

2 cups fresh or frozen blueberries

2 cups fresh or frozen blackberries

1 peach, peeled and thinly sliced

1. Preheat oven to 450°F. Coat 9-inch pie pan or tart pan with nonstick cooking spray. Carefully place pie crust on bottom of pan. Turn edges of pie crust inward to form ½-inch thick edge. Press edges firmly against side of pan. Using fork, pierce several times over entire bottom of pan to prevent crust from puffing up while baking. Bake 12 minutes or until golden brown. Cool completely on wire rack.

2. For glaze, heat fruit spread in small saucepan over high heat; stir until completely melted. Immediately remove from heat; stir in ginger and set aside to cool slightly.

3. Combine blueberries, blackberries and all but 2 tablespoons glaze; set aside.

4. Brush remaining 2 tablespoons glaze over bottom of cooled crust. Arrange peach slices on top of crust and mound berries on top of peach slices. Refrigerate 2 hours. *Makes 8 servings*

Peanut Crumb Apple Pie

1 cup all-purpose flour

½ cup SMUCKER'S® Creamy Natural Peanut Butter or LAURA SCUDDER'S® Smooth Old-Fashioned Peanut Butter

½ cup firmly packed light brown sugar

¼ cup butter or margarine, softened

¼ teaspoon salt

1 can (30-ounce) apple pie filling

1 (9-inch) unbaked pie shell

Blend flour, peanut butter, brown sugar, butter and salt until mixture is crumbly. Spoon apple pie filling into unbaked crust; sprinkle peanut butter mixture over pie filling.

Bake at 400°F for 30 to 35 minutes or until filling is hot and pastry is browned.
Makes 6 to 8 servings

Mixed Berry Tart with Ginger-Raspberry Glaze

Honey Pumpkin Pie

1 can (16 ounces) solid pack pumpkin

1 cup evaporated low-fat milk

¾ cup honey

3 eggs, slightly beaten

2 tablespoons all-purpose flour

1 teaspoon ground cinnamon

½ teaspoon ground ginger

½ teaspoon rum extract

Pastry for single 9-inch pie crust

Combine all ingredients except pastry in large bowl; beat until well blended. Pour into pastry-lined 9-inch pie plate. Bake at 400°F 45 minutes or until knife inserted near center comes out clean.

Makes 8 servings

Favorite recipe from **National Honey Board**

Fudgy Pecan Pie

2 (1-ounce) squares unsweetened chocolate

¼ cup (½ stick) butter or margarine

1 (14-ounce) can EAGLE® BRAND Sweetened Condensed Milk (NOT evaporated milk)

½ cup hot water

2 eggs, well beaten

1¼ cups pecan halves or pieces

1 teaspoon vanilla extract

⅛ teaspoon salt

1 (9-inch) unbaked pastry shell

1. Preheat oven to 350°F. In medium saucepan over low heat, melt chocolate and butter. Stir in Eagle Brand, hot water and eggs; mix well.

2. Remove from heat; stir in pecans, vanilla and salt. Pour into pastry shell. Bake 40 to 45 minutes or until center is set. Cool slightly. Serve warm or chilled. Garnish as desired. Store covered in refrigerator. *Makes 1 (9-inch) pie*

Prep Time: 15 minutes
Bake Time: 40 to 45 minutes

Honey Pumpkin Pie

Nestlé® Toll House® Chocolate Chip Pie

2 eggs

½ cup all-purpose flour

½ cup granulated sugar

½ cup packed brown sugar

¾ cup (1½ sticks) butter, softened

1 cup (6 ounces) NESTLÉ® TOLL HOUSE® Semi-Sweet Chocolate Morsels

1 cup chopped nuts

1 unbaked 9-inch (4-cup volume) pie shell*

Sweetened whipped cream or ice cream (optional)

*If using frozen pie shell, use deep-dish style, thawed completely. Bake on baking sheet; increase baking time slightly.

BEAT eggs in large mixer bowl on high speed until foamy. Beat in flour, granulated sugar and brown sugar. Beat in butter. Stir in morsels and nuts. Spoon into pie shell.

BAKE in preheated 325°F. oven for 55 to 60 minutes or until knife inserted halfway between outside edge and center comes out clean. Cool on wire rack. Serve with whipped cream. *Makes 8 servings*

Southern Peanut Pie

3 eggs

1½ cups dark corn syrup

½ cup granulated sugar

¼ cup butter, melted

½ teaspoon vanilla extract

¼ teaspoon salt

1½ cups chopped roasted peanuts

1 (9-inch) unbaked deep-dish pastry shell

Beat eggs until foamy. Add corn syrup, sugar, butter, vanilla and salt; continue to beat until thoroughly blended. Stir in peanuts. Pour into unbaked pastry shell. Bake in preheated 375°F oven 50 to 55 minutes. Serve warm or cold. Garnish with whipped cream or ice cream, if desired. *Makes 6 servings*

Favorite recipe from **Texas Peanut Producers Board**

Tarte Tatin

8 Granny Smith apples (about 3 pounds)

½ cup granulated sugar

Pastry for single crust 9-inch pie

½ cup butter

½ cup dark brown sugar, loosely packed

1 tablespoon Calvados or other apple brandy

Sweetened whipped cream and fresh mint leaves (optional)

1. Preheat oven to 375°F.

2. Peel and core apples; cut into halves. Place apple halves, core sides up, in 13×9-inch baking dish. Sprinkle with granulated sugar. Bake 45 minutes; remove from oven. *Increase oven temperature to 425°F.* (Bake apples immediately after cutting to prevent browning.)

3. Roll pie pastry on lightly floured surface with lightly floured rolling pin into circle at least 1 inch larger than inverted 9-inch pie plate.

4. Melt butter in small saucepan over medium heat. Pour into 9-inch pie pan.

Quickly spread brown sugar over butter. Sprinkle with Calvados. Arrange cooked apples, core sides up, in concentric circles. Carefully lift dough and place over apples. Gently press dough around fruit. Trim crust even with edge of pie plate. Turn under edge of crust to seal. Prick several holes in crust with fork to release steam.

5. Bake 20 to 25 minutes until crust is golden brown and apples are tender. Let tart stand 10 minutes before inverting onto serving platter. Garnish with whipped cream and mint, if desired. Serve immediately. *Makes 8 servings*

Cook's Tip: *A tarte Tatin is a French upside-down apple tart made by covering the bottom of the pie plate with butter and sugar, then apples and the crust. After baking, the tarte is inverted onto a serving platter.*

Cranberry Cobbler

2 (16-ounce) cans sliced peaches in light syrup, drained
1 (16-ounce) can whole berry cranberry sauce
1 package DUNCAN HINES® Cinnamon Swirl Muffin Mix
½ cup chopped pecans
⅓ cup butter or margarine, melted
Whipped topping or ice cream

Preheat oven to 350°F.

Cut peach slices in half lengthwise. Combine peach slices and cranberry sauce in *ungreased* 9-inch square pan. Knead swirl packet from Mix for 10 seconds. Squeeze contents evenly over fruit.

Combine muffin mix, contents of topping packet from mix and pecans in large bowl. Add melted butter. Stir until thoroughly blended (mixture will be crumbly). Sprinkle crumbs over fruit. Bake 40 to 45 minutes or until lightly browned and bubbly. Serve warm with whipped topping. *Makes 9 servings*

Tip: Store leftovers in the refrigerator. Reheat in microwave oven to serve warm.

Upside-Down Pear Tart

½ cup sugar
2 tablespoons butter or margarine
2 teaspoons grated lemon peel
5 medium (2½ to 3 pounds) firm Northwest winter pears, peeled, cored and cut into eighths
1 tablespoon lemon juice
Pastry for 9-inch single crust pie
Vanilla yogurt

Heat sugar over medium heat in heavy 10-inch skillet with oven-safe handle until syrupy and light brown in color. Remove from heat and add butter and lemon peel; stir until butter melts. Arrange pears in two layers over hot sugar mixture in skillet. Fill open spaces with pear slices; sprinkle with lemon juice. Roll pastry to 10-inch round and place over pears. Bake at 425°F 25 to 30 minutes or until pastry is golden brown. Cool, in pan, 30 minutes. If there is too much sauce in pan, reserve to serve over tart. Invert tart onto shallow serving dish. Serve warm with yogurt. *Makes 6 to 8 servings*

*Favorite recipe from **Pear Bureau Northwest***

Cranberry Cobbler

Amazing White Chocolate Coconut Custard Pie

3 squares BAKER'S® Premium White Baking Chocolate, melted

2 cups milk

4 eggs

½ cup sugar

½ cup buttermilk baking mix

¼ cup (½ stick) butter or margarine, softened

2 teaspoons vanilla

1⅓ cups BAKER'S® ANGEL FLAKE® Coconut (3½ ounces)

HEAT oven to 350°F. Grease 9-inch pie plate.

PLACE melted chocolate, milk, eggs, sugar, baking mix, butter and vanilla in blender container; cover. Blend on low speed 3 minutes.

POUR into prepared pie plate. Sprinkle with coconut.

BAKE in lower third of oven for 45 minutes or until pie is set and top is golden brown. Cool completely on wire rack. *Makes 8 servings*

Prep Time: 10 minutes
Bake Time: 45 minutes

Country Fruit Pie

2 pie crust sticks

5 fresh California peaches or nectarines, each cut into 8 slices (about 3 cups)

3 fresh California plums, each cut into 6 slices (about 1 cup)

⅓ cup honey

3 tablespoons all-purpose flour

½ teaspoon almond extract

Preheat oven to 400°F. Roll out 1 pie crust stick according to package directions to fit 8-inch pie dish. Roll out remaining pie crust stick; cut out about 35 leaf shapes with small leaf-shaped cutter. Gently toss fruit, honey, flour and almond extract in large bowl. Spoon fruit mixture into crust. Place 8 leaf cut-outs over fruit; press remaining leaves onto rim of pie crust with small amount of water. Bake 25 to 30 minutes or until crust is browned and fruit is easily pierced with knife.

Makes 8 servings

Favorite recipe from **California Tree Fruit Agreement**

Libby's® Famous Pumpkin Pie

1 *unbaked* 9-inch (4-cup volume) deep-dish pie shell

¾ cup granulated sugar

1 teaspoon ground cinnamon

½ teaspoon salt

½ teaspoon ground ginger

¼ teaspoon ground cloves

2 eggs

1¾ cups (15-ounce can) LIBBY'S® 100% Pure Pumpkin

1½ cups (12 fluid-ounce can) NESTLÉ® CARNATION® Evaporated Milk*

*For lower fat/calorie pie, substitute CARNATION® Evaporated Lowfat Milk or Evaporated Fat Free Milk.

COMBINE sugar, cinnamon, salt, ginger and cloves in small bowl. Beat eggs lightly in large bowl. Stir in pumpkin and sugar-spice mixture. Gradually stir in evaporated milk. Pour into pie shell.

BAKE in preheated 425°F. oven for 15 minutes. *Reduce temperature to 350°F.* Bake 40 to 50 minutes or until knife inserted near center comes out clean. Cool on wire rack for 2 hours. Serve immediately or chill (do not freeze as this will cause filling to separate from crust).

FOR 2 SHALLOW PIES, substitute two 9-inch (2-cup volume) pie shells. Bake in preheated 425°F. oven for 15 minutes. *Reduce temperature to 350°F.; bake for 20 to 30 minutes or until pies test done.*

Makes 8 servings

Southern Custard Pecan Pie

1 cup packed light brown sugar

1 cup sugar

¾ cup egg substitute

2 tablespoons margarine

1 teaspoon vanilla extract

1 cup PLANTERS® Pecan Halves

1 (9-inch) unbaked pastry crust

1. Beat sugars, egg substitute, margarine and vanilla with electric mixer at medium speed until well blended; stir in pecan halves. Pour into pastry crust.

2. Bake at 400°F for 15 minutes; *reduce temperature to 350°F.* Bake for 20 to 25 more minutes or until lightly browned and completely puffed across top of pie. Cool completely on wire rack. Garnish as desired.

Makes 10 servings

Praline Pie

1 (6-ounce) HONEY MAID®
 Graham Pie Crust

1 egg white, slightly beaten

¼ cup margarine or butter, melted

1 cup packed light brown sugar

¾ cup all-purpose flour

1 egg

1 teaspoon baking powder

1 teaspoon vanilla extract

1 cup PLANTERS® Pecans, coarsely
 chopped, divided

 Prepared whipped topping, for
 garnish

1. Brush pie crust with egg white. Bake at 375°F for 5 minutes; set aside. *Reduce oven temperature to 350°F.*

2. Beat margarine or butter and brown sugar in medium bowl with mixer at low speed until blended. Mix in flour, egg, baking powder and vanilla until well combined. Stir in ¾ cup pecans. Spread filling into prepared crust; sprinkle top with remaining ¼ cup pecans.

3. Bake at 350°F for 25 to 30 minutes or until lightly browned and filling is set. Cool on wire rack. Garnish with whipped topping. *Makes 6 servings*

Blueberry Granola Crumble Pie

1 package (16 ounces) frozen
 unsweetened blueberries

¼ cup sugar

2 tablespoons lemon juice

1 tablespoon plus 1½ teaspoons
 cornstarch

2 teaspoons vanilla

1 frozen reduced-fat pie crust

1 cup low-fat granola

1. Preheat oven 425°F. Place baking sheet in oven while preheating.

2. Toss blueberries with sugar, lemon juice, cornstarch and vanilla to coat. Spoon blueberry mixture into pie crust; place on heated baking sheet.

3. Bake 20 minutes; sprinkle granola evenly over pie. Bake an additional 20 minutes or until pie is bubbly.
Makes 8 servings

Tip: If pie is allowed to stand 4 hours or overnight, the flavors will blend making a sweeter-tasting dessert. This is true with most fruit pies, especially blueberry, cherry and peach pies.

Praline Pie

Apple and Walnut Strudel

1 package (17¼-ounces) frozen puff pastry

1 cup sour cream

1 egg, separated

1 tablespoon water

1 can (21 ounces) apple pie filling

1 cup coarsely chopped walnuts

1. Thaw the puff pastry according to package directions.

2. Preheat oven to 375°F. Spray 2 baking sheets with nonstick cooking spray.

3. Combine sour cream and egg yolk in small bowl; set aside. In separate small bowl, mix egg white and water; set aside.

4. On lightly floured board, roll 1 sheet pastry into 12×10-inch rectangle. Spread ½ can pie filling vertically down center ⅓ of pastry. Spread ½ cup sour cream mixture over apples; sprinkle with ½ cup walnuts.

5. Fold one long side of pastry over apple mixture then fold the other side over filling overlapping edges. Press edges together to seal. Place on baking sheet, seam side down, tucking under ends. Using a sharp knife, make 7 diagonal slits on the top, then brush with egg white mixture. Repeat with remaining pastry, apple filling, sour cream mixture and walnuts. Bake for 30 to 35 minutes or until golden brown.

Makes 16 servings

Caramel-Pecan Pie

3 eggs

⅔ cup sugar

1 cup (12-ounce jar) SMUCKER'S® Caramel Topping

¼ cup butter or margarine, melted

1½ cups pecan halves

1 (9-inch) unbaked pie shell

In mixing bowl, beat eggs slightly with fork. Add sugar, stirring until dissolved. Stir in topping and butter; mix well. Stir in pecan halves. Pour filling into pie shell.

Bake at 350°F for 45 minutes or until knife inserted near center comes out clean. Cool thoroughly on rack before serving. Cover and store in refrigerator.

Makes 6 to 8 servings

Apple and Walnut Strudel

Spiced Peach Pie

Pastry for double-crust 9-inch pie

1 egg, separated

5 cups peeled sliced fresh peaches or
frozen unsweetened sliced
peaches, thawed and well drained

2 tablespoons cornstarch

2 teaspoons ground cinnamon

½ teaspoon ground nutmeg

⅛ teaspoon salt

½ cup thawed frozen unsweetened
apple juice concentrate

1 teaspoon vanilla

1 tablespoon butter or margarine

1 teaspoon cold water

Preheat oven to 400°F. Roll out half of
pastry to 11-inch circle. Place in 9-inch
pie plate. Beat egg white until frothy;
brush lightly onto bottom of pastry. Set
aside. Place peaches in large bowl.
Combine cornstarch, cinnamon, nutmeg
and salt; mix well. Blend in apple juice
concentrate and vanilla. Pour over
peaches; toss lightly to coat. Spoon into
pie shell; dot with butter. Cut remaining
pastry into ½-inch wide strips; form into
lattice design over peaches. Beat together
egg yolk and water; brush lightly over
pastry. Bake 50 minutes or until pastry is
golden brown and filling is hot and
bubbly.* Cool on wire rack. Serve warm,
at room temperature or chilled.

Makes 8 servings

*Pie may be covered loosely with foil after
30 minutes of baking to prevent overbrowning,
if desired.

Chocolate-Topped Raspberry Cheese Pie

2 (3-ounce) packages cream cheese,
softened

1 (14-ounce) can EAGLE® BRAND
Sweetened Condensed Milk
(NOT evaporated milk)

1 egg

3 tablespoons REALEMON® Lemon
Juice From Concentrate

1 teaspoon vanilla extract

1 cup fresh or frozen raspberries

1 (6-ounce) ready-made chocolate
crumb pie crust

Chocolate Glaze (recipe page 267)

1. Preheat oven to 350°F. In medium
bowl, beat cream cheese until fluffy.
Gradually beat in Eagle Brand until
smooth. Add egg, ReaLemon and vanilla;
mix well.

2. Arrange raspberries on bottom of crust. Slowly pour cheese mixture over fruit.

3. Bake 30 to 35 minutes or until center is almost set. Cool.

4. Prepare Chocolate Glaze and spread over cheesecake; chill. Garnish as desired. Store covered in refrigerator.

Makes 1 pie

Chocolate Glaze: In small saucepan over low heat, melt 2 (1-ounce) squares semi-sweet chocolate with ¼ cup whipping cream. Cook and stir until thickened and smooth. Remove from heat; cool slightly.

Prep Time: 15 minutes
Bake Time: 30 to 35 minutes

> **Cook's Tip:** *When rolling out pie dough, carefully fold the dough into quarters and place it in the pie pan. Unfold it and gently press into place. Be careful not to pull or stretch the dough because this will cause it to shrink during baking.*

Country Pecan Pie

Pie pastry for single 9-inch pie crust
1¼ **cups dark corn syrup**
4 **eggs**
½ **cup packed light brown sugar**
¼ **cup butter or margarine, melted**
2 **teaspoons all-purpose flour**
1½ **teaspoons vanilla**
1½ **cups pecan halves**

Preheat oven to 350°F. Roll pastry on lightly floured surface to form 13-inch circle. Fit into 9-inch pie plate. Trim edge; flute. Set aside.

Combine corn syrup, eggs, brown sugar and melted butter in large bowl; beat with electric mixer on medium speed until well blended. Stir in flour and vanilla until blended. Pour into unbaked pie crust. Arrange pecans on top.

Bake 40 to 45 minutes until center of filling is puffed and golden brown. Cool completely on wire rack. Garnish as desired.

Makes one 9-inch pie

Maple Walnut Pie

1 cup maple-flavored syrup

3 eggs

½ cup firmly packed dark brown
    sugar

1 tablespoon butter, melted

1 teaspoon vanilla extract

¼ teaspoon salt

1 cup coarsely chopped walnuts

1 (9-inch) unbaked deep-dish pie shell

Non-dairy whipped topping or
    whipped cream (optional)

1. Preheat oven to 350°F.

2. Beat syrup, eggs, brown sugar, butter,
vanilla and salt in large bowl with electric
mixer on medium speed until well
blended. Stir in walnuts. Pour filling into
unbaked crust.

3. Bake 40 to 45 minutes or until center is
firm. Cool 2 hours on wire rack. Top with
dollops of whipped topping, if desired.
Store in refrigerator.   *Makes 8 servings*

Coconut Peach Crunch Pie

1 (6-ounce) READY CRUST®
    Shortbread Pie Crust

1 egg yolk, beaten

1 (21-ounce) can peach pie filling

1 cup flaked coconut

½ cup all-purpose flour

½ cup sugar

¼ cup wheat germ

¼ cup margarine, melted

1. Preheat oven to 375°F. Brush bottom
and sides of crust with egg yolk; bake on
baking sheet 5 minutes or until golden
brown.

2. Spoon peach filling into crust. Combine
coconut, flour, sugar, wheat germ and
margarine in small bowl. Mix until well
blended. Spread over peach filling.

3. Bake on baking sheet 30 to 35 minutes
or until filling is bubbly and topping is
light brown. Cool on wire rack.

Makes 8 servings

Preparation Time: 15 minutes
Baking Time: 35 to 40 minutes

Maple Walnut Pie

Pumpkin Pie

Pastry for single crust 9-inch pie

1 can (16 ounces) pumpkin

1 can (12 ounces) evaporated skim milk

3 eggs

5½ teaspoons EQUAL® FOR RECIPES *or* 18 packets EQUAL® sweetener *or* ¾ cup EQUAL® SPOONFUL™

1 teaspoon ground cinnamon

½ teaspoon ground ginger

¼ teaspoon salt

¼ teaspoon ground nutmeg

⅛ teaspoon ground cloves

• Roll pastry on floured surface into circle 1 inch larger than inverted 9-inch pie pan. Ease pastry into pan; trim and flute edge.

• Beat pumpkin, evaporated milk and eggs in medium bowl; beat in remaining ingredients. Pour into pastry shell. Bake in preheated 425°F oven 15 minutes. *Reduce heat to 350°F;* bake until knife inserted near center comes out clean, about 40 minutes. Cool on wire rack.

Makes 8 servings

Quick & Easy Chocolate Chip Cherry Pie

1 can (21 ounces) cherry pie filling

1 tablespoon cornstarch

1 extra serving-size packaged graham cracker crumb crust (9 ounces)

1 package (8 ounces) cream cheese, softened

2 eggs

¼ cup sugar

½ teaspoon vanilla extract

½ teaspoon almond extract

½ cup HERSHEY'S Semi-Sweet Chocolate Chips or HERSHEY'S MINI CHIPS™ Semi-Sweet Chocolate Chips

1. Heat oven to 350°F.

2. Stir together pie filling and cornstarch in medium bowl until blended; pour into crust. Beat cream cheese, eggs, sugar, vanilla and almond extract in small bowl until blended; pour over pie filling. Sprinkle chocolate chips evenly over top.

3. Bake 35 to 40 minutes or until almost set in center. Cool completely on wire rack. Refrigerate until firm.

Makes 8 to 10 servings

Nectarine and Berry Pie

Pastry for single crust 9-inch pie

5 cups sliced nectarines (about 5 medium)

1 cup raspberries or sliced strawberries

1 cup fresh or frozen blueberries, partially thawed

2 teaspoons lemon juice

3 tablespoons cornstarch

7¼ teaspoons EQUAL® FOR RECIPES *or* 24 packets EQUAL® sweetener *or* 1 cup EQUAL® SPOONFUL™

1 teaspoon grated lemon peel

¼ teaspoon ground allspice

• Roll pastry on floured surface into 12-inch circle; transfer to ungreased cookie sheet.

• Toss nectarines and berries with lemon juice in large bowl; sprinkle fruit with combined cornstarch, Equal®, lemon peel and allspice and toss to coat. Arrange fruit on pastry, leaving 2-inch border around edge. Bring edge of pastry to center, overlapping as necessary. Bake pie in preheated 425°F oven until pastry is golden and fruit is tender, 35 to 40 minutes. Cool on wire rack. *Makes 8 servings*

Planters® Perfect Pecan Pie

3 eggs

1 cup light corn syrup

1 cup sugar

2 tablespoons margarine or butter, melted

1 teaspoon vanilla extract

⅛ teaspoon salt

1 cup PLANTERS® Pecan Halves

1 (9-inch) unbaked pastry shell

COOL WHIP® Whipped Topping and PLANTERS® Pecan Halves, for garnish

1. Beat eggs slightly. Stir in corn syrup, sugar, margarine or butter, vanilla and salt until blended.

2. Stir in pecan halves; pour into pastry shell.

3. Bake at 400°F for 15 minutes. *Reduce temperature to 350°F;* bake for 25 to 30 minutes more or until lightly browned and completely puffed across top. Cool completely.

4. Serve garnished with whipped topping and pecan halves if desired.

Makes 8 servings

Della Robbia Cake (page 306)

Easiest Ever Cakes

❧ ❧ ❧

Win over family and friends with delicious cakes and cupcakes that look and taste like they took hours to make. Whether it's a delicate angel food cake or a flavorful spice cake, you'll find fabulous recipes in this collection of mouthwatering, contemporary cakes.

For a great ending to a simple supper serve Fudgy Ripple Cake (page 287), or create a grand finale with an elegant Fantasy Angel Food Cake (page 307). Take one of these easy-to-transport cakes to a party, work or special event and be assured you'll come home with an empty plate.

Carrot Cake with Easy Cream Cheese Frosting

1 package (2-layer size) carrot cake mix

1 package (8 ounces) PHILADELPHIA® Cream Cheese, softened

⅓ cup granulated or powdered sugar

¼ cup cold milk

1 tub (8 ounces) COOL WHIP® Whipped Topping, thawed

PREPARE cake mix as directed on package for 13×9-inch pan. Cool completely.

BEAT cream cheese, sugar and milk in medium bowl with wire whisk until smooth. Gently stir in whipped topping. Spread over top of cake.

REFRIGERATE until ready to serve. Garnish as desired. *Makes 10 servings*

Note: Substitute your favorite carrot cake recipe for carrot cake mix.

Prep Time: 20 minutes

Lemony Pound Cake

1 (4-serving size) package lemon-flavor gelatin

¾ cup boiling water

1 package DUNCAN HINES® Moist Deluxe® Classic Yellow Cake Mix

4 eggs

¾ cup vegetable oil

1 (6-ounce) can frozen lemonade concentrate, thawed

½ cup granulated sugar

Preheat oven to 350°F. Grease and flour 10-inch tube pan.

Dissolve gelatin in water in large mixing bowl; cool. Stir in cake mix, eggs and oil. Beat at medium speed with electric mixer for 2 minutes. Spoon into prepared pan. Bake 50 minutes or until toothpick inserted near center comes out clean. Mix lemonade concentrate and sugar in small bowl. Pour over hot cake; cool in pan 1 hour. Remove from pan. Cool completely. *Makes 12 to 16 servings*

Tip: Serve this cake with fresh or thawed frozen strawberries for a special dessert.

Carrot Cake with Easy Cream Cheese Frosting

Double Chocolate Bundt Cake

1 package (about 18 ounces) chocolate cake mix

1 package (4-serving size) instant chocolate pudding mix

4 eggs, beaten

¾ cup water

¾ cup sour cream

½ cup oil

6 ounces (1 cup) semisweet chocolate chips

Powdered sugar

1. Preheat oven to 350°F. Spray 10-inch Bundt or tube pan with nonstick cooking spray.

2. Beat cake mix, pudding mix, eggs, water, sour cream and oil in large bowl with electric mixer at medium speed until ingredients are blended. Stir in chocolate chips; pour into prepared pan.

3. Bake 55 to 60 minutes or until cake springs back when lightly touched. Cool 1 hour in pan on wire rack. Invert cake onto serving plate; cool completely. Sprinkle with powdered sugar before serving. *Makes 10 to 12 servings*

Cinnamon Ripple Cake

1 package DUNCAN HINES® Angel Food Cake Mix

2¼ teaspoons ground cinnamon, divided

1½ cups frozen whipped topping, thawed

1. Preheat oven to 350°F.

2. Prepare cake following package directions. **Spoon** one-third of batter into ungreased 10-inch tube pan. **Spread** evenly. **Sprinkle** 1 teaspoon cinnamon over batter with small fine sieve. **Repeat. Top** with remaining cake batter. **Bake** and cool following package directions.

3. Combine whipped topping and ¼ teaspoon cinnamon in small bowl. **Serve** with cake slices.

Makes 12 to 16 servings

Tip: To slice cake, use a serrated knife and cut in a sawing motion.

Double Chocolate Bundt Cake

Easy Cappuccino Cake

1 package (2-layer size) white cake mix

4 tablespoons MAXWELL HOUSE® Instant Coffee, divided

¼ cup milk plus 1 tablespoon milk, divided

4 squares BAKER'S® Semi-Sweet Baking Chocolate, melted

2 tubs (8 ounces each) COOL WHIP® Whipped Topping, thawed, divided

HEAT oven to 350°F.

PREPARE and bake cake mix as directed on package for 8- or 9-inch round pans, adding 2 tablespoons instant coffee to cake mix.

POUR ¼ cup milk and 1 tablespoon instant coffee into small bowl, stirring until coffee is dissolved. Slowly stir into melted chocolate until smooth. Cool completely. Gently stir in 1 tub of whipped topping. Refrigerate 20 minutes, or until well chilled.

MEANWHILE, mix 1 tablespoon milk and 1 tablespoon coffee until dissolved. Gently stir into remaining tub of whipped topping.

COVER one cake layer with chocolate mixture. Place second cake layer on top. Frost top and side of cake with coffee-flavored whipped topping. Refrigerate until ready to serve.

Makes 14 servings

Variation: If desired, omit the coffee for a delicious plain chocolate filled layer cake.

Prep Time: 25 minutes

Cook's Tip: When baking cakes, place the cake pans in the center of a preheated oven. Oven racks may need to be set lower for cakes baked in tube or Bundt pans. If two racks are used, arrange them so they divide the oven into thirds and then stagger the pans so they are not directly over each other.

Golden Apple Cupcakes

1 package (18 to 20 ounces) yellow
    cake mix
1 cup MOTT'S® Chunky Apple Sauce
3 eggs
⅓ cup vegetable oil
¼ cup firmly packed light brown
    sugar
¼ cup chopped walnuts
½ teaspoon ground cinnamon
    Vanilla Frosting (recipe follows)

Heat oven to 350°F. In bowl, combine
cake mix, apple sauce, eggs and oil; blend
according to package directions. Spoon
batter into 24 paper-lined muffin pan
cups. Mix brown sugar, walnuts and
cinnamon; sprinkle over prepared batter
in muffin cups. Bake 20 to 25 minutes or
until toothpick inserted into centers
comes out clean. Cool in pan 10 minutes.
Remove from pan; cool completely on
wire rack. Frost cupcakes with Vanilla
Frosting. *Makes 24 cupcakes*

Vanilla Frosting: In large bowl, beat
1 package (8 ounces) softened cream
cheese until light and creamy; blend in
¼ teaspoon vanilla extract. Beat ½ cup
heavy cream until stiff; fold into cream
cheese mixture.

Spice Cake with Rum Caramel Sauce

1 package DUNCAN HINES® Moist
    Deluxe® Spice Cake Mix
¾ cup prepared caramel topping
1 tablespoon rum or water
1 teaspoon ground cinnamon
½ cup milk chocolate English toffee
    chips
    Whipped cream for garnish

Preheat oven to 350°F. Grease and flour
13×9-inch pan.

Prepare and bake cake as directed on
package. Cool cake 10 minutes. Combine
topping, rum and cinnamon in small
bowl. Spread over warm cake. Top with
chips. Serve warm with whipped cream, if
desired. *Makes 12 to 16 servings*

I Think You're "Marbleous" Cupcakes

1 box (18½ ounces) pudding-in-the-mix cake mix, any flavor

1¼ cups water

3 eggs

¼ cup oil

1 container (16 ounces) vanilla frosting

1 tube (4¼ ounces) red decorating icing

Supplies

Decorating tips to fit tube of icing

1. Preheat oven to 350°F. Grease or paper-line 24 (2½-inch) muffin cups.

2. Prepare cake mix according to package directions with water, eggs and oil. Spoon batter into prepared pans, filling each ⅔ full.

3. Bake 20 to 25 minutes or until toothpick inserted into centers comes out clean. Cool in pans 20 minutes. Remove to wire rack and cool completely.

4. Spread 1½ to 2 tablespoons frosting over each cupcake. Fit round tip onto tube of icing. Squeeze 4 to 5 dots icing over each cupcake. Swirl toothpick through icing and frosting in continuous motion to make marbleized pattern or heart shapes. *Makes 2 dozen cupcakes*

Butterscotch Pudding Cake

1 package DUNCAN HINES® Moist Deluxe® Yellow Cake Mix

1 (15¾-ounce) can prepared butterscotch pudding

1⅓ cups water

3 eggs

3 tablespoons vegetable oil

1½ cups chopped pecans

1 (12-ounce) package butterscotch chips

Preheat oven to 325°F. Grease and flour 13×9-inch pan.

Combine cake mix, pudding, water, eggs and oil in large mixing bowl. Beat at medium speed with electric mixer for 2 minutes. Pour into prepared pan. Top with pecans and chips. Bake 45 to 50 minutes or until toothpick inserted into center comes out clean. Cool completely in pan.

Makes 12 to 16 servings

I Think You're "Marbleous" Cupcakes

Luscious Lemon Poke Cake

2 baked 8- or 9-inch round white
  cake layers, cooled completely

2 cups boiling water

1 package (8-serving size) *or*
  2 packages (4-serving size)
  JELL-O® Brand Lemon Flavor
  Gelatin Dessert

1 tub (8 or 12 ounces) COOL WHIP®
  Whipped Topping, thawed

PLACE cake layers, top sides up, in
2 clean 8- or 9-inch round cake pans.
Pierce cake with large fork at ½-inch
intervals.

STIR boiling water into gelatin in
medium bowl at least 2 minutes until
completely dissolved. Carefully pour
1 cup of the gelatin over 1 cake layer.
Pour remaining gelatin over second cake
layer. Refrigerate 3 hours.

DIP 1 cake pan in warm water
10 seconds; unmold onto serving plate.
Spread with about 1 cup of the whipped
topping. Unmold second cake layer;
carefully place on first cake layer. Frost
top and side of cake with remaining
whipped topping.

REFRIGERATE at least 1 hour or until
ready to serve. Decorate as desired.

Makes 12 servings

Preparation Time: 30 minutes
Refrigerating Time: 4 hours

Cherry-Mallow Cake

4 cups miniature marshmallows
  (about ¾ of 10½-ounce package)

1 (about 18-ounce) package yellow
  cake mix plus ingredients to
  prepare mix

1 (21-ounce) can cherry pie filling

Spray 13×9×2-inch baking pan with
vegetable cooking spray. Place
marshmallows evenly in bottom of pan.

Prepare cake mix according to package
directions. Pour batter over
marshmallows. Spoon cherry filling
evenly over cake batter.

Bake in preheated 350°F oven 30 to
40 minutes. Top of cake will be bubbly
and marshmallows will be sticky. Let cool
before serving.   *Makes 15 servings*

Favorite recipe from **Cherry Marketing Institute**

Luscious Lemon Poke Cake

Easy Cream Cake

1 package DUNCAN HINES® Moist Deluxe® Classic White Cake Mix

1⅓ cups half-and-half

3 egg whites

1 cup flaked coconut, finely chopped

½ cup finely chopped pecans

2 tablespoons vegetable oil

2 containers DUNCAN HINES® Creamy Home-Style Cream Cheese Frosting

1. Preheat oven to 350°F. Grease and flour three 8-inch round pans.

2. Combine cake mix, half-and-half, egg whites, coconut, pecans and oil in large bowl. Beat at low speed with electric mixer until moistened. Beat at medium speed 2 minutes. Pour into pans. Bake at 350°F 22 to 25 minutes or until toothpick inserted into centers comes out clean. Cool following package directions.

3. To assemble, place one cake layer on serving plate. Spread with ¾ cup Cream Cheese frosting. Place second cake layer on top. Spread with ¾ cup frosting. Top with third layer. Spread ¾ cup frosting on top only.   *Makes 12 to 16 servings*

Creamy Banana Toffee Dessert

1 package DUNCAN HINES® Moist Deluxe® Butter Recipe Golden Cake Mix

1 (4-serving size) package banana cream-flavor instant pudding and pie filling mix

1½ cups milk

1 (8-ounce) container frozen non-dairy whipped topping, thawed

3 medium bananas, sliced

¾ cup English toffee bits

Preheat oven to 375°F. Grease and flour 10-inch tube pan.

Prepare, bake and cool cake as directed on package. Meanwhile, combine pudding mix and milk in medium bowl. Chill 5 minutes. Fold in whipped topping. Chill while cake cools.

To assemble, cut cake into 12 slices. Place 6 cake slices in 3-quart clear glass bowl. Top with half of bananas, pudding and toffee bits. Repeat layering. Chill until ready to serve.

Makes 12 to 14 servings

Easy Cream Cake

Punch Bowl Party Cake

1 package (18¼ ounces) yellow cake mix plus ingredients to prepare mix

1 package (4-serving size) vanilla flavor instant pudding and pie filling mix plus milk to prepare the mix

2 cans (21 ounces each) cherry pie filling

1 cup chopped pecans

1 container (12 ounces) frozen nondairy whipped topping, thawed

1. Prepare cake mix and bake according to package directions for 13×9-inch cake; cool completely.

2. Prepare pudding mix according to package directions.

3. Crumble ½ of cake into bottom of small punch bowl. Cover with ½ of pudding.

4. Reserve a few cherries from cherry pie filling. Top pudding with layers of cherry pie filling, nuts and whipped topping.

5. Repeat layers, using remaining cake, pudding and cherry pie filling. Top with remaining nuts and whipped topping. Garnish with reserved cherries.

Makes 16 servings

Orange Glazed Pound Cake

1 package DUNCAN HINES® Moist Deluxe® Butter Recipe Golden Cake Mix

4 eggs

1 cup sour cream

⅓ cup vegetable oil

¼ cup plus 1 to 2 tablespoons orange juice

2 tablespoons grated orange peel

1 cup confectioners' sugar

Preheat oven to 375°F. Grease and flour 10-inch tube pan.

Combine cake mix, eggs, sour cream, oil, ¼ cup orange juice and orange peel in large bowl. Beat at medium speed with electric mixer for 2 minutes. Pour into prepared pan. Bake 45 to 50 minutes or until toothpick inserted near center comes out clean. Cool in pan 25 minutes. Invert onto cooling rack. Cool completely.

Combine sugar and remaining 1 to 2 tablespoons orange juice in small bowl; stir until smooth. Drizzle over cake. Garnish as desired.

Makes 12 to 16 servings

Fudgy Ripple Cake

1 package (about 18 ounces) yellow cake mix plus ingredients to prepare mix

1 package (3 ounces) cream cheese, softened

2 tablespoons unsweetened cocoa powder

Fudgy Glaze (recipe follows)

½ cup "M&M's"® Chocolate Mini Baking Bits

Preheat oven to 350°F. Lightly grease and flour 10-inch Bundt or ring pan; set aside. Prepare cake mix as package directs. In medium bowl combine 1½ cups prepared batter, cream cheese and cocoa powder until smooth. Pour half of yellow batter into prepared pan. Drop spoonfuls of chocolate batter over yellow batter in pan. Top with remaining yellow batter. Bake about 45 minutes or until toothpick inserted near center comes out clean. Cool completely on wire rack. Unmold cake onto serving plate. Prepare Fudgy Glaze; spread over top of cake, allowing some glaze to run over side. Sprinkle with "M&M's"® Chocolate Mini Baking Bits. Store in tightly covered container.

Makes 10 servings

Fudgy Glaze

1 square (1 ounce) semi-sweet chocolate

1 cup powdered sugar

⅓ cup unsweetened cocoa powder

3 tablespoons milk

½ teaspoon vanilla extract

Place chocolate in small microwave-safe bowl. Microwave at HIGH 30 seconds; stir. Repeat as necessary until chocolate is completely melted, stirring at 10-second intervals; set aside. In medium bowl combine powdered sugar and cocoa powder. Stir in milk, vanilla and melted chocolate until smooth.

Dump Cake

1 (20-ounce) can crushed pineapple
with juice, undrained

1 (21-ounce) can cherry pie filling

1 package DUNCAN HINES® Moist
Deluxe® Yellow Cake Mix

1 cup chopped pecans or walnuts

½ cup (1 stick) butter or margarine,
cut into thin slices

Preheat oven to 350°F. Grease
13×9-inch pan.

Dump pineapple with juice into pan.
Spread evenly. Dump in pie filling. Spread
evenly. Sprinkle cake mix evenly over
cherry layer. Sprinkle pecans over cake
mix. Dot with butter. Bake 50 minutes or
until top is lightly browned. Serve warm
or at room temperature.

Makes 12 to 16 servings

Tip: You can use DUNCAN HINES®
Moist Deluxe® Pineapple Supreme Cake
Mix in place of Moist Deluxe® Yellow
Cake Mix.

Little Banana Upside Down Cakes

3 tablespoons margarine, melted

3 tablespoons flaked coconut, toasted

3 tablespoons chopped almonds,
toasted

2 tablespoons brown sugar

1 firm large DOLE® Banana, sliced

¼ cup cake flour

¼ teaspoon baking powder
Pinch salt

1 egg

3 tablespoons granulated sugar

1 teaspoon rum extract

• Divide margarine, coconut, almonds,
brown sugar and banana among 3 (¾-cup)
soufflé dishes.

• Combine flour, baking powder and salt.

• Beat egg and granulated sugar until
thick and pale. Beat in rum extract. Fold
in flour mixture. Pour batter evenly into
prepared dishes.

• Bake in 350°F oven 15 to 20 minutes.
Invert onto serving plates.

Makes 3 servings

Dump Cake

Cherry Cupcakes

1 (18¾-ounce) box chocolate cake mix

1⅓ cups water

3 eggs

½ cup vegetable oil

1 (21-ounce) can cherry pie filling

1 (16-ounce) can vanilla frosting

Prepare cake mix according to package directions, adding water, eggs and oil. Pour batter into 24 paper-lined muffin-pan cups, filling two-thirds full.

Remove 24 cherries from cherry filling; set aside. Spoon a generous teaspoon of remaining cherry filling onto the center of each cupcake.

Bake in preheated 350°F oven 20 to 25 minutes. Cool in pans on wire racks 10 minutes. Remove from pan. Let cool completely. Frost cupcakes with vanilla frosting. Garnish cupcakes with reserved cherries.   *Makes 24 cupcakes*

Favorite recipe from **Cherry Marketing Institute**

Applesauce Walnut Cake

1 package DUNCAN HINES® Moist Deluxe® Butter Recipe Golden Cake Mix

1⅓ cups applesauce

3 eggs

½ cup butter or margarine, melted

1 teaspoon ground cinnamon

½ cup chopped walnuts

Confectioners' sugar, for garnish

1. Preheat oven to 375°F. Grease and flour 10-inch Bundt or tube pan.

2. Combine cake mix, applesauce, eggs, melted butter and cinnamon in large bowl. Beat at low speed with electric mixer until moistened. Beat at medium speed for 4 minutes. Stir in walnuts. Pour into pan. Bake at 375°F for 45 to 55 minutes or until toothpick inserted near center comes out clean. Cool in pan 25 minutes. Invert cake onto serving plate. Cool completely. Dust with confectioners' sugar.

Makes 12 to 16 servings

Tip: Also delicious using chopped pecans instead of walnuts.

Cherry Cupcakes

Lemon Sour Cream Pound Cake with Lemon Glaze

Cake

- 1 package (2-layer size) yellow cake mix or cake mix with pudding in the mix
- 1 package (2.9 ounces) JELL-O® Lemon Flavor Cook & Serve Pudding & Pie Filling (not Instant)
- 1 container (8 ounces) BREAKSTONE'S® Sour Cream
- 4 eggs
- ⅓ cup oil

Glaze

- 1 cup powdered sugar
- ¼ cup lemon juice
- 2 tablespoons butter or margarine, melted
- 1 teaspoon water

HEAT oven to 350°F.

PLACE cake mix, pudding mix, sour cream, eggs and oil in large bowl. Beat with electric mixer on medium speed 4 minutes. Pour into greased and floured 10-inch tube or fluted tube pan.

BAKE 55 to 60 minutes or until toothpick inserted near center comes out clean. Meanwhile, mix powdered sugar, lemon juice, butter and water until smooth.

REMOVE cake from oven. Cool 15 minutes; remove from pan. Place on wire rack. Poke cake all over with skewer. Spoon glaze over warm cake. Dust cooled cake with additional powdered sugar, if desired. *Makes 12 servings*

Preparation Time: 30 minutes
Baking Time: 1 hour

Marbled Angel Cake

1 package (16 ounces) angel food cake mix

¼ cup HERSHEY'S Cocoa
Chocolate Glaze (recipe follows)

1. Place oven rack in lowest position. Heat oven to 375°F.

2. Prepare cake batter as directed on package. Transfer 4 cups batter to medium bowl; gradually fold in cocoa until well blended, being careful not to deflate batter. Alternately pour vanilla and chocolate batters into ungreased 10-inch tube pan. With knife or metal spatula, cut through batters for marble effect.

3. Bake 30 to 35 minutes or until top crust is firm and looks very dry. *Do not underbake.* Invert pan on heatproof funnel or bottle; cool completely, at least 1½ hours. Carefully run knife along side of pan to loosen cake; remove from pan. Place on serving plate; drizzle with Chocolate Glaze. Let stand until set. Store, covered, at room temperature.

Makes 16 servings

Chocolate Glaze: In small saucepan, combine ⅓ cup sugar and ¼ cup water. Cook over medium heat, stirring constantly, until mixture comes to a boil. Stir until sugar dissolves; remove from heat. Immediately add 1 cup HERSHEY'S MINI CHIPS® Semi-Sweet Chocolate; stir until chips are melted and mixture is smooth. Cool to desired consistency; use immediately. Makes about ⅔ cup glaze.

> **Cook's Tip:** *To cut an angel food cake, use a long serrated knife and cut with a sawing motion.*

Banana Fudge Layer Cake

1 package DUNCAN HINES® Moist
   Deluxe® Yellow Cake Mix

1⅓ cups water

3 eggs

⅓ cup vegetable oil

1 cup mashed ripe bananas (about
   3 medium)

1 container DUNCAN HINES®
   Chocolate Frosting

Preheat oven to 350°F. Grease and flour
two 9-inch round cake pans.

Combine cake mix, water, eggs and oil in
large bowl. Beat at low speed with electric
mixer until moistened. Beat at medium
speed 2 minutes. Stir in bananas.

Pour into prepared pans. Bake 28 to
31 minutes or until toothpick inserted
into centers comes out clean. Cool in pans
15 minutes. Remove from pans; cool
completely.

Fill and frost cake with frosting. Garnish
as desired.   *Makes 12 to 16 servings*

Easy Lemon Cake

1 package (2-layer size) lemon cake
   mix

1½ cups cold milk

2 packages (4-serving size each)
   JELL-O® Lemon or Vanilla
   Flavor Instant Pudding & Pie
   Filling

1 tub (8 ounces) COOL WHIP®
   Whipped Topping, thawed

PREPARE cake mix as directed on
package for 2 (8-inch) round cake layers.
Cool completely.

POUR milk into medium bowl. Add
pudding mixes. Beat with wire whisk
2 minutes. Immediately spread over top of
both cake layers.

PLACE one cake layer on top of the
other. Frost top and side of cake with
whipped topping. Refrigerate until ready
to serve. Garnish as desired.
                          Makes 10 servings

Prep Time: 20 minutes

Banana Fudge Layer Cake

Double Berry Layer Cake

1 package DUNCAN HINES® Moist Deluxe® Strawberry Supreme Cake Mix

⅔ cup strawberry jam, divided

2½ cups fresh blueberries, rinsed, drained and divided

1 container (8 ounces) frozen whipped topping, thawed and divided

Fresh strawberry slices, for garnish

1. Preheat oven to 350°F. Grease and flour two 9-inch round cake pans.

2. Prepare, bake and cool cake following package directions for basic recipe.

3. Place one cake layer on serving plate. Spread with ⅓ cup strawberry jam. Arrange 1 cup blueberries on jam. Spread half the whipped topping to within ½ inch of cake edge. Place second cake layer on top. Repeat with remaining ⅓ cup strawberry jam, 1 cup blueberries and remaining whipped topping. Garnish with strawberry slices and remaining ½ cup blueberries. Refrigerate until ready to serve. *Makes 12 servings*

Tip: For best results, cut cake with serrated knife; clean knife after each slice.

Saucy Bake

1 package (2-layer size) yellow or devil's food cake mix or cake mix with pudding in the mix

2 cups water

2 cups milk

2 packages (4-serving size) JELL-O® Chocolate Flavor Instant Pudding & Pie Filling

⅓ cup sugar

¼ to ½ teaspoon ground cinnamon

HEAT oven to 350°F.

PREPARE cake mix as directed on package. Pour batter into greased 13×9-inch baking pan. Pour water and milk into large bowl. Add pudding mixes, sugar and cinnamon. Beat with electric mixer on low speed 1 to 2 minutes or until well blended. Pour over cake batter in pan.

BAKE 1 hour or until cake tester inserted into center comes out clean. Garnish as desired. Serve warm.

Makes 15 servings

Prep Time: 30 minutes
Bake Time: 1 hour

Double Berry Layer Cake

Pineapple Upside Down Cake

Topping

½ cup butter or margarine

1 cup firmly packed brown sugar

1 can (20 ounces) pineapple slices, well drained

Maraschino cherries, halved and drained

Walnut halves

Cake

1 package DUNCAN HINES® Moist Deluxe® Pineapple Supreme Cake Mix

1 package (4-serving size) vanilla instant pudding and pie filling mix

4 eggs

1 cup water

½ cup oil

1. Preheat oven to 350°F.

2. For topping, melt butter over low heat in 12-inch cast-iron skillet or skillet with ovenproof handle. Remove from heat. Stir in brown sugar. Spread to cover bottom of skillet. Arrange pineapple slices, maraschino cherries and walnut halves in skillet. Set aside.

3. For cake, combine cake mix, pudding mix, eggs, water and oil in large mixing bowl. Beat at medium speed with electric mixer for 2 minutes. Pour batter evenly over fruit in skillet. Bake at 350°F for 1 hour or until toothpick inserted into center comes out clean. Invert onto serving plate.   *Makes 16 to 20 servings*

Cook's Tip: *Cake can be made in a 13×9×2-inch pan. Bake at 350°F for 45 to 55 minutes or until toothpick inserted into center comes out clean. Cake is also delicious using Duncan Hines® Moist Deluxe Yellow Cake Mix.*

Pineapple Upside Down Cake

Sensibly Delicious Chocolate Chip Snacking Cake

2 cups all-purpose flour

¾ cup granulated sugar

1 teaspoon baking soda

½ teaspoon ground cinnamon

¼ teaspoon salt

¾ cup unsweetened applesauce

¼ cup nonfat milk

¼ cup margarine, melted

1 egg white

2 teaspoons vanilla extract

2 cups (12-ounce package) NESTLE® TOLL HOUSE® Semi-Sweet Chocolate Morsels, divided

COMBINE flour, sugar, baking soda, cinnamon and salt in large bowl. Stir in applesauce, milk, margarine, egg white and vanilla just until blended. Stir in 1 cup morsels. Spoon into greased 9×9-inch baking pan. Sprinkle with remaining morsels.

BAKE in preheated 350°F. oven for 25 to 35 minutes or until wooden pick inserted into center comes out clean. Cool in pan. Cut into squares. *Makes 16 servings*

Luscious Lime Angel Food Cake Rolls

1 package (16 ounces) angel food cake mix

2 drops green food coloring (optional)

2 containers (8 ounces each) lime-flavored nonfat sugar-free yogurt

Lime slices (optional)

1. Preheat oven to 350°F. Line two 17×11¼-inch jelly-roll pans with parchment or waxed paper; set aside.

2. Prepare angel food cake mix according to package directions. Divide batter evenly between prepared pans. Draw knife through batter to remove large air bubbles. Bake 12 minutes or until cakes are lightly browned and toothpick inserted into centers comes out clean.

3. Invert each cake onto separate clean towel. Starting at short end, roll up warm cake, jelly-roll fashion, with towel inside. Cool cakes completely.

4. Place 1 to 2 drops green food coloring in each container of yogurt, if desired; stir well. Unroll cake; remove towel. Spread each cake with 1 container yogurt, leaving 1-inch border. Roll up cake; place seam side down. Slice each cake roll into 8 pieces. Garnish with lime slices, if desired. Serve immediately or refrigerate.

Makes 16 servings

Strawberry Stripe Refrigerator Cake

Cake

    1 package DUNCAN HINES® Moist Deluxe® Classic White Cake Mix

    2 packages (10 ounces) frozen sweetened strawberry slices, thawed

Topping

    1 package (4-serving) vanilla instant pudding and pie filling mix

    1 cup milk

    1 cup whipping cream, whipped

    Fresh strawberries, for garnish (optional)

1. Preheat oven to 350°F. Grease and flour 13×9×2-inch pan.

2. For cake, prepare, bake and cool following package directions. Poke holes 1 inch apart in top of cake using handle of wooden spoon. Purée thawed strawberries with juice in blender or food processor.

Spoon evenly over top of cake, allowing mixture to soak into holes.

3. For topping, combine pudding mix and milk in large bowl. Stir until smooth. Fold in whipped cream. Spread over cake. Decorate with fresh strawberries, if desired. Refrigerate at least 4 hours.

Makes 12 to 16 servings

Tip: For a Neapolitan Refrigerator Cake, replace the White Cake Mix with Duncan Hines® Moist Deluxe® Devil's Food Cake Mix and follow directions listed above.

Berry Cobbler Cake

2 cups (1 pint) fresh or frozen berries (blueberries, blackberries, and/or raspberries)
1 package (1-layer size) yellow cake mix
1 teaspoon cinnamon
1 egg
1 cup water, divided
¼ cup sugar
1 tablespoon cornstarch
  Ice cream (optional)

1. Preheat oven to 375°F.

2. Place berries in 9×9-inch baking pan; set aside.

3. Combine cake mix and cinnamon in large bowl. Add egg and ¼ cup water; stir to combine. Spoon over berries.

4. Combine sugar and cornstarch in small bowl. Stir in remaining ¾ cup water until sugar mixture dissolves; pour over cake batter and berry mixture.

5. Bake 40 to 45 minutes or until lightly browned. Serve warm or cool with ice cream, if desired.   *Makes 6 servings*

Easy Carrot Cake

1¼ cups MIRACLE WHIP® Salad Dressing
1 (2-layer size) yellow cake mix
4 eggs
¼ cup cold water
2 teaspoons ground cinnamon
2 cups finely shredded carrots
½ cup chopped PLANTERS® Walnuts
1 (16-ounce) container ready-to-spread cream cheese frosting

• Beat salad dressing, cake mix, eggs, water and cinnamon in large bowl with electric mixer at medium speed until well blended. Stir in carrots and walnuts.

• Pour batter into greased 13×9-inch baking pan.

• Bake at 350°F for 35 to 40 minutes or until wooden toothpick inserted into center comes out clean. Cool completely. Spread cake with frosting. Garnish as desired.   *Makes 12 servings*

Prep Time: 15 minutes
Bake Time: 35 minutes

Berry Cobbler Cake

Chocolate Cream Torte

1 package DUNCAN HINES® Moist
  Deluxe® Devil's Food Cake Mix

1 package (8 ounces) cream cheese,
  softened

½ cup sugar

1 teaspoon vanilla extract

1 cup finely chopped pecans

1 cup whipping cream, chilled
  Strawberry halves for garnish
  Mint leaves for garnish

1. Preheat oven to 350°F. Grease and flour two 8- or 9-inch round cake pans.

2. Prepare, bake and cool cake following package directions for basic recipe. Chill layers for ease in splitting.

3. Place cream cheese, sugar and vanilla extract in small bowl. Beat at low speed with electric mixer until smooth. Add pecans; stir until blended. Set aside. Beat whipping cream in small bowl until stiff peaks form. Fold whipped cream into cream cheese mixture.

4. To assemble, split each cake layer in half horizontally (see Tip). Place one cake layer on serving plate. Spread top with one fourth of filling. Repeat with remaining layers and filling. Garnish with strawberry halves and mint leaves, if desired. Refrigerate until ready to serve.

Makes 12 to 16 servings

Tip: To split layers evenly, measure cake with ruler. Divide into 2 equal layers. Mark with toothpicks. Cut through layers with serrated knife, using toothpicks as guide.

Angel Almond Cupcakes

1 package DUNCAN HINES® Angel
  Food Cake Mix

1¼ cups water

2 teaspoons almond extract

1 container DUNCAN HINES® Wild
  Cherry Vanilla Frosting

Preheat oven to 350°F.

Combine cake mix, water and almond extract in large mixing bowl. Beat at low speed with electric mixer until moistened. Beat at medium speed for 1 minute. Line medium muffin pans with paper baking cups. Fill muffin cups two-thirds full. Bake 20 to 25 minutes or until golden brown, cracked and dry. Remove from muffin pans. Cool completely. Frost with frosting.   *Makes 30 to 32 cupcakes*

Chocolate Cream Torte

Coconut Jam Cake

1 package (2-layer size) yellow cake mix

1 package (7 ounces) BAKER'S® ANGEL FLAKE® Coconut, divided

½ cup strawberry jam

1 tub (8 ounces) COOL WHIP® Whipped Topping, thawed

½ cup apricot jam

Sliced fresh strawberries

Canned apricot halves, drained

Fresh mint leaves

HEAT oven to 350°F.

PREPARE and bake cake mix as directed on package for 2 (9-inch) round cake layers, gently stirring 1 cup coconut into batter just before pouring into pans. Cool 10 minutes; remove from pans. Cool completely on wire racks.

PLACE 1 cake layer on serving plate; spread top with strawberry jam. Spread ¾ cup whipped topping over jam; top with second cake layer. Spread top of cake with apricot jam. Frost top and side of cake with remaining whipped topping. Pat remaining coconut onto side of cake.

REFRIGERATE. Garnish just before serving. *Makes 12 servings*

Della Robbia Cake

1 package DUNCAN HINES® Angel Food Cake Mix

1½ teaspoons grated lemon peel

1 cup water

6 tablespoons granulated sugar

1½ tablespoons cornstarch

1 tablespoon lemon juice

½ teaspoon vanilla extract

Few drops red food coloring

6 cling peach slices

6 medium strawberries, sliced

Preheat oven to 375°F.

Prepare cake mix as directed on package, adding lemon peel. Bake and cool cake as directed on package.

Combine water, sugar and cornstarch in small saucepan. Cook on medium-high heat until mixture thickens and clears. Remove from heat. Stir in lemon juice, vanilla extract and food coloring.

Alternate peach slices with strawberry slices around top of cake. Pour glaze over fruit and top of cake.

Makes 12 to 16 servings

Tip: For angel food cakes, use a totally grease-free cake pan for the best volume.

Fantasy Angel Food Cake

1 package DUNCAN HINES® Angel
Food Cake Mix

Red and green food coloring

1 container DUNCAN HINES®
Creamy Home-Style Cream
Cheese Frosting

1. Preheat oven to 350°F.

2. Prepare cake following package directions. Divide batter into thirds and place in 3 different bowls. Add a few drops red food coloring to one. Add a few drops green food coloring to another. Stir each until well blended. Leave the third one plain. Spoon pink batter into ungreased 10-inch tube pan. Cover with white batter and top with green batter. Bake and cool following package directions.

3. To make Cream Cheese glaze, heat frosting in microwave at HIGH (100% power) 20 to 30 seconds. Do not overheat. Stir until smooth. Set aside ¼ cup warm glaze. Spoon remaining glaze on top and sides of cake to completely cover. Divide remaining glaze in half and place in 2 different bowls. Add a few drops red food coloring to one. Add a few drops green food coloring to the other. Stir each until well blended. Using a teaspoon, drizzle green glaze around edge of cake so it will run down sides. Repeat with pink glaze.   *Makes 16 servings*

Tip: For marble cake, drop batter by spoonfuls, alternating colors frequently.

Cook's Tip: To make a cake with a high volume, avoid opening the oven door during the first half of the baking time. The oven temperature must remain constant in order for the cake to rise properly.

Sweetheart Layer Bars
(page 312)

Holiday Celebrations

❧ ❧ ❧

*F*estive gatherings call for plenty of fun foods that will be the showpiece of any holiday affair. Prepare for happy occasions with this delightful collection of breads, cookies, cakes and pies, especially selected for holidays throughout the year.

Bake special treats like Sweetheart Layer Bars (page 312) or Celebration Pumpkin Cake (page 320) ahead of time. When the guests arrive, you'll be celebrating the memorable event with everyone else ... enjoy!

Sweetheart Cheesecake

1¼ cups chocolate cookie crumbs

¼ cup butter, melted

2 packages (8 ounces each) cream
   cheese, softened

½ cup plus 1 tablespoon sugar,
   divided

1 teaspoon vanilla, divided

2 eggs

1 cup sour cream

1 can (21 ounces) cherry pie filling

Preheat oven to 350°F.

For crust, combine cookie crumbs and
butter until well blended. Press mixture
onto bottom of 9-inch springform pan.
Bake 8 minutes; cool.

For filling, beat cream cheese, ½ cup sugar
and ½ teaspoon vanilla in medium bowl
with electric mixer until well blended.
Beat in eggs. Pour into cooled crust; bake
about 40 minutes or until center is almost
set. Cool.

For topping, combine sour cream,
remaining 1 tablespoon sugar and
remaining ½ teaspoon vanilla in small
bowl. Spread evenly over top of
cheesecake. Drop teaspoonfuls of sauce
from cherry pie filling onto sour cream

topping; carefully pull tip of knife or
wooden skewer through cherry sauce to
form hearts. Cover and refrigerate 3 hours
or overnight. Serve remaining cherry pie
filling over slices of cheesecake.

Makes 10 servings

Strawberry Hearts

1 roll (17 to 18 ounces) refrigerated
   sugar cookie dough

2 packages (8 ounces each) cream
   cheese, softened

⅔ cup powdered sugar

1 teaspoon vanilla

2 cups sliced fresh strawberries

Remove dough from wrapper. Roll out
dough, cut out hearts and bake as directed
on package.

Combine cream cheese, powdered sugar
and vanilla; mix well.

Spread evenly onto cooled hearts; top
evenly with strawberries.

Makes about 2 dozen hearts

Sweetheart Cheesecake

Sweetheart Layer Bars

1 cup (2 sticks) butter or margarine, divided

1½ cups finely crushed unsalted thin pretzels or pretzel sticks

1 cup HERSHEY'S MINI KISSES™ Milk Chocolates or Semi-Sweet Chocolates

1 can (14 ounces) sweetened condensed milk (not evaporated milk)

¾ cup HERSHEY'S Cocoa

2 cups MOUNDS® Sweetened Coconut Flakes, tinted*

*To tint coconut: Place 1 teaspoon water and ½ teaspoon red food color in small bowl; stir in 2 cups coconut flakes. With fork, toss until evenly coated.

1. Heat oven to 350°F.

2. Put ¾ cup butter in 13×9×2-inch baking pan; place in oven just until butter melts. Remove from oven. Stir in crushed pretzels; press evenly into bottom of pan. Sprinkle Mini Kisses™ over pretzel layer.

3. Place sweetened condensed milk, cocoa and remaining ¼ cup butter in small microwave-safe bowl. Microwave at HIGH (100%) 1 to 1½ minutes or until mixture is melted and smooth when stirred; carefully pour over pretzel layer in pan. Top with coconut; press firmly down onto chocolate layer.

4. Bake 25 to 30 minutes or until lightly browned around edges. Cool completely in pan on wire rack. Cut into heart-shaped pieces with cookie cutters or cut into bars. *Makes about 36 bars*

Cupid's Cherry Cheesecakes

12 NILLA® Wafers

2 (8-ounce) packages cream cheese, softened

¾ cup sugar

2 eggs

Cherry pie filling

Place 1 wafer in bottom of each of 12 (2½-inch) paper-lined muffin-pan cups; set aside.

Beat cream cheese, sugar and eggs in large bowl with electric mixer at medium speed until light and fluffy. Spoon filling into each cup, filling about ⅔ full.

Bake at 350°F for 30 minutes. Turn off oven; open door slightly. Let cool in oven for 30 minutes. Remove from oven; cool completely. Top with pie filling. Chill at least 1 hour. *Makes 12 cheesecakes*

Black & White Hearts

1 cup butter, softened

¾ cup sugar

1 package (3 ounces) cream cheese, softened

1 egg

1½ teaspoons vanilla

3 cups all-purpose flour

1 cup semisweet chocolate chips

2 tablespoons shortening

1. Beat butter, sugar, cream cheese, egg and vanilla in large bowl with electric mixer at medium speed, scraping bowl often, until light and fluffy. Add flour; beat until well blended. Divide dough in half; wrap each half in waxed paper. Refrigerate 2 hours or until firm.

2. Preheat oven to 375°F. Roll dough to ⅛-inch thickness on lightly floured surface. Cut dough with lightly floured 2-inch heart-shaped cookie cutters. Place cutouts 1 inch apart on *ungreased* cookie sheets. Bake 7 to 10 minutes or until edges are lightly browned. Remove immediately to wire racks; cool completely.

3. Melt chips and shortening in small saucepan over low heat 4 to 6 minutes until melted. Dip half of each heart into melted chocolate. Refrigerate on cookie sheets or trays lined with waxed paper until chocolate is set. Store, covered, in refrigerator.   *Makes about 3½ dozen*

Easter Basket Cupcakes

24 REYNOLDS® Easter Baking Cups

1 package (about 18 ounces) white cake mix

1 container (16 ounces) white ready-to-spread frosting

Flaked coconut

Green food color

Tiny jelly beans

Licorice twists

PREHEAT oven to 350°F. Place Reynolds Easter Baking Cups in muffin pans; set aside. Prepare cake mix following package directions for 24 cupcakes. Spoon batter into baking cups. Bake as directed. Cool.

FROST cupcakes; set aside.

TINT coconut green by mixing with food color. Make a coconut nest on top of each cupcake. Fill coconut nests with tiny jelly beans. For basket handles, with a knife, cut licorice twists in half lengthwise; cut halves into 6-inch pieces. Attach basket handles by inserting ends of licorice into cupcakes.   *Makes 24 cupcakes*

Edible Easter Baskets

1 package (about 18 ounces) refrigerated sugar cookie dough

1 cup "M&M's"® Milk Chocolate Mini Baking Bits, divided

1 teaspoon water

1 to 2 drops green food coloring

¾ cup sweetened shredded coconut

¾ cup any flavor frosting

Red licorice whips, cut into 3-inch lengths

Lightly grease 36 (1¾-inch) mini muffin cups. Cut dough into 36 equal pieces; roll into balls. Place 1 ball in each muffin cup. Press dough onto bottom and up side of each muffin cup; chill 15 minutes. Press ⅓ cup "M&M's"® Milk Chocolate Mini Baking Bits into bottoms and sides of dough cups. Preheat oven to 350°F. Bake cookies 8 to 9 minutes. Cookies will be puffy. Remove from oven; gently press down center of each cookie. Return to oven 1 minute. Cool cookies in muffin cups 5 minutes. Remove to wire racks; cool completely. In medium bowl combine water and food coloring. Add coconut; stir until evenly tinted. In each cookie cup, layer 1 teaspoon frosting, 1 teaspoon tinted coconut and 1 teaspoon "M&M's"® Milk Chocolate Mini Baking

Bits. Push both licorice ends into frosting to make basket handle. Store in tightly covered container.

Makes 3 dozen baskets

Cook's Tip: *Use Edible Easter Baskets to make a spectacular table setting. Prop up festive place cards against baskets or arrange baskets on a special platter for a center piece. Complete the arrangement by surrounding the platter with tiny vases of spring flowers.*

Edible Easter Baskets

Fourth of July Cherry Pie

5 cups Northwest fresh sweet cherries, pitted

2 tablespoons cornstarch

Pastry for 2-crust (9-inch) pie

2 tablespoons butter or margarine

⅓ cup sifted powdered sugar

1 tablespoon fresh lemon juice

1 teaspoon grated lemon peel

Preheat oven to 425°F.

Sprinkle cornstarch over cherries; toss to coat. Turn into pastry-lined 9-inch pie pan. Dot with butter. Roll remaining pastry into 10-inch circle. Cut into ¾-inch-wide strips. Arrange lattice-fashion over filling; seal and flute edges. Bake 35 to 45 minutes or until filling bubbles. Combine powdered sugar, lemon juice and peel; drizzle over warm pie.

Makes one 9-inch pie

Combination Method: Preheat oven to 425°F. Prepare pie as above in microwave/ovenproof pie plate. Microwave at HIGH 10 minutes or until filling bubbles; remove to conventional oven and bake 10 to 15 minutes or until crust is golden.

*Favorite recipe from **Northwest Cherry Growers***

Ghostly Delights

1 package (18 ounces) refrigerated cookie dough, any flavor

1 cup prepared vanilla frosting

¾ cup marshmallow creme

32 chocolate chips for decoration

1. Preheat oven to 350°F. Using about 1 tablespoon dough for body and about 1 teaspoon dough for head, form cookie dough into ghost shapes on greased cookie sheets. Bake 10 to 11 minutes or until browned. Cool 1 minute on cookie sheet; place warm cookies on serving plates.

2. While cookies are baking, combine frosting and marshmallow creme in small bowl until well blended.

3. Frost each ghost with frosting mixture. Press 2 chocolate chips, points up, into frosting mixture to create eyes on each ghost. Decorate with additional candy, if desired.

Makes 16 servings

Serving Suggestion: These cookies are excellent served with a tall glass of cold milk.

Prep and Cook Time: 25 minutes

Maple Pumpkin Pie

1⅓ cups all-purpose flour

⅓ cup plus 1 tablespoon sugar, divided

¾ teaspoon salt, divided

2 tablespoons vegetable shortening

2 tablespoons margarine

4 to 5 tablespoons ice water

1 can (15 ounces) solid-pack pumpkin

1 cup evaporated skim milk

⅓ cup maple syrup

2 egg whites

1 teaspoon ground cinnamon

½ teaspoon ground ginger

Light nondairy whipped topping (optional)

1. Combine flour, 1 tablespoon sugar and ¼ teaspoon salt in medium bowl. Cut in shortening and margarine with pastry blender or two knives until mixture forms coarse crumbs. Mix in ice water, 1 tablespoon at a time, until mixture comes together and forms a soft dough. Wrap in plastic wrap. Refrigerate 30 minutes.

2. Preheat oven to 425°F. Roll out pastry on floured surface to ⅛-inch thickness. Cut into 12-inch circle. Ease pastry into 9-inch pie plate; turn edges under and flute edge.

3. Combine pumpkin, milk, remaining ⅓ cup sugar, syrup, egg whites, cinnamon, ginger and remaining ½ teaspoon salt in large bowl; mix well. Pour into unbaked pie shell. Bake 15 minutes; *reduce oven temperature to 350°F.* Continue baking 45 to 50 minutes or until center is set. Transfer to wire cooling rack; let stand at least 30 minutes before serving. Serve warm, at room temperature or chilled with whipped topping, if desired.

Makes 8 servings

Note: Use pastry for single (9-inch) pie crust in place of ingredients in Step 1. Proceed with pastry as directed in Step 2.

Tombstone Brownies

1 package (about 21 ounces) brownie mix plus ingredients to prepare mix

1 cup chocolate fudge frosting (about ½ of 16-ounce container)

2 milk chocolate candy bars (1.55 ounces each)

Creamy Decorator's Frosting (recipe follows)

¾ cup flaked coconut, tinted green

12 pumpkin candies

1. Preheat oven to 350°F. Line 13×9-inch baking pan with foil, extending foil beyond edges of pan; grease foil.

2. Prepare brownie mix according to package directions. Spread in prepared pan. Bake 30 to 35 minutes. *Do not overbake.* Cool in pan on wire rack.

3. Using foil as handles, remove brownies from pan; peel off foil. Frost with chocolate frosting. Cut brownies into twelve 4×2-inch bars.

4. Break chocolate bars into pieces along scored lines. Using Creamy Decorator's Frosting, write "R.I.P." on chocolate pieces. Let stand until set.

5. Press 1 chocolate piece into end of each brownie for tombstone. Sprinkle tinted coconut on each brownie for grass. Place 1 pumpkin candy on coconut.

Makes 12 servings

Note: To tint coconut, dilute a few drops of food color with ½ teaspoon water in a large plastic bag. Add 1 to 1⅓ cups flaked coconut. Close the bag and shake well until the coconut is evenly coated. If a deeper color is desired, add more diluted food color and shake again.

Creamy Decorator's Frosting

1½ cups vegetable shortening

1½ teaspoons lemon, coconut, almond or peppermint extract

7½ cups sifted powdered sugar

⅓ cup milk

Beat shortening and extract in large bowl with electric mixer on medium speed until fluffy. Slowly add half of sugar, ½ cup at a time, beating well after each addition. Beat in milk and remaining sugar. Beat one minute more until smooth and fluffy. Store in refrigerator.

Tombstone Brownies

Celebration Pumpkin Cake

1 package (18 ounces) spice cake mix
1 can (16 ounces) pumpkin
3 eggs
¼ cup butter, softened
1½ containers (16 ounces each) cream
    cheese frosting
⅓ cup caramel topping
    Pecan halves for garnish

Preheat oven to 350°F. Grease and flour 3 (9-inch) round cake pans. Combine cake mix, pumpkin, eggs and butter in large bowl; beat with electric mixer at medium speed 2 minutes. Divide batter evenly among prepared pans. Bake 20 to 25 minutes or until toothpick inserted into centers comes out clean. Cool 5 minutes on wire rack; remove from pans and cool completely.

Place one cake layer on serving plate; cover with frosting. Repeat layers, ending with frosting. Frost side of cake. Spread caramel topping over top of cake, letting some caramel drip down side. Garnish with pecan halves. *Makes 16 servings*

Golden Kolacky

½ cup butter, softened
4 ounces cream cheese, softened
1 cup all-purpose flour
    Fruit preserves

Combine butter and cream cheese in large bowl; beat until smooth. Gradually add flour to butter mixture, blending until mixture forms soft dough. Divide dough in half; wrap each half in plastic wrap. Refrigerate until firm.

Preheat oven to 375°F. Roll out dough, half at a time, on floured surface to ⅛-inch thickness. Cut into 3-inch squares. Spoon 1 teaspoon preserves into center of each square. Bring up two opposite corners to center; pinch together tightly to seal. Fold sealed tip to one side; pinch to seal. Place 1 inch apart on *ungreased* cookie sheets. Bake 10 to 15 minutes or until lightly browned. Remove to wire racks; cool completely.

Makes about 2½ dozen cookies

Celebration Pumpkin Cake

Dreidel Cake

1 package (2-layer size) cake mix, any flavor

1¼ cups water

3 eggs

¾ cup sliced or slivered almonds, toasted* and finely ground

¼ cup vegetable oil

½ teaspoon almond extract

1½ containers (16 ounces each) cream cheese frosting

Yellow and blue food colors

Supplies

1 large tray or (15×10-inch) cake board, covered

Pastry bag and medium star tip

*To toast almonds, place in single layer on baking sheet. Bake at 350°F 7 to 10 minutes or until golden brown, stirring occasionally. Cool completely.

1. Preheat oven to 350°F. Grease and flour 13×9-inch baking pan.

2. Combine cake mix, water, eggs, almonds, oil and extract in medium bowl. Beat at low speed of electric mixer until blended. Beat at medium speed 2 minutes. Pour batter into prepared pan.

3. Bake 35 to 40 minutes until wooden toothpick inserted into center comes out clean. Cool in pan on wire rack 10 minutes. Remove from pan; cool completely on rack.

4. If cake top is rounded, trim horizontally with long serrated knife. Cut cake and position cake pieces on tray as shown in photo, connecting pieces with small amount of frosting. Frost center of cake with about ½ cup white frosting as shown in photo.

5. Tint about ¾ cup frosting yellow. To tint frosting, add small amount of desired food color; stir well. Slowly add more color until frosting is desired shade. Spread onto top and sides of cake as shown in photo.

6. Tint remaining frosting blue. Spoon frosting into pastry bag fitted with star tip. Pipe stars around top edge of cake and make symbol as shown in photo.

Makes 12 servings

Dreidel Cake

Philadelphia® Snowmen Cookies

1 package (8 ounces)
   PHILADELPHIA® Cream
   Cheese, softened
1 cup powdered sugar
¾ cup (1½ sticks) butter or margarine
½ teaspoon vanilla
2¼ cups flour
½ teaspoon baking soda
   Sifted powdered sugar
   Miniature peanut butter cups
   (optional)

MIX cream cheese, 1 cup sugar, butter and vanilla with electric mixer on medium speed until well blended. Add flour and baking soda; mix well.

SHAPE dough into equal number of ½-inch and 1-inch diameter balls. Using 1 small and 1 large ball for each snowman, place balls, slightly overlapping, on ungreased cookie sheets. Flatten to ¼-inch thickness with bottom of glass dipped in additional flour. Repeat with remaining balls.

BAKE at 325°F for 19 to 21 minutes or until light golden brown. Cool on wire racks. Sprinkle each snowman with sifted powdered sugar. Decorate with icing as desired. Cut peanut butter cups in half for hats.   *Makes about 3 dozen cookies*

Prep Time: 20 minutes
Bake Time: 21 minutes

Chocolate-Pecan Angels

1 cup mini semisweet chocolate chips
1 cup chopped pecans, toasted
1 cup sifted powdered sugar
1 egg white

Preheat oven to 350°F. Grease cookie sheets. Combine chips, pecans and powdered sugar in medium bowl. Add egg white; mix well. Drop batter by teaspoonfuls 2 inches apart onto prepared cookie sheets.

Bake 11 to 12 minutes or until edges are light golden brown. Let cookies stand on cookie sheets 1 minute. Remove cookies to wire racks; cool completely.
          Makes about 3 dozen cookies

Philadelphia® Snowmen Cookies

Festive Mincemeat Tartlets

Pastry for double pie crust

1½ cups prepared mincemeat

½ cup chopped peeled cored tart apple

⅓ cup golden raisins

⅓ cup chopped walnuts

3 tablespoons brandy or frozen apple juice concentrate, thawed

1 tablespoon grated lemon peel

Preheat oven to 400°F. Divide pastry in half. Refrigerate one half. Roll remaining half on lightly floured surface to form 13-inch circle. Cut six 4-inch rounds. Fit each pastry round into 2¾-inch muffin cup. Prick inside of crust with fork; set aside. Repeat with remaining pastry.

Bake unfilled pastry crusts 8 minutes. Meanwhile, combine mincemeat, apple, raisins, walnuts, brandy and lemon peel in medium bowl until well blended. Remove crusts from oven; fill each with rounded tablespoonful of mincemeat mixture. Press lightly into crust with back of spoon.

Bake 18 to 20 minutes more or until crust edges are golden. Cool in pan 5 minutes. Carefully remove from pan to wire rack. Serve warm or cool completely.

Makes 12 tartlets

Cinnamon Stars

2 tablespoons sugar

¾ teaspoon ground cinnamon

¾ cup butter or margarine, softened

2 egg yolks

1 teaspoon vanilla extract

1 package DUNCAN HINES® Moist Deluxe® French Vanilla Cake Mix

1. Preheat oven to 375°F. Combine sugar and cinnamon in small bowl. Set aside.

2. Combine butter, egg yolks and vanilla extract in large bowl. Blend in cake mix gradually. Roll to ⅛-inch thickness on lightly floured surface. Cut with 2½-inch star cookie cutter. Place 2 inches apart on ungreased baking sheet.

3. Sprinkle cookies with cinnamon-sugar mixture. Bake at 375°F for 6 to 8 minutes or until edges are light golden brown. Cool 1 minute on baking sheet. Remove to cooling rack. Cool completely. Store in airtight container.

Makes 3 to 3½ dozen cookies

Tip: You can use your favorite cookie cutter in place of the star cookie cutter.

Pretty in Pink Peppermint Cupcakes

1 package (about 18 ounces) white cake mix

1⅓ cups water

3 large egg whites

2 tablespoons vegetable oil or melted butter

½ teaspoon peppermint extract

3 to 4 drops red liquid food coloring *or* ¼ teaspoon gel food coloring

1 container (16 ounces) prepared vanilla frosting

½ cup crushed peppermint candies (about 16 candies)

1. Preheat oven to 350°F. Line 30 regular-size (2½-inch) muffin pan cups with pink or white paper muffin cup liners.

2. Beat cake mix, water, egg whites, oil, peppermint extract and food coloring with electric mixer at low speed 30 seconds. Beat at medium speed 2 minutes.

3. Spoon batter into prepared cups filling ¾ full. Bake 20 to 22 minutes or until toothpick inserted into centers comes out clean. Cool in pans on wire racks 10 minutes. Remove cupcakes to racks; cool completely. (At this point, cupcakes

may be frozen up to 3 months. Thaw at room temperature before frosting.)

4. Spread cooled cupcakes with frosting; top with crushed candies. Store at room temperature up to 24 hours or cover and refrigerate up to 3 days before serving.

Makes about 30 cupcakes

Santa's Thumbprints

1 cup (2 sticks) margarine, softened

½ cup firmly packed brown sugar

1 whole egg

1 teaspoon vanilla

1½ cups QUAKER® Oats (quick or old fashioned, uncooked)

1½ cups all-purpose flour

1 cup finely chopped nuts

⅓ cup jelly or preserves

Preheat oven to 350°F. Beat margarine and sugar until fluffy. Blend in egg and vanilla. Add combined oats and flour; mix well. Shape to form 1-inch balls; roll in chopped nuts. Place 2 inches apart on ungreased cookie sheets. Press center of each ball with thumb. Fill each thumbprint with about ¼ teaspoon jelly. Bake 12 to 15 minutes or until light golden brown. Cool completely on wire rack. *Makes about 3 dozen cookies*

Christmas Rainbow Cake

1 package (2-layer size) white cake mix

1 package (4-serving size) JELL-O® Brand Lime Flavor Gelatin

1 package (4-serving size) JELL-O® Brand Strawberry Flavor Gelatin

2 tubs (8 ounces each) COOL WHIP® Whipped Topping, thawed

HEAT oven to 350°F.

PREPARE cake mix as directed on package. Divide batter equally between 2 bowls. Add lime gelatin to one bowl and strawberry gelatin to the other bowl. Stir until well blended. Pour each color batter into separate greased and floured 9-inch round cake pans.

BAKE 25 to 30 minutes or until toothpick inserted into centers comes out clean. Cool 10 minutes; remove from pans. Cool to room temperature on wire racks.

SLICE each cooled cake layer in half horizontally. Place 1 lime-flavored cake layer on serving plate; frost with whipped topping. Top with 1 strawberry-flavored cake layer; frost with whipped topping.

Repeat layers. Frost top and side of cake with remaining whipped topping.

Makes 10 to 12 servings

Storage Know-How: Store cakes frosted with COOL WHIP® Whipped Topping in the refrigerator.

Great Substitute: Use any two flavors of JELL-O® Brand Gelatin to fit your favorite holiday.

Prep Time: 30 minutes
Bake Time: 30 minutes

Cook's Tip: To evenly cut a cake horizontally in half, remove the cake from the pan and place it on a flat surface. Measure the height of the cake with a ruler and mark a cutting line with toothpicks. Cut through the cake with a long serrated knife, just above the toothpicks.

Christmas Rainbow Cake

Holiday Thumbprint Cookies

1 package (8 ounces) sugar-free low-fat yellow cake mix

3 tablespoons orange juice

2 teaspoons grated orange peel

½ teaspoon vanilla

4 teaspoons strawberry all-fruit spread

2 tablespoons pecans, chopped

Preheat oven to 350°F. Spray baking sheets with nonstick cooking spray.

Beat cake mix, orange juice, orange peel and vanilla in medium bowl with electric mixer at medium speed for 2 minutes until mixture looks crumbly. Increase speed to medium and beat 2 minutes or until smooth dough forms. *Dough will be very sticky.*

Coat hands with nonstick cooking spray. Roll dough into 1-inch balls. Place balls 2½ inches apart on prepared baking sheets. Press center of each ball with thumb. Fill each thumbprint with ¼ teaspoon fruit spread. Sprinkle with nuts.

Bake 8 to 9 minutes or until cookies are light golden brown and lose their shininess. *Do not overbake.* Remove to wire racks; cool. *Makes 20 cookies*

Cranberry Pecan Muffins

1¾ cups all-purpose flour

½ cup firmly packed light brown sugar

2½ teaspoons baking powder

½ teaspoon salt

¾ cup milk

¼ cup butter, melted

1 egg, beaten

1 cup chopped fresh cranberries

⅓ cup chopped pecans

1 teaspoon grated lemon peel

Preheat oven to 400°F. Grease or paper-line 36 (1¾-inch) mini-muffin cups.

Combine flour, brown sugar, baking powder and salt in large bowl. Combine milk, butter and egg in small bowl until blended; stir into flour mixture just until moistened. Fold in cranberries, pecans and lemon peel. Spoon into prepared muffin cups, filling almost full.

Bake 15 to 17 minutes or until toothpick inserted into centers comes out clean. Remove from pans. Cool on wire racks. *Makes 36 mini muffins*

Holiday Thumbprint Cookies

Reindeer Cupcakes

38 Holiday OREO® Chocolate
  Sandwich Cookies, divided

1 (18.25-ounce) package white cake
  mix with pudding

1¼ cups water

3 egg whites

¼ cup vegetable oil

48 mini pretzel twists

4 ounces BAKER'S® Premium White
  Baking Chocolate, melted

Red hot candies, white chocolate
  chips and miniature chocolate
  chips, for decorating

1 (16-ounce) can prepared chocolate
  frosting

1. Coarsely chop 14 cookies. Mix cake mix, water, egg whites and oil in large bowl with electric mixer at low speed until moistened. Beat 2 minutes at high speed. Stir in chopped cookies. Spoon batter into 24 paper-lined 2½-inch muffin-pan cups.

2. Bake at 350°F for 20 to 25 minutes or until toothpick inserted into centers comes out clean. Remove from pans; cool on wire rack.

3. Cut a "V"-shaped portion off each remaining cookie to form reindeer face.

Attach two pretzel twists to cookies using some melted chocolate for antlers. Decorate face using red hot candies and chocolate chips. Refrigerate until set.

4. To serve, frost cupcakes with chocolate frosting. Stand reindeer faces on edge on each cupcake.   *Makes 24 cupcakes*

Preparation Time: 45 minutes
Cook Time: 20 minutes
Cooling Time: 1 hour
Total Time: 2 hours and 5 minutes

Easy Egg Nog Pound Cake

1 (18¼-ounce) package yellow cake mix

1 (4-serving size) package instant vanilla flavor pudding and pie filling mix

¾ cup BORDEN® Egg Nog

¾ cup vegetable oil

4 eggs

½ teaspoon ground nutmeg

Powdered sugar (optional)

1. Preheat oven to 350°F.

2. In large mixing bowl, combine cake mix, pudding mix, Borden Egg Nog and oil; beat at low speed until moistened. Add eggs and nutmeg; beat at medium-high speed 4 minutes.

3. Pour into greased and floured 10-inch fluted or tube pan.

4. Bake 40 to 45 minutes or until toothpick inserted near center comes out clean.

5. Cool 10 minutes; remove from pan. Cool completely. Sprinkle with powdered sugar, if desired.

Makes 1 (10-inch) cake

Prep Time: 10 minutes
Bake Time: 40 to 45 minutes

Philadelphia® Sugar Cookies

1 package (8 ounces) PHILADELPHIA® Cream Cheese, softened

1 cup (2 sticks) butter or margarine, softened

⅔ cup sugar

¼ teaspoon vanilla

2 cups flour

Colored sugar, sprinkles and colored gels

BEAT cream cheese, butter, ⅔ cup sugar and vanilla with electric mixer on medium speed until well blended. Mix in flour. Refrigerate several hours or overnight.

ROLL dough to ¼-inch thickness on lightly floured surface. Cut into desired shapes; sprinkle with colored sugar. Place on ungreased cookie sheets.

BAKE at 350°F for 12 to 15 minutes or until edges are lightly browned. Cool on wire racks. Decorate as desired with colored sugar, sprinkles and colored gels.

Makes 3½ dozen

Prep Time: 10 minutes plus refrigerating
Bake Time: 15 minutes

White Chocolate Cranberry Tart

1 refrigerated pie crust (half of 15-ounce package)

1 cup sugar

2 eggs

¼ cup butter, melted

2 teaspoons vanilla

½ cup all-purpose flour

1 package (6 ounces) white chocolate baking bar, chopped

½ cup chopped macadamia nuts, lightly toasted*

½ cup dried cranberries, coarsely chopped

*Toast chopped macadamia nuts in hot skillet about 3 minutes or until fragrant.

1. Preheat oven to 350°F. Line 9-inch tart pan with removable bottom or pie pan with pie crust (refrigerate or freeze other crust for another use).

2. Combine sugar, eggs, butter and vanilla in large bowl; mix well. Stir in flour until well blended. Add white chocolate, nuts and cranberries.

3. Pour filling into unbaked crust. Bake 50 to 55 minutes or until top of tart is crusty and deep golden brown and knife inserted into center comes out clean.

4. Cool completely on wire rack. Cover and store at room temperature until serving time. *Makes 8 servings*

Serve It With Style!: Top each serving with a dollop of whipped cream flavored with ground cinnamon, a favorite liqueur and grated orange peel.

Make-Ahead Time: up to 2 days before serving

> ***Cook's Tip:*** *White chocolate is a mixture of cocoa butter with added sugar, milk and flavorings (often vanilla or vanillin). It is more delicate than other chocolates and burns easily.*

White Chocolate Cranberry Tart

Individual Cheesecake Cups

Crust

1 package DUNCAN HINES® Moist Deluxe® Classic Yellow or Devil's Food Cake Mix

¼ cup margarine or butter, melted

Cheese Filling

2 packages (8 ounces each) cream cheese, softened

3 eggs

¾ cup sugar

1 teaspoon vanilla extract

Topping

1½ cups dairy sour cream

¼ cup sugar

1 can (21 ounces) cherry pie filling (optional)

1. Preheat oven to 350°F. Place 2½-inch foil or paper liners in 24 muffin cups.

2. For crust, combine cake mix and melted ¼ cup margarine in large bowl. Beat at low speed with electric mixer for 1 minute. Mixture will be crumbly. Divide mixture evenly among muffin cups. Level but do not press.

3. For filling, combine cream cheese, eggs, ¾ cup sugar and vanilla extract in medium bowl. Beat at medium speed with electric mixer until smooth. Spoon evenly into muffin cups. Bake at 350°F for 20 minutes or until set.

4. For topping, combine sour cream and ¼ cup sugar in small bowl. Spoon evenly over cheesecakes. Return to oven for 5 minutes. Cool completely. Garnish each cheesecake with cherry pie filling, if desired. Refrigerate until ready to serve.

Makes 24 servings

Individual Cheesecake Cups

Cherry Eggnog Quick Bread

2½ cups all-purpose flour

¾ cup sugar

1 tablespoon baking powder

½ teaspoon ground nutmeg

1¼ cups prepared dairy eggnog

2 eggs, slightly beaten

6 tablespoons butter, melted and cooled

1 teaspoon vanilla

½ cup chopped pecans

½ cup chopped candied red cherries

Preheat oven to 350°F. Grease three 5½×3-inch mini-loaf pans.

Combine flour, sugar, baking powder and nutmeg in large bowl. Blend eggnog, eggs, melted butter and vanilla in medium bowl. Add eggnog mixture to flour mixture. Mix just until moistened. Stir in pecans and cherries. Spoon into pans.

Bake 35 to 40 minutes or until wooden toothpick inserted into centers comes out clean. Cool in pans 15 minutes. Remove from pans; cool completely on wire racks. Store tightly wrapped in plastic wrap at room temperature.

Makes 3 mini loaves

Holiday Wreath Cookies

1 package (20 ounces) refrigerated sugar cookie dough

2 cups shredded coconut

2 to 3 drops green food color

1 container (16 ounces) French vanilla frosting

Green sugar and small cinnamon candies

1. Preheat oven to 350°F. Remove dough from wrapper according to package directions. Divide dough in half; wrap half of dough in plastic wrap and refrigerate. Roll out remaining half of dough on well-floured surface to ⅛-inch thickness. Cut with cookie cutters to resemble wreaths. Repeat with remaining half of dough.

2. Place cookies about 2 inches apart on *ungreased* baking sheets. Bake 7 to 9 minutes or until edges are lightly browned. Remove cookies from baking sheets to wire racks to cool completely.

3. Place coconut in resealable plastic food storage bag. Add food color; seal bag and shake until coconut is evenly tinted. Frost cookies with frosting and decorate with coconut, green sugar and cinnamon candies.   *Makes about 2 dozen cookies*

Snowman Cupcakes

1 package (about 18 ounces) yellow or white cake mix plus ingredients to prepare mix

2 containers (16 ounces each) vanilla frosting

4 cups flaked coconut

15 large marshmallows

15 miniature chocolate covered peanut butter cups, unwrapped

Small red candies and pretzel sticks for decoration

Green and red decorating gel

Preheat oven to 350°F. Line 15 regular-size (2½-inch) muffin pan cups and 15 small (about 1-inch) muffin pan cups with paper muffin cup liners. Prepare cake mix according to package directions. Spoon batter into muffin cups.

Bake 10 to 15 minutes for small cupcakes and 15 to 20 minutes for large cupcakes or until cupcakes are golden and toothpick inserted into centers comes out clean. Cool in pans on wire racks 10 minutes. Remove from pans to racks; cool completely. Remove paper liners.

For each snowman, frost bottom and side of 1 large cupcake; coat with coconut. Repeat with 1 small cupcake. Attach small cupcake to large cupcake with frosting to form snowman body. Attach marshmallow to small cupcake with frosting to form snowman head. Attach inverted peanut butter cup to marshmallow with frosting to form snowman hat. Use pretzels for arms and small red candies for buttons. Pipe faces with decorating gel. Repeat with remaining cupcakes.

Makes 15 snowmen

Banana Split Cupcakes
(page 346)

Especially for Kids

❦ ❦ ❦ ❦

With this collection of fun-filled treats, any aspiring baker can create these delightful desserts. Begin with prepared mixes and roll into fanciful shapes. Creamy frostings, colorful jelly beans, licorice and gumdrops magically turn cookies and cupcakes into yummy treats.

You won't want to wait for a special occasion to make these simple-to-bake goodies. Recipes like Handprints (page 358) and Ice Cream Cone Cakes (page 348) are a quick and easy—and delicious—way to make any day brighter.

Cookie Pizza

- 1 (18-ounce) package refrigerated sugar cookie dough
- 2 cups (12 ounces) semi-sweet chocolate chips
- 1 (14-ounce) can EAGLE® BRAND Sweetened Condensed Milk (NOT evaporated milk)
- 2 cups candy-coated milk chocolate candies
- 2 cups miniature marshmallows
- ½ cup peanuts

1. Preheat oven to 375°F. Press cookie dough into 2 *ungreased* 12-inch pizza pans. Bake 10 minutes or until golden. Remove from oven.

2. In medium-sized saucepan, melt chips with Eagle Brand. Spread over crusts. Sprinkle with milk chocolate candies, marshmallows and peanuts.

3. Bake 4 minutes or until marshmallows are lightly toasted. Cool. Cut into wedges.
Makes 2 pizzas (24 servings)

Prep Time: 15 minutes
Bake Time: 14 minutes

Kids' Cookie Dough

- 1 cup butter, softened
- 2 teaspoons vanilla
- ½ cup powdered sugar
- 2¼ cups all-purpose flour
- ¼ teaspoon salt
- Assorted colored glazes, frostings, sugars and small candies

1. Preheat oven to 350°F. Grease cookie sheets.

2. Beat butter and vanilla in large bowl at high speed of electric mixer until fluffy. Add sugar and beat at medium speed until blended. Combine flour and salt in small bowl. Gradually add to butter mixture.

3. Divide dough into 10 equal sections. Form shapes directly on prepared cookie sheets as desired.

4. Bake 15 to 18 minutes or until edges are lightly browned. Cool completely on cookie sheets.

5. Decorate cookies with glazes, frostings, sugars and small candies as desired.
Makes 10 (4-inch) cookies

Cookie Pizza

Peanut Butter and Jelly Cookies

1 cup Butter Flavor CRISCO® all-vegetable shortening or 1 Butter Flavor CRISCO® Stick

1 cup JIF® Creamy Peanut Butter

1 teaspoon vanilla

⅔ cup firmly packed light brown sugar

⅓ cup granulated sugar

2 large eggs

2 cups all-purpose flour

1 cup strawberry preserves or any flavor

1. Heat oven to 350°F.

2. Combine shortening, peanut butter and vanilla in food processor fitted with metal blade. Process until well blended and smooth. Add sugars; process until incorporated completely. Add eggs, beat just until blended. Add flour; pulse until it begins to form ball. *Do not over process.*

3. Place dough in medium bowl. Roll ½ tablespoon dough into ball for each cookie. Place 1½ inches apart on ungreased cookie sheets. Press thumb into center of each ball to create deep well. Fill each well with about ½ teaspoon preserves. Bake at 350°F for 10 minutes or until lightly browned and firm. Cool on cookie sheets 4 minutes; transfer to cooling racks. Leave on racks about 30 minutes or until completely cool.

Makes about 5 dozen cookies

Chocolate Sundae Cupcakes

24 REYNOLDS® Baking Cups

1 package (about 18 ounces) devil's food cake mix

1 container (16 ounces) ready-to-spread chocolate frosting

½ cup caramel ice cream topping

1½ cups frozen whipped topping, thawed

24 maraschino cherries with stems, drained

PREHEAT oven to 350°F. Place Reynolds Baking Cups in muffin pans; set aside. Prepare cake mix following package directions for 24 cupcakes. Spoon batter into baking cups. Bake as directed. Cool.

FROST cupcakes. Top each cupcake with 1 teaspoon caramel topping and 1 tablespoon whipped topping. Garnish each cupcake with a cherry. Refrigerate until serving time.   *Makes 24 cupcakes*

Peanut Butter and Jelly Cookies

Banana Split Cupcakes

1 (about 18 ounces) yellow cake mix, divided

1 cup water

1 cup mashed ripe bananas

3 eggs

1 cup chopped drained maraschino cherries

1½ cups miniature semi-sweet chocolate chips, divided

1½ cups prepared vanilla frosting

1 cup marshmallow creme

1 teaspoon shortening

30 whole maraschino cherries, drained and patted dry

1. Preheat oven to 350°F. Line 30 regular-size (2½-inch) muffin cups with paper muffin cup liners.

2. Reserve 2 tablespoons cake mix. Combine remaining cake mix, water, bananas and eggs in large bowl. Beat at low speed of electric mixer until moistened, about 30 seconds. Beat at medium speed 2 minutes. Combine chopped cherries and reserved cake mix in small bowl. Stir chopped cherry mixture and 1 cup chocolate chips into batter.

3. Spoon batter into prepared muffin cups. Bake 15 to 20 minutes or until toothpick inserted into centers comes out clean. Cool in pans on wire racks 10 minutes. Remove to wire racks; cool completely.

4. Combine frosting and marshmallow creme in medium bowl until well blended. Frost each cupcake with frosting mixture.

5. Combine remaining ½ cup chocolate chips and shortening in small microwavable bowl. Microwave at HIGH 30 to 45 seconds, stirring after 30 seconds, or until smooth. Drizzle chocolate mixture over cupcakes. Place one whole cherry on each cupcake.

Makes 30 cupcakes

Note: If desired, omit chocolate drizzle and top cupcakes with colored sprinkles.

Cookie Cups

1 package (20 ounces) refrigerated
  sugar cookie dough

All-purpose flour (optional)

Prepared pudding, nondairy
  whipped topping, maraschino
  cherries, jelly beans, assorted
  sprinkles and small candies

1. Grease 12 (2¾-inch) muffin cups.

2. Remove dough from wrapper according to package directions. Sprinkle dough with flour to minimize sticking, if necessary.

3. Cut dough into 12 equal pieces; roll into balls. Place 1 ball in bottom of each muffin cup. Press dough halfway up sides of muffin cups, making indentation in centers.

4. Freeze muffin cups 15 minutes. Preheat oven to 350°F.

5. Bake 15 to 17 minutes or until golden brown. Cookies will be puffy. Remove from oven; gently press indentations with teaspoon.

6. Return to oven 1 to 2 minutes. Cool cookies in muffin cups 5 minutes. Remove to wire rack; cool completely.

7. Fill each cookie cup with desired fillings. Decorate as desired.

Makes 12 cookie cups

Giant Cookie Cups Variation: Grease 10 (3¾-inch) muffin cups. Cut dough into 10 pieces; roll into balls. Complete recipe according to regular Cookie Cups directions. Makes 10 giant cookie cups.

Cook's Tip: *Add some pizzazz to your cookie cups by filling with a mixture of prepared fruit-flavored gelatin combined with prepared pudding or nondairy whipped topping. For convenience, snack-size gelatins and puddings can be found at the supermarket, so there is no need to make them from scratch.*

Ice Cream Cone Cakes

1 package DUNCAN HINES® Moist Deluxe® Cake Mix (any flavor)

1 container DUNCAN HINES® Creamy Home-Style Chocolate Frosting

1 container DUNCAN HINES® Creamy Home-Style Vanilla Frosting

Chocolate sprinkles

Assorted decors

Jelly beans

2 maraschino cherries, for garnish

1. Preheat oven to 350°F. Grease and flour one 8-inch round cake pan and one 8-inch square pan.

2. Prepare cake following package directions for basic recipe. Pour about 2 cups batter into round pan. Pour about 3 cups batter into square pan. Bake at 350°F 30 to 35 minutes or until toothpick inserted into centers comes out clean. Cool following package directions.

3. To assemble, cut cooled cake and arrange as shown in photo. Frost "cone" with Chocolate frosting, reserving ½ cup. Place writing tip in pastry bag. Fill with remaining ½ cup Chocolate frosting. Pipe waffle pattern onto "cones." Decorate with chocolate sprinkles. Spread Vanilla frosting on "ice cream" parts. Decorate with assorted decors and jelly beans. Top each with maraschino cherry.

Makes 12 to 16 servings

Hint: Use tip of knife to draw lines in frosting for waffle pattern as guide for piping chocolate frosting.

> **Cook's Tip:** *Create a party theme around Ice Cream Cone Cakes. Send invitations shaped like ice cream cones. For a party activity, let kids finish decorating frosted cupcakes with sprinkles, jelly beans and decors.*

Ice Cream Cone Cakes

Berry Surprise Cupcakes

1 package DUNCAN HINES® Moist
   Deluxe® White Cake Mix

1⅓ cups water

3 egg whites

2 tablespoons vegetable oil

3 sheets (0.5 ounce each) strawberry
   chewy fruit snacks

1 container DUNCAN HINES®
   Vanilla Frosting

2 pouches (0.9 ounce each) chewy
   fruit snack shapes, for garnish
   (optional)

1. Preheat oven to 350°F. Place
24 (2½-inch) paper liners in muffin cups.

2. Combine cake mix, water, egg whites
and oil in large bowl. Beat at low speed
with electric mixer until moistened. Beat
at medium speed 2 minutes. Fill each liner
half full with batter.

3. Cut three fruit snack sheets into 9 equal
pieces. (You will have 3 extra squares.)
Place each fruit snack piece on top of
batter in each cup. Pour remaining batter
equally over each. Bake at 350°F 18 to
23 minutes or until toothpick inserted
into centers comes out clean. Cool in pans
5 minutes. Remove to cooling racks. Cool
completely. Frost cupcakes with Vanilla
frosting. Decorate with fruit snack shapes,
if desired.   *Makes 12 to 16 servings*

Tip: To make a Berry Surprise Cake,
prepare cake following package directions.
Pour half the batter into prepared
13×9×2-inch pan. Place 4 fruit snack
sheets evenly on top. Pour remaining
batter over all. Bake and cool as directed
on package. Frost and decorate as
described above.

Berry Surprise Cupcakes

Surprise Cookies

**1 package (18 ounces) refrigerated
sugar cookie dough**

All-purpose flour (optional)

**Any combination of walnut halves,
whole almonds, chocolate-
covered raisins or caramel candy
squares for filling**

Assorted colored sugars

1. Grease cookie sheets. Remove dough
from wrapper according to package
directions. Divide dough into 4 equal
sections. Reserve 1 section; cover and
refrigerate remaining 3 sections.

2. Roll reserved dough to ¼-inch
thickness. Sprinkle with flour to minimize
sticking, if necessary. Cut out 3-inch
square cookie with sharp knife. Transfer
cookie to prepared cookie sheet.

3. Place desired "surprise" filling in center
of cookie. (If using caramel candy square,
place so that caramel forms diamond
shape within square.)

4. Bring up 4 corners of dough towards
center; pinch gently to seal. Repeat steps
with remaining dough and fillings, placing
cookies about 2 inches apart on prepared
cookie sheets. Sprinkle with colored

sugar, if desired. Freeze cookies
20 minutes. Preheat oven to 350°F.

5. Bake 9 to 11 minutes or until edges are
lightly browned. Remove to wire racks;
cool completely.

Makes about 14 cookies

Cook's Tip: *Make extra batches of
these simple cookies and store in the
freezer in heavy-duty freezer bags. Take
out a few at a time for your kids' after-
school treats.*

Chocolate Teddy Bears

1 recipe Chocolate Cookie dough
**White and colored frostings,
  decorator gels, coarse sugars and
  assorted small candies**

1. Prepare Chocolate Cookie Dough (see Tip). Cover; refrigerate about 2 hours or until firm.

2. Preheat oven to 325°F. Grease cookie sheets. Divide dough in half. Reserve 1 half; refrigerate remaining dough.

3. Divide reserved dough into 8 equal balls. Cut 1 ball in half; roll 1 half into ball for body. Cut other half into 2 equal pieces; roll 1 piece into 4 small balls for paws.

4. Divide second piece into thirds. Roll two-thirds of dough into ball for head. Divide remaining one-third of dough in half; roll into 2 small balls for ears.

5. Place balls together to form bear directly on prepared cookie sheet. Repeat steps with remaining dough.

6. Bake 13 to 15 minutes or until set. Cool completely on cookie sheets. Decorate with frostings, gels, sugars and assorted candies as desired.

Makes 16 (4-inch) teddy bears

Tip: For easy-to-make Bears, substitute refrigerated chocolate cookie dough for homemade chocolate cookie dough. Shape dough as directed in steps 3, 4 and 5. Bake according to package directions.

Chocolate Cookie Dough

1 cup butter, softened
1 cup sugar
1 egg
1 teaspoon vanilla
2 ounces semisweet chocolate, melted
2¼ cups all-purpose flour
1 teaspoon baking powder
¼ teaspoon salt

1. Beat butter and sugar in large bowl at high speed of electric mixer until fluffy. Beat in egg and vanilla. Add melted chocolate; mix well.

2. Add flour, baking powder and salt; mix well. Cover; refrigerate about 2 hours or until firm.

Smushy Cookies

1 package (20 ounces) refrigerated cookie dough, any flavor
All-purpose flour (optional)

Fillings
    Peanut butter, multi-colored miniature marshmallows, assorted colored sprinkles, chocolate-covered raisins and caramel candy squares

1. Preheat oven to 350°F. Grease cookie sheets.

2. Remove dough from wrapper according to package directions. Cut into 4 equal sections. Reserve 1 section; refrigerate remaining 3 sections.

3. Roll reserved dough to ¼-inch thickness. Sprinkle with flour to minimize sticking, if necessary. Cut out cookies using 2½-inch round cookie cutter. Transfer to prepared cookie sheets. Repeat with remaining dough, working with 1 section at a time.

4. Bake 8 to 11 minutes or until edges are light golden brown. Remove to wire racks; cool completely.

5. To make sandwich, spread about 1½ tablespoons peanut butter on underside of 1 cookie to within ¼ inch of edge. Sprinkle with miniature marshmallows and candy pieces. Top with second cookie, pressing gently. Repeat with remaining cookies and fillings.

6. Just before serving, place sandwiches on paper towels. Microwave at HIGH 15 to 25 seconds or until fillings become soft.

Makes about 9 sandwich cookies

Cook's Tip: *Invite the neighbor kids over on a rainy day to make these fun Smushy Cookies. Be sure to have lots of filling choices available so each child can create his own unique cookies.*

Smushy Cookies

Ice Cream Cone Cupcakes

1 package (18¼ ounces) white cake mix plus ingredients to prepare

2 tablespoons nonpareils*

2 packages (1¾ ounces each) flat-bottomed ice cream cones (about 24 cones)

1 container (16 ounces) vanilla or chocolate frosting

Candies and other decorations

*Nonpareils are tiny, round, brightly colored sprinkles used for cake and cookie decorating.

1. Preheat oven to 350°F.

2. Prepare cake mix according to package directions. Stir in nonpareils.

3. Spoon ¼ cup batter into each ice cream cone.

4. Stand cones on cookie sheet. Bake cones until toothpick inserted into centers of cake comes out clean, about 20 minutes. Cool on wire racks.

5. Frost each filled cone. Decorate as desired. *Makes 24 cupcakes*

Note: Cupcakes are best served the day they are prepared. Store loosely covered.

Chocolate Pretzel Cookies

Chocolate Cookie Dough (recipe page 353)

White and colored rock or coarse sugar

1. Prepare Chocolate Cookie Dough. Cover; refrigerate about 2 hours or until firm.

2. Preheat oven to 325°F. Grease cookie sheets.

3. Divide dough into 4 equal sections. Reserve 1 section; refrigerate remaining 3 sections. Divide reserved dough into 5 equal pieces. Shape each dough piece on lightly floured surface to 12-inch rope; sprinkle with rock or coarse sugar.

4. Transfer 1 rope at a time to prepared cookie sheets. Form each rope into pretzel shape. Repeat steps with remaining dough pieces.

5. Bake 12 to 14 minutes or until edges begin to brown. Cool cookies on cookie sheets 1 minute. Remove to wire racks; cool completely.

Makes about 20 cookies

Ice Cream Cone Cupcakes

Handprints

1 package (20 ounces) refrigerated cookie dough, any flavor

All-purpose flour (optional)

Cookie glazes, frostings, nondairy whipped topping, peanut butter and assorted candies

1. Grease cookie sheets. Remove dough from wrapper according to package directions.

2. Cut dough into 4 equal sections. Reserve 1 section; refrigerate remaining 3 sections. Sprinkle reserved dough with flour to minimize sticking, if necessary.

3. Roll dough on prepared cookie sheet to 5×7-inch rectangle.

4. Place hand, palm-side down, on dough. Carefully, cut around outline of hand with knife. Remove scraps. Separate fingers as much as possible using small spatula. Pat fingers outward to lengthen slightly. Repeat steps with remaining dough.

5. Freeze dough 15 minutes. Preheat oven to 350°F.

6. Bake 7 to 13 minutes or until cookies are set and edges are golden brown. Cool completely on cookie sheets.

7. Decorate as desired.

Makes 5 adult handprint cookies

Cook's Tip: *To get the kids involved, let them use their hands to make the handprints. Be sure that an adult is available to cut around the outline with a knife. The kids will enjoy seeing how their handprints bake into big cookies.*

Handprints

Smucker's® Spider Web Tartlets

1 (16-ounce) package refrigerated
 sugar cookie dough

¾ cup flour

 Nonstick cooking spray or
 parchment paper

1 cup (12-ounce jar) SMUCKER'S®
 Apricot Preserves

1 tube black cake decorating gel

1. Preheat the oven to 375°F. Unwrap cookie dough and place in medium mixing bowl. With floured hands, knead flour into cookie dough. Roll dough back into log shape, place on clean cutting board and cut into eight equal slices. With floured fingers, place dough circles on baking sheet lined with parchment paper or sprayed with nonstick spray.

2. Gently press dough circles, flattening each one to approximately 4 inches in diameter. With thumb and forefinger, pinch edge of each dough circle to create a ridge all around. Pinch each dough circle along the ridge to make eight points.

3. Spread 2 tablespoons of Smucker's® Jam (or Simply Fruit) onto each dough circle, making sure to spread it all the way to the edges and into the points. Refrigerate for 20 minutes. Bake 12 to 14 minutes or until edges are lightly browned.

4. Remove tartlets from baking sheet and cool on wire rack. When cool, use black decorating gel to make a spider web design.   *Makes 8 servings*

Butter Pretzel Cookies

 Butter Cookie Dough (recipe page
 361)

 White, rainbow or colored rock or
 coarse sugar

1. Prepare Butter Cookie Dough. Cover; refrigerate about 4 hours or until firm.

2. Preheat oven to 350°F. Grease cookie sheets.

3. Divide dough into 4 equal sections. Reserve 1 section; refrigerate remaining 3 sections. Divide reserved dough into 4 equal pieces. Shape each dough piece on lightly floured surface to 12-inch rope; sprinkle with rock or coarse sugar.

4. Transfer 1 rope at a time to prepared cookie sheets. Form each rope into pretzel shape. Repeat steps with remaining dough pieces.

5. Bake 14 to 18 minutes or until edges begin to brown. Cool cookies on cookie sheets 1 minute. Remove to wire racks; cool completely. *Makes 16 cookies*

Butter Cookie Dough

¾ cup butter, softened

¼ cup granulated sugar

¼ cup packed light brown sugar

1 egg yolk

1¾ cups all-purpose flour

¾ teaspoon baking powder

⅛ teaspoon salt

1. Combine butter, granulated sugar, brown sugar and egg yolk in medium bowl. Add flour, baking powder and salt; mix well.

2. Cover; refrigerate about 4 hours or until firm.

Brownie Rainbow Pie

1 (6-ounce) READY CRUST® Graham Cracker Pie Crust

1 egg yolk, beaten

2 eggs

⅛ teaspoon salt

½ cup brown sugar

3 (1-ounce) squares semi-sweet baking chocolate, melted

½ teaspoon vanilla

1 cup chopped KEEBLER® Rainbow Chips Deluxe® cookies

1. Preheat oven to 350°F.

2. Brush bottom and sides of crust with egg yolk. Bake on baking sheet 5 minutes or until light brown.

3. Beat eggs and salt in medium bowl 5 minutes or until thick. Gradually beat in sugar, chocolate and vanilla. Stir in cookies, reserving some for topping. Pour into crust on baking sheet. Top with reserved chopped cookies. Bake 20 minutes. Cool on wire rack. Refrigerate leftovers.

Makes 8 servings

Prep Time: 15 minutes
Bake Time: 25 minutes

Brownie Gems

1 package DUNCAN HINES® Chocolate Lover's® Double Fudge Brownie Mix

2 eggs

⅓ cup vegetable oil

2 tablespoons water

28 miniature peanut butter cups or chocolate kiss candies

1 container of your favorite Duncan Hines frosting

Preheat oven to 350°F. Spray (1¾ inch) mini-muffin pans with vegetable cooking spray.

Combine brownie mix, fudge packet from Mix, eggs, oil and water in large bowl. Stir with spoon until well blended, about 50 strokes. Drop 1 heaping teaspoonful of batter into each muffin cup; top with candy. Cover candy with more batter. Bake 15 to 17 minutes.

Cool 5 minutes. Carefully loosen brownies from pan. Remove to cool completely. Frost and decorate as desired.

Makes 30 brownie gems

Raindrop Cupcakes

1 package (2-layer size) white cake mix

1 package (4-serving size) JELL-O® Brand Berry Blue Flavor Gelatin

1 cup boiling water

1 tub (8 ounces) COOL WHIP® Whipped Topping, thawed

Decorating gel

Colored sugar (optional)

HEAT oven to 350°F.

PREPARE cake mix as directed on package, using egg whites. Spoon batter into paper-lined muffin pan, filling each cup ½ full. Bake as directed on package. Cool cupcakes in pan 15 minutes, then pierce with large fork at ¼-inch intervals.

DISSOLVE gelatin completely in boiling water in small bowl. Gradually spoon over cupcakes.

REFRIGERATE 3 to 4 hours. Frost with whipped topping. Draw umbrellas on cupcakes with decorating gel. Sprinkle with colored sugar. Store cupcakes in refrigerator. *Makes 24 cupcakes*

Brownie Gems

Mini Pizza Cookies

1 (20-ounce) tube of refrigerated
   sugar cookie dough
2 cups (16 ounces) prepared pink
   frosting
   "M&M's"® Chocolate Mini Baking
   Bits
   Variety of additional toppings such
   as shredded coconut, granola,
   raisins, nuts, small pretzels,
   snack mixes, sunflower seeds,
   popped corn and mini
   marshmallows

Preheat oven to 350°F. Lightly grease
cookie sheets; set aside. Divide dough into
8 equal portions. On lightly floured
surface, roll each portion of dough into
¼-inch-thick circle; place about 2 inches
apart onto prepared cookie sheets. Bake
10 to 13 minutes or until golden brown
on edges. Cool completely on wire racks.
Spread top of each pizza with frosting;
sprinkle with "M&M's"® Chocolate Mini
Baking Bits and 2 or 3 suggested toppings.

Makes 8 cookies

Clown Cupcakes

1 package DUNCAN HINES® Moist
   Deluxe® Classic Yellow Cake Mix
12 scoops vanilla ice cream
12 sugar ice cream cones
1 container (7 ounces) refrigerated
   aerosol whipped cream
   Assorted colored decors
   Assorted candies for eyes, nose and
   mouth

1. Preheat oven to 350°F. Place 2½-inch
paper liners in 24 muffin cups.

2. Prepare, bake and cool cupcakes
following package directions.

3. Remove paper from cupcakes. Place
top-side down on serving plates. Top with
scoops of ice cream. Place cones on ice
cream for hats. Spray whipped cream
around bottom of cupcakes for collar.
Spray three small dots up front on cones.
Sprinkle whipped cream with assorted
colored decors. Use candies to make
clowns' faces.   *Makes 12 cupcakes*

Note: This recipe makes 24 cupcakes:
12 to make into "clowns" and 12 to freeze
for later use.

Mini Pizza Cookies

Domino Cookies

1 package (20 ounces) refrigerated
sugar cookie dough
All-purpose flour (optional)
½ cup semisweet chocolate chips

1. Preheat oven to 350°F. Grease cookie sheets.

2. Remove dough from wrapper according to package directions. Cut dough into 4 equal sections. Reserve 1 section; refrigerate remaining 3 sections.

3. Roll reserved dough to ⅛-inch thickness. Sprinkle with flour to minimize sticking, if necessary. Cut out 9 (2½×1¾-inch) rectangles using sharp knife. Place 2 inches apart on prepared cookie sheets.

4. Score each cookie across middle with sharp knife. Gently press chocolate chips, point side down, into dough to resemble various dominos. Repeat with remaining dough, scraps and chocolate chips.

5. Bake 8 to 10 minutes or until edges are light golden brown. Remove to wire racks; cool completely.

Makes 3 dozen cookies

Cook's Tip: *Use these adorable cookies as a learning tool for kids. They can count the number of chocolate chips in each cookie and arrange them in lots of ways: highest to lowest, numerically or even solve simple math problems. As a treat, they can eat the cookies afterwards.*

Our House

1 package (18 ounces) refrigerated cookie dough, any flavor

All-purpose flour (optional)

Blue, green, white and purple icings, granulated sugar, yellow-colored sugar, green gumdrops, red licorice, small decors and hard candies

1. Preheat oven to 350°F. Line large cookie sheet with parchment paper.

2. Remove dough from wrapper according to package directions. Roll small piece of dough into 1½-inch square; reserve.

3. Press remaining dough into 12×9-inch rectangle on prepared cookie sheet. Sprinkle with flour to minimize sticking, if necessary.

4. Place reserved dough at top of rectangle to make chimney. Press to seal.

5. Bake 10 to 12 minutes or until edges are lightly browned. Cool on baking sheet 5 minutes. Slide house and parchment paper onto wire rack; cool completely.

6. Decorate using flat decorating tip for clapboards and shingles, yellow colored sugar for windows, star decorating tip for columns and steps and gumdrops for bushes. *Makes 1 cookie house*

Cook's Tip: This is a perfect rainy-day project. Keep your kids entertained by decorating this cookie house as directed or let their minds go wild and decorate it however they like.

Chocolate Peanut Butter Cookies

1 package DUNCAN HINES® Moist Deluxe® Devil's Food Cake Mix

¾ cup crunchy peanut butter

2 eggs

2 tablespoons milk

1 cup candy-coated peanut butter pieces

Preheat oven to 350°F. Grease cookie sheets.

Combine cake mix, peanut butter, eggs and milk in large mixing bowl. Beat at low speed with electric mixer until blended. Stir in peanut butter pieces.

Drop dough by slightly rounded tablespoonfuls onto prepared cookie sheets. Bake 7 to 9 minutes or until lightly browned. Cool 2 minutes on cookie sheets. Remove to cooling racks.

Makes about 3½ dozen cookies

Tip: You can use 1 cup peanut butter chips in place of peanut butter pieces.

Fruity Cookie Rings and Twists

1 package (20 ounces) refrigerated sugar cookie dough

3 cups fruit-flavored cereal, crushed and divided

1. Remove dough from wrapper according to package directions. Combine dough and ½ cup crushed cereal in large bowl. Divide dough into 32 balls. Refrigerate 1 hour.

2. Preheat oven to 375°F. Shape dough balls into 6- to 8-inch-long ropes. Roll ropes in remaining cereal to coat; shape into rings or fold in half and twist.

3. Place cookies 2 inches apart on ungreased cookie sheets.

4. Bake 10 to 11 minutes or until lightly browned. Remove to wire racks; cool completely. *Makes 32 cookies*

Chocolate Peanut Butter Cookies

Caramel Apple Cupcakes

1 package (about 18 ounces) butter-recipe yellow cake mix plus ingredients to prepare
1 cup chopped dried apples
   Caramel Frosting (recipe follows)
   Chopped nuts (optional)

1. Preheat oven to 375°F. Line 24 regular-size (2½-inch) muffin pan cups with paper muffin cup liners.

2. Prepare cake mix according to package directions. Stir in apples. Spoon batter into prepared muffin pans.

3. Bake 15 to 20 minutes or until toothpick inserted into centers comes out clean. Cool in pans on wire racks 10 minutes. Remove to racks; cool completely.

4. Prepare Caramel Frosting. Frost cupcakes. Sprinkle cupcakes with nuts, if desired.   *Makes 24 cupcakes*

Caramel Frosting

3 tablespoons butter
1 cup packed brown sugar
½ cup evaporated milk
⅛ teaspoon salt
3¾ cups powdered sugar
¾ teaspoon vanilla

1. Melt butter in 2-quart saucepan. Stir in brown sugar, evaporated milk and salt. Bring to a boil, stirring constantly. Remove from heat; cool to lukewarm.

2. Beat in powdered sugar until frosting is of spreading consistency. Blend in vanilla.

Caramel Apple Cupcakes

Acknowledgments

The publisher would like to thank the companies and organizations listed below for the use of their recipes and photographs in this publication.

Birds Eye®

Blue Diamond Growers®

Bob Evans®

California Tree Fruit Agreement

Cherry Marketing Institute

CHIPS AHOY!® Chocolate Chip Cookies

ConAgra Grocery Products Company

Cream of Wheat® Cereal

Dole Food Company, Inc.

Duncan Hines® and Moist Deluxe® are registered trademarks of Aurora Foods Inc.

Eagle® Brand

Equal® sweetener

General Mills, Inc.

Grandma's® is a registered trademark of Mott's, Inc.

Hershey Foods Corporation

The Hidden Valley® Food Products Company

HONEY MAID® Honey Grahams

Kahlúa® Liqueur

Keebler® Company

Kraft Foods Holdings

Lawry's® Foods, Inc.

© Mars, Incorporated 2002

McIlhenny Company (TABASCO® brand Pepper Sauce)

Mott's® is a registered trademark of Mott's, Inc.

National Honey Board

Nestlé USA

NILLA® Wafers

Norseland, Inc. Lucini Italia Co.

North American Blueberry Council

Northwest Cherry Growers

OREO® Chocolate Sandwich Cookies

Peanut Advisory Board

Pear Bureau Northwest

PLANTERS® Nuts

The Procter & Gamble Company

The Quaker® Oatmeal Kitchens

Reckitt Benckiser

Reynolds Consumer Products, A Business of Alcoa Inc.

The J.M. Smucker Company

Sonoma® Dried Tomatoes

Southeast United Dairy Industry Association, Inc.

Texas Peanut Producers Board

Unilever Bestfoods North America

Walnut Marketing Board

Washington Apple Commission

Wisconsin Milk Marketing Board

METRIC CONVERSION CHART

VOLUME MEASUREMENTS (dry)

1/8 teaspoon = 0.5 mL
1/4 teaspoon = 1 mL
1/2 teaspoon = 2 mL
3/4 teaspoon = 4 mL
1 teaspoon = 5 mL
1 tablespoon = 15 mL
2 tablespoons = 30 mL
1/4 cup = 60 mL
1/3 cup = 75 mL
1/2 cup = 125 mL
2/3 cup = 150 mL
3/4 cup = 175 mL
1 cup = 250 mL
2 cups = 1 pint = 500 mL
3 cups = 750 mL
4 cups = 1 quart = 1 L

VOLUME MEASUREMENTS (fluid)

1 fluid ounce (2 tablespoons) = 30 mL
4 fluid ounces (1/2 cup) = 125 mL
8 fluid ounces (1 cup) = 250 mL
12 fluid ounces (1 1/2 cups) = 375 mL
16 fluid ounces (2 cups) = 500 mL

WEIGHTS (mass)

1/2 ounce = 15 g
1 ounce = 30 g
3 ounces = 90 g
4 ounces = 120 g
8 ounces = 225 g
10 ounces = 285 g
12 ounces = 360 g
16 ounces = 1 pound = 450 g

DIMENSIONS

1/16 inch = 2 mm
1/8 inch = 3 mm
1/4 inch = 6 mm
1/2 inch = 1.5 cm
3/4 inch = 2 cm
1 inch = 2.5 cm

OVEN TEMPERATURES

250°F = 120°C
275°F = 140°C
300°F = 150°C
325°F = 160°C
350°F = 180°C
375°F = 190°C
400°F = 200°C
425°F = 220°C
450°F = 230°C

BAKING PAN SIZES

Utensil	Size in Inches/Quarts	Metric Volume	Size in Centimeters
Baking or Cake Pan (square or rectangular)	8×8×2	2 L	20×20×5
	9×9×2	2.5 L	23×23×5
	12×8×2	3 L	30×20×5
	13×9×2	3.5 L	33×23×5
Loaf Pan	8×4×3	1.5 L	20×10×7
	9×5×3	2 L	23×13×7
Round Layer Cake Pan	8×1½	1.2 L	20×4
	9×1½	1.5 L	23×4
Pie Plate	8×1¼	750 mL	20×3
	9×1¼	1 L	23×3
Baking Dish or Casserole	1 quart	1 L	—
	1½ quart	1.5 L	—
	2 quart	2 L	—